CREATING *and* GROWING REAL ESTATE WEALTH

CREATING *and*
GROWING
REAL ESTATE
WEALTH

The 4 Stages to a Lifetime of Success

William J. Poorvu
with Jeffrey L. Cruikshank

Vice President, Publisher: Tim Moore
Associate Publisher and Director of Marketing: Amy Neidlinger
Executive Editor: Jim Boyd
Editorial Assistant: Pamela Boland
Development Editor: Russ Hall
Digital Marketing Manager: Julie Phifer
Marketing Coordinator: Megan Colvin
Cover Designer: Alan Clements
Managing Editor: Gina Kanouse
Project Editor and Proofreader: Chelsey Marti
Copy Editor: Keith Cline
Indexer: Lisa Stumpf
Compositor: ICC Macmillan Inc.
Manufacturing Buyer: Dan Uhrig

© 2008 by Pearson Education, Inc.
Publishing as FT Press
Upper Saddle River, New Jersey 07458

FT Press offers excellent discounts on this book when ordered in quantity for bulk purchases or special sales. For more information, please contact U.S. Corporate and Government Sales, 1-800-382-3419, corpsales@pearsontechgroup.com. For sales outside the U.S., please contact International Sales at international@pearsoned.com.

Company and product names mentioned herein are the trademarks or registered trademarks of their respective owners.

Printed in the United States of America
This product is printed digitally on demand.
First Printing February 2008
ISBN-10: 0-13-243453-9
ISBN-13: 978-0-13-243453-9

Pearson Education Ltd., London
Pearson Education Australia PTY, Limited.
Pearson Education Singapore, Pte. Ltd.
Pearson Education North Asia, Ltd.
Pearson Education Canada, Ltd.
Pearson Educatión de Mexico, S.A. de C.V.
Pearson Education—Japan
Pearson Education Malaysia, Pte. Ltd.

Library of Congress Cataloging-in-Publication Data

Poorvu, William J., 1935–

  Creating and growing real estate wealth : an insider's guide to the many paths to success / William Poorvu.

    p. cm.

  ISBN 0-13-243453-9 (pbk. : alk. paper) 1. Real estate business. 2. Real estate investment.
3. Entrepreneurship—Psychological aspects. 4. Success in business. 5. Work and family.
I. Title.
  HD1375.P6637 2008
  333.33068—dc22

                                                        2007039362

To many generations of students, who have
taught me so much

Contents

Acknowledgements

Creating and Growing Real Estate Wealth is about how to craft a successful long-term career in real estate. But because there is no single path to follow into real estate, this book seeks to present multiple paths, which in turn reflect the wisdom of many skilled people with a variety of backgrounds.

I have conducted more than one hundred in-depth interviews with real estate entrepreneurs in the U.S. and abroad, and I greatly appreciate their candor and insights. Similarly, I need to thank the people at all those real estate companies—of all sizes and configurations—about which I've written cases, over the years.

Besides my experience as a practitioner over many decades, I also have benefited from the students I have taught, and learned from, during 35 years of teaching at Harvard Business School. Many have continued to come to me for career counseling, and again, their stories, comments, and questions have taught me even more about my field.

Over the decades, I have served on three REIT Boards: Connecticut General Mortgage and Realty Investors, Trammell Crow Realty Investors, and CBL Associate Properties. In recent years, Charles and Steven Lebovitz and John Foy, the chief executives at CBL, have given me innumerable insights into the effective management of a public company. As an advisory board member to the Shorenstein Company, I learned from Walter and Doug Shorenstein what it is like to adapt your strategy to attract institutional investors. In writing cases about the Hines Company over the years, I discovered that a properly structured entrepreneurial company can continue to thrive over a number of economic cycles.

This book started with an inquiry from Jim Boyd, Executive Editor of Pearson Education. He and his associates have continued to support and advise me. Jim even convinced me that I could say more in 80,000 than 115,000 words. Former teaching colleagues, Don Brown, Arthur Segel, and John Vogel added their input at various stages of the manuscript. Seth Klarman, Marilyn Yalom, and Stuart

Lucas effectively challenged numerous points they thought were unclear. Bob Glauber gave me a reality check on the financial markets.

My real estate partner, son Jonathan, politely made me aware of sections that did not tie together. My daughter, Alison Jaffe, did the same, even if she had to remind me that she had made similar comments earlier, and I should have listened to her the first time. My mother who passed away a few months ago just short of her 97th birthday encouraged me for 72 years to *do better*; she also served as my grammarian of last resort. My wife Lia has supported me not only through the writing of this, my fourth book, but through 50 years of marriage—truly a mind-boggling example of perseverance.

Tyler Kim typed more drafts than either of us would like to count with patience, good will, and endless cheerfulness. This is the second book I have collaborated on with Jeff Cruikshank. By now, I can't tell which of us has written or rewritten what. The key is we are still speaking, and, I believe, continue to be energized by our dialogue.

About the Author

William J. Poorvu managed the real estate program and taught real estate courses at Harvard Business School for 35 years. He has personally trained many of today's most successful leaders in the real estate industry. He is a successful real estate entrepreneur himself and also a professional investor, both on his own behalf and for various endowment boards on which he serves. He also authored *The Real Estate Game: The Intelligent Guide to Decision-Making and Investment.*

Introduction:
The Many Paths to Success

Real estate is a wonderful business.

It is as pure and enjoyable a form of entrepreneurship as you can find on the planet. You will come in contact with amazing people from all walks of life—people from whom you will learn more than the nuts and bolts of real estate. You have the chance to be creative, to find a niche where the competition doesn't already have an advantage of greater knowledge, better contacts, or a deeper skill set. More than most endeavors, it lets you define what's important to *you,* and then go after it.

And, of course, it can reward you very well financially. However, this book is not a "get rich quick in real estate" book—the kind that have spilled off the bookstore shelves in recent years. As I see it, those books are written by people who don't really understand the field, or who are simply trying to cash in on whatever is the current fad in real estate. The truth is, there are many real estate success stories, more than in most other businesses. But, few of them came easily or quickly. Most involved years of hard work: acquiring experience and building relationships with the many people you will need to help you achieve your goals.

Many of these books focus on a particular path to success—one that presumably has worked well for the author—and then prescribe that *everybody* go down that same path. Several things are wrong with that approach. First, there's no single aspect of the real estate business in which everybody can be a winner. To cite just one example of an option that I've seen proposed in some books, there aren't enough foreclosure auctions to go around if everybody tries to specialize in buying properties at them.

Second, there are many different ways to be successful. Although real estate is often considered a single industry, it is for most participants a local business—one that is, in fact, incredibly fragmented. This fragmentation can be good news. You just have to be opportunistic enough to find the approach that suits you best, and then work hard. If you get a little lucky along the way, that won't hurt either.

You also have to find out what you *don't* want to do. Foreclosure auctions aren't for everybody. They certainly weren't, and aren't, for me. If someone had told me five decades ago that success in real estate could only come from snapping up homes that families in distress were forced to abandon, I would have found something else to do, *quickly*. I wouldn't be writing this book today.

A "Typical" Life in Real Estate

What does a "typical" life in real estate look like? What are the milestones, pitfalls, and rewards? How can you create, grow, and use wealth successfully? How do your challenges and opportunities change over time? How can you make a difference? When is your product a commodity, with price being the key criterion? Alternatively, when can you add value through your skills at assembling the parts and providing services to your customers?

This book sets out to answer those questions. In the process, it describes exactly how the real estate industry works, what has changed, and what has stayed the same. It tells you how to get into the real estate business, and—if you choose—how to *stay* and *grow* in that business. It tells you how to spot opportunities, and how to respond to them. It explains the wide range of roles you might play—either as an active or passive participant—and helps you figure out which role might be most appropriate for you. Again, one of the main themes of this book is that there's no one way to succeed in real estate. You can't point to a single path and say, "This is the right way to do it."

In my previous book, *The Real Estate Game*, I explained how projects get built and how deals are put together. My central theme was that to succeed in the real estate game, you have to take into account several key factors: the people, the property, and the deal. You have to be immersed in the process. You have to get the details right and adapt them to the environment in which you operate.

A major objective of this book is to help you be more strategic: to define for yourself what makes a successful real estate career, and how to go about making it a reality. For many people, a job in this field is primarily a means to make a good salary (and perhaps earn a sizeable bonus) that will enable them to support their family. Others see their career as an opportunity to achieve responsibilities in an organization—a way to acquire not just money, but power and influence. Then, of course, there is the wealth-building aspect, whereby you can build an equity base by acquiring, improving, holding, and selling properties.

For still others, a career in real estate becomes a *way of life*. The deal-making, and the excitement of developing new projects, turns them on. For most of these people, retirement is not something they look forward to. Fortunately, retirement is something you can easily postpone when the business is yours and you call the shots.

Others have loftier aspirations. In their mind's eye, they have a compelling picture of a better world. They hope to make the physical environment a more satisfying place to live in.

Most real estate people, myself included, fit into more than one of these categories. The questions for you to answer are, *where do you fit, or want to fit? What are your goals?*

Even if you are not looking at a career in real estate for yourself—for example, if you are a passive investor, a service provider to the industry, or a student of business—you can use this book to derive a better understanding of how the real estate world works.

There are a number of questions asked for which there is no one right answer. Your challenge is to decide the answer that works best for you.

A Career in Four Stages

Think about a career in real estate as having four stages:

- **Starting out.** This is about building your foundation—your first job, your first deal. How and where can you add value? Are you coming into the field cold, or are you a lawyer, a contractor, or someone who's already providing services to players in the industry? How, exactly, do you do your first deal? (Did you inherit a property?) Where can you get the money that you may not have, and how do you deploy it? How much of your time will this new enterprise take? Most likely at this stage, you will be working for someone else. Getting the right job or training should be high on your priority list. You may begin doing your own deals on the side, but often as a sidebar to your day job.

- **Scaling up.** This focuses on finding your way through the forest—the deals after your first deal. First of all, *do* you get bigger, or do you stay small? Do you expand geographically, by product type, or by project size? If you get bigger, how do you build an organization that will help you succeed, and not swallow you up in all the complexities of finding, motivating, and managing people? How do you find the capital to do multiple projects? When do you give up your day job? When do you leave a position in someone else's real estate company and start your own firm, either alone or with others?

- **Hedging your bets.** This is my way of reinforcing the notion that real estate is *risky*. It gives a reality to the stock disclaimer, so prevalent in the mutual fund industry, that "past performance is not necessarily indicative of future results." There are a number of "X" factors that you cannot control and that will affect your outcome. As a highly cyclical business, it is vulnerable to externalities that can do you in if you're not careful (and sometimes even if you *are* careful). Some of these cycles may be related to your local or regional market, others can be macroeconomic, political, technological, or product-driven.

  To survive is like surfing: No matter how much you practice, you still have to be willing to take risks. You have to alter your plans to take advantage of new realities. At the end of the day, you may have gotten a great ride, falling and getting up again . . . or you can get wiped out. In real estate, there are winners and losers. Whether or not you are good at market timing, there are ways to minimize potential damage and to take advantage of the potential turnarounds in each cycle. You have to practice a form of "preventive maintenance" to prepare yourself for such times.

- **Taking stock.** This fourth and final career stage has to do with understanding your later career options in today's world and deciding what to do about them. It's not just about harvesting or not harvesting profits (although that's a piece of it). Depending on your circumstances, it may be about jumping back into the game in a new way. It may be about involving your family in the business, possibly over multiple generations. Conversely, it may be about encouraging your children to go out and do their own thing.

You may want to increase your charitable giving, perhaps to give your family a platform in the community to grow from. You may want your projects to be not only successful financially, but to have broader significance. You may worry more about how the environment is changed. Although it might seem counterintuitive, as you grow older—and as you start thinking about your legacy—your perspective may start becoming longer term.

This book is divided into four parts, with each part corresponding to one of these four stages. I open each part with some introductory comments and questions, and list a number of generalizations or takeaways that emphasize the major points in that section. I then introduce a series of characters who are going through that particular stage of their career. All of these characters are real people. I have known almost all of them personally. Some I have met through my academic work, I have done business with several, and served on boards for others. Their stories should be fascinating to anyone interested in real estate, no matter what his or her level of experience.

I don't claim that these people are "typical" or that they collectively represent all the different types you can find out there. In a field this diversified and fragmented, that would be impossible. I've chosen them because I believe their careers—individually and as a group—illustrate a variety of problems, opportunities, and situations you might encounter at some point in your career. Some stay small, buying properties opportunistically, whereas others establish large companies. Without exception, however, they gain experience, work hard, remain flexible, and attempt to manage risk—traits I have found in virtually all the successful real estate entrepreneurs I know.

Although many of these characters started in real estate decades ago—which means we can trace their careers over the four stages in this book—their earlier experiences are still relevant today. For example, real estate is a cyclical business, and being able to anticipate and then manage in the downturns is essential for survival. This involves managing both the asset and liability sides of the balance sheet: the property on one side, and the financial structure on the other. Whether the cycle occurred 10 or 20 years ago is not important. The key is to expect and prepare yourself for such changes and be ready to capitalize on them.

Many decades ago, I realized that I was unlikely to win the U.S. Open tennis tournament. With some help and practice, however, I could learn to play a better game, and maybe even make fewer mistakes. When you are young, you tend to hit the ball harder and try for more outright winners. As you get older, you try to become a more strategic player, perhaps lobbing the ball over your opponent's head a little more often. You adapt to your own physical condition and to your external environment. In both tennis and real estate, *playing smarter increases your chances for success*. It is not so much about winning each point as it is ending up on top, at the end of the match. Helping you to play smarter at every stage is the goal of this book.

Part I

Starting Out

How do you get started in real estate? How do you become an active player? How should you think about your career? How do you gain experience? How do you decide to go out on your own—either by yourself or with others?

There are many answers; in part because real estate is such a huge and fragmented industry. There is no shortage of opportunity waiting out there, and people seize those opportunities in an extraordinary variety of ways. My objective in this opening part is to help you examine your options, and encourage you to define the right strategy for yourself in this exciting field.

1

The Starting Line

Is real estate a good personal fit for you? If so, how do you find your first job? After that, how do you find your first deal?

Most likely, you have no experience, very little knowledge, not much money, no relationships, and no credibility out there in the world—in other words, none of the things that you'll eventually need to succeed in a real estate venture. So, why should you consider a career in real estate?

There are many advantages to being in this field, financial and otherwise. The industry has almost unlimited points of entry. You can practice your craft in any community in the country. The product comes in all sizes, shapes, and price points. Each property can be owned in a separate entity, with the ownership apportioned to reward specific contributions. You can be in the business owning one property or hundreds.

Real estate is the poster-child industry for entrepreneurs. You don't need substantial capital of your own to start. Financing is available for individual properties, based *primarily on the income from the property* rather than the net worth of the owner. You can outsource the services required to build, lease, and operate the property, allowing you to keep your own organization small and your overhead minimal.

What do we know about entrepreneurs? The ideal entrepreneur can be described as visionary, driven, energetic, flexible, persistent, detail oriented, good at negotiation, quick with numbers, and able to manage risk. The simple truth, however, is that few of us possess all these traits. (We'd probably be impossible to live with if we did.) In any case, it's really not necessary to be all these things at once. It is more important to be intimately aware of the market, understand the financing options, and maintain a healthy network of contacts and professional resources—achievable goals for most of us.

In many cases, the most successful entrepreneurs are life-long learners. They are people who are willing to listen, and who don't need to prove they are the smartest in the room.

The Job Search

Finding your first job is always daunting. Pick an area of real estate that relates to your strengths—one that will give you a point of entry and an opportunity to gain experience.

You might begin by working for a property owner directly, but such jobs are relatively hard to come by. In terms of sheer numbers, there are many more entry-level jobs in firms that provide services to property owners. These firms usually specialize by function, locale, and product type. *Functions* can include real estate brokerage, law, accounting, financing, building management, design, construction services, and so on. *Product type* can mean residential, office, industrial, warehouse, retail, hotel—or, in some parts of the country, self storage, parking, agriculture, or ranching.

Think about which functional area plays to your strengths—for example, your sales skills, your accounting background, or perhaps even your computer skills (in this day of Internet listings and virtual tours of properties). That will not only help you get your first job, but also put you in a position where you can excel and have more to offer to your next employer. Use your contacts: families, friends, alumni groups, and so on. Talk to as many people as will see you. Word of mouth is vitally important. Firms don't necessarily do their hiring to accommodate your graduation schedule, so be prepared to discover that your job search may take time.

Before you start your job search in earnest, try to learn more about your own strengths and weaknesses. You might want to do some online research, or borrow some books from the library, to get a sense as to what makes you tick. Some online personality tests can expand your thinking, and you can follow up these general tests with more targeted research.

Meanwhile, try to look at the landscape around you with new eyes. Where does opportunity lie? Where are new buildings going up? Can you get a summer job at one of these building sites?

For most of us, *where we live* is where we start looking for a job. In other words, we usually don't pick the location of our first real estate job search based on its inherent real estate potential. Our day job, our desire to be near where we or our spouse grew up, the sheer accident of where we were discharged from the service or where we went to school—these are far more often the determinants of location.

As it turns out, there's usually nothing particularly wrong with being in one location versus another. Each area has its own subsets of communities, neighborhoods, and streets. It has its own social, economic, zoning, and transportation dynamics. Even though, as a rule, it is better to be in a faster-growing market, even slow or no-growth markets have their opportunities. And without a doubt, we tend to have better contacts in the town where we grew up or where we spent our college years. Great contacts can make up for a less-than-hot local real estate market, especially when your goal is to gain experience.

Make your resumé a strong tool. Have a friend—or even better, someone who has experience hiring people—look at it and give you honest feedback as to what this all-important self-introduction is likely to tell a prospective employer.

Don't be afraid to include something offbeat at the bottom of your resumé, such as running a painting crew during the summer, working in another country, or excelling at a sport, second language, or musical instrument. You want to demonstrate to your potential employer that you have some kind of *spark*—and of course, give that person something to talk about at your interview. (Here's where having had that summer construction job will definitely be a plus.)

Do research on the person who's agreed to interview you, and on the company that he or she represents. This will demonstrate your initiative and seriousness, allow you to ask better questions, and perhaps flatter the interviewer. Google is an easy starting point.

Yes, this adds up to a lot of work, which can sometimes be frustrating. You need persistence and patience. Keep in mind, however, that the first success is often the hardest to achieve.

When you finally do get a job, try to perform multiple tasks within that company. The more experiences you get, the better. Talk to your coworkers about your interest in learning as much as possible. They often will be happy to share if they see you are eager to help, and to learn. Again, people may be flattered if you show a genuine interest in what they do and how they do it.

This raises an important and related point: *The person whom you are going to work for is just as important as the work you'll be doing,* and maybe even more so. In an ideal scenario, your boss will spend time with you, share experiences, challenge you, and introduce you to others. If he or she has a great reputation in the industry, that reputation may well rub off on you.

Timing is also important. Sometimes it is better to go into real estate when real estate is out of fashion, when people are flocking to other trendy fields—say, Internet start-ups or private equity firms. There may be fewer openings in real estate at those points in the cycle, but there is also less competition in the tough times, you'll get better training, and you'll be well positioned to take advantage of the eventual upswing in the market.

One Real Estate Career

Gordon Smith, a friend who graduated in 1959 from business school, decided early on to go into real estate. His story illustrates just how personal, and how particular, the starting-up decision can be.

Gordon grew up in a small Midwestern town, with part of his early education taking place in a one-room schoolhouse. He decided while at business school that he wanted to be a homebuilder. Without exception, his professors and friends told him that taking this path would be a waste of his graduate education. The homebuilding field, as they saw it, was a bunch of guys in pickup trucks with hammers, subject to the wild cyclical swings in the housing sector—in other words, low margins and high volatility.

Gordon loved the sound of all this. Something like a million and a half houses a year were being built in the United States back then. (The total is not too different today.) Couldn't he use his skills and smarts to grab a piece of that market? And, the fact that no one else in his MBA class of hundreds of equally smart people wanted to go into homebuilding was a plus: Gordon would be the only one in his class who would be applying what he had learned to the housing market. He picked a good locale—the rapidly growing suburbs around Washington, D.C.—where he made himself into one of the area's premier homebuilders. Half a century later, his firm—now run by his son—is still building something like 500 homes each year.

Gordon's world of 50 years ago is not the same as today's. But that's always the case. The world is always changing. The one reliable constant is that this is a cyclical industry—one in which playing a contrarian game and swimming against the tide can have great advantages over the long term. Even as you start your real estate career, and you're preoccupied by the demands of the moment, try to start thinking long term. Think like a contrarian. What can you do that not everyone else is doing?

Your First Deal

Not too long ago, I took a call from a reporter at the *Los Angeles Times* who was doing a story on a session at which Donald Trump, the ultimate real estate salesman, was speaking. The writer later wrote, in essence, that *Donald Trump said you can make it quickly, whereas Bill Poorvu, the Harvard Business School professor, said, "Not so fast; go more slowly."*

I realize that some people approach the real estate industry the same way they approach the stock market: looking for the quick hit. They hang on the words of a (self-described) billionaire. And of course, Donald Trump wasn't, and isn't, dumb. He was getting free publicity for a session in which he was getting paid a big fee. Meanwhile, I was giving an interview for nothing.

Still, I'll hold my ground. Because real estate is *not* like the stock market, the same answers don't apply. When you dabble in stocks, you can buy an index, such as the S&P 500, and be certain that your performance will mimic the averages, with low transaction costs. Buying individual real estate is much more complicated, and there is much more to learn, in part because it is a less-efficient market with much higher transaction costs.

You hope your first deal will be a financial success. In truth, however, it's more likely to be a good learning experience, in which you discover how the process actually works.

For example, it isn't just about gaining control of a property and sitting on it. Most people who succeed in real estate find a way to *take a property from a less valuable use to a more valuable one.* You can add value in many ways, some of which are listed here:

- Repositioning (that is, changing the use, condition, or pricing).
- Using excess land for new or extended purposes, especially if most of the initial cost can be allocated to the primary use.
- Adding new uses to existing development, such as a shopping center next to a residential subdivision.
- Buying properties at auctions, whether from lenders or distressed sellers, at prices that reflect a lack of liquidity in the financial markets rather than a permanent loss of value.
- Building on one's own tenancy. For example, your retail firm may anchor a shopping center. Your occupancy may fill an office building. In both cases, why not own the building? It is your lease that is creating much of the value of that property.
- Leasing rather than buying land, which is a way of reducing your up-front cash requirements.
- Pre-leasing, which means filling a vacant building with suitable tenants either before or soon after you acquire or construct it.
- Financing/leveraging. As noted, using other people's money is a necessity for most of us. The availability and cost of money will affect your cash flow, *big time.*
- Design/construction. Creative architecture, efficient layouts, cost control, and on-time delivery are keys to good execution.
- Customer service. Understanding and satisfying your existing tenants' needs leads to higher occupancy and lower turnover.

Here's an important point to keep in mind, as you think about deals: Strictly in terms of a percentage return, the *greatest increase in a property's value often comes in the early stages of owning that property,* when your influence or specialized knowledge has its greatest impact.

For example, if you can make a $100,000 purchase that is worth $150,000 after a year, that first-year gain is 50 percent. After the property is repositioned, stabilized, and financed, it's unlikely that the annual return will be anything like that in subsequent years. We've already talked about the idea of buying at distressed prices. The corollary is to sell in times when the risk is lower, there is an overabundance of money anxious to come into the market, and the capitalization rate is more favorable.[1]

The example is made even more compelling if you assume that you only had to put up $10,000 of the initial $100,000, and could borrow the rest. If you sold the building for $150,000, your return on sale would be $50,000 on your $10,000: a very satisfying 500 percent return! You have bought wholesale and sold at retail.

But what if you don't sell at that point? Going forward, if you assume you have, after the first year, a theoretical equity of $60,000—that is, your $10,000 initial cash plus the $50,000 potential gain—you won't make anything like that kind of annual return on the higher equity. You will likely only receive an annual cash flow of $5,000 or $6,000 on that $60,000.

So selling, especially early in your career, may make good sense. You might be in a lower-income tax bracket, and taxes might not be a huge issue if you sell the property. In addition, you're likely to need to sell your first property to have the cash to do your second deal. You'll read in subsequent parts of this book that in later stages of your career, *holding the property may be the best long-term strategy.* But, what you do starting out may be very different from what you do later on.

The downside in all this is that *your risk level goes up* as a result of your greater dependency on short-term activities—whether those risks are market related, the result of cost overruns on renovations, or whatever. You may assume that the interest rate is less important because you see yourself selling or refinancing the property in the near future. If you are heavily leveraged, you might need larger reserves to cover higher financing costs.[2] If it takes longer than you projected to generate revenues, you can quickly find yourself in deep trouble.

The Deal Search

Nearly all the deals that I've gone into have come from people who wanted more than just a commission for bringing me a deal. They wanted to be partners, architects, lawyers, or rental brokers in the project. If you treat others fairly, good deals are likely to be offered to you. But, getting the right help through building relationships and networks takes time. *Work at it.*

At some point, you have to pull the trigger and do your first deal. There's no easy answer to the question, "When should I be willing to make a purchase?" Chances are, you won't get it exactly right, or you'll get it right for the wrong reason. If you're lucky, however, a favorable market can make up for a lot of miscalculations.

Speaking personally, if I had known then what I know now, I would likely *never* have done many of my early deals—most of which turned out to be very profitable! As Mark Twain put it in his autobiography, "It is strange the way the ignorant and inexperienced so often and so undeservedly succeed."

Picking a Location

As with your job search, there's no one place to start. Usually, however, you will start in the area where you work or live, picking a property type you understand at a price level you can afford.

You can begin to explore your options simply by looking at maps. (It is amazing how much you can learn by looking at maps—all kinds of maps!) These days, the Internet is making available a wealth of detailed aerial maps that in the past were accessible to only the biggest companies.

You can continue your education by walking or driving around. You can visit apartments, houses, stores, and offices. Try to spot where change is occurring. What areas are in or out? Where are the artists moving? Where are the trendy shops and hot restaurants—the streets with "buzz?" Where are the areas with architecturally interesting structures that might be renovated attractively? What companies, and which brokers, are operating in this area?

Think of yourself as a comparison shopper. You would think nothing of asking the proprietor the price of a particular item in a store. Think the same way about property that goes up for sale. In real estate, it is much more difficult to "find the proprietor," and you might not know how much to believe when you do hear a price, but it is crucial that you begin to understand value. Thinking simultaneously in qualitative *and* quantitative terms about a property is not easy, but it is crucial to successful investment. The size and physical condition, the legal restrictions, the rent structure, the availability and cost of financing—all enter into the equation. There may be a big difference between the asking and the real price.

One of your toughest problems, starting out, is deciding which deals are worth spending time to investigate. Especially if you have a day job, this will be a limiting factor. This is why it's better to focus early on a specific neighborhood or property type where your learning will be cumulative. It is like buying a house. Until you have seen several, preferably in the same neighborhood, you will not have the confidence needed to act quickly when the right deal comes along.

Building Relationships

Real estate is a field with myriad players. They perform a number of services, many of which will be essential to your success. Most operate at the local level. At the same time that you are becoming knowledgeable about your local markets, therefore, you should be cultivating relationships and building your own reputation. At all points in your career, you need help from others, but this is especially crucial when you're starting out.

In particular, brokers are a wonderful source of information. It is not easy to find the right ones—that is, those who will spend time with you, and show you their best listings in a timely way. It often depends on the broker. As in every field, there are good brokers and bad ones. Keep in mind that 1) they are being paid by the seller, and 2) they only get paid if the deal goes through. Obviously, then, you have to assess how much weight you should put on their advice. But the better brokers take a longer-term view, hoping to build long-term relationships. After all, they might someday be selling a building for *you*.

Most brokers specialize in particular property types or markets. You need to find out which brokers fit *your* needs. Not surprisingly, brokers spend more time with their repeat customers. The problem for most of us starting out is that we're not (yet) repeat customers, nor are we flush with cash, nor are we blessed with ready access to credit. The broker has to look past those limitations and see our potential.

One sensible question to ask and answer is this: Do you pick a broker based on the individual's reputation, track record, and willingness to show you around, or on the reputation of the firm with which the broker is affiliated? Personally, I go for the individual—and that's pretty much my rule of thumb in *all* aspects of real estate. If your people judgment is good, picking someone with time to spend who, like you, is just starting out may be a good compromise (at least for most simple transactions).

If you are buying a house, you can turn up a great deal of information online, including specific properties for sale. But because each commercial property is different, and because many property owners desire confidentiality for various reasons, few investment properties are listed this way. Nevertheless, you can often uncover a great deal of general market information online, as well as information about nearby buildings. Comparative real estate tax assessments can be a good starting point. Sale prices are generally public information, although you should keep in mind that a stated price may have been affected by the terms of the transaction. If the seller took back a mortgage at an interest rate favorable to the buyer, for example, that might have led to a higher-than-normal sales price.

Although the transparency of information in the real estate industry is gradually improving, much of that improvement shows up in the single-family home market and—at the other end of the spectrum—properties that are large enough to be attractive to institutional investors. These larger properties are rarely the right fit for those just starting out. Smaller properties will simply require more detective work.

After you've found a promising prospect, be prepared to do a detailed inspection and analysis before you sign a binding purchase and sales (P&S) agreement. If you've purchased a home, you're familiar with the basics here. But most likely, as the stakes are higher and the buildings more complex in a commercial transaction, a higher level of diligence is in order. Make sure you have adequate time between the signing of your P&S agreement and the closing date to arrange for your financing. (Your lender needs processing time.) In some cases, you might make your offer contingent on your obtaining that financing. This may be a negative to the seller, but it is something to consider.

At this stage of your career, if you do not have much cash, you may attempt to limit the amount of your deposit. The seller may take the opposite view, looking at the size of your deposit as evidence of your commitment to the deal. Be careful how you negotiate, especially in a competitive market. The amount of deposit you're willing to put down may determine whether you get the deal.

Lawyers and Other Resources

The P&S and other legal agreements raise the issue of the selection and role of real estate lawyers.

Some real estate professionals believe that signing a P&S confirming the acceptance of your offer to purchase is standard, and therefore doesn't require the services of an attorney. But generally speaking, because *you don't know what you don't know,* that's not true.

What happens if you don't get your financing, or you find major structural problems in the property? Under what circumstances can you cancel the deal and get your deposit back? Is there a time frame within which you can raise certain objections, such as the physical condition of the property? It's important to spell out these and all other conditions in the P&S.

After the P&S is signed, your attorney will help you navigate the next stages of your due diligence process: assessing the condition of the land and the property; examining the terms and conditions of existing leases; confirming compliance with zoning, environmental, and other code restrictions; checking the validity of the owner's title; investigating options for financing; and forming the legal entity that will own the property.[3]

In short, you will need a lot of help from real estate attorneys, who represent a separate, specialized breed within the legal profession. The key here, as with brokers, is to find the one who *fits your needs.* The person within the firm who actually will do much of your work is much more important to you than the partner who brought in your business. Again, don't be afraid to ask for references.

A good lawyer knows the difference between providing *legal* advice and providing *business* advice—although if you're just starting out, you may need some of both. He or she will know which points are important to negotiate, and which ones are unlikely to be an issue in purchase and sales agreements, tenant leases, loan documents, and other contracts. If you are working with a junior attorney in a larger firm—as is often the case when you're starting out—make sure your attorney is not spending your time and money to impress the senior partners by preparing the "perfect" legal brief. (There's no such thing, and you probably don't need it.) Most agreements are variations upon forms that may already be in your attorney's computers, although you can get in a lot of trouble if you and your attorney don't understand the nuances.

Over time, you'll find that from deal to deal, many of the same legal points come up again and again. You will still need your attorney, but you eventually should be able to do much of your negotiating with tenants and contractors yourself.

For really important matters, I often find that it is more cost-efficient to pay the higher hourly fees for an experienced, busy attorney than to work with one who, like you, is just starting out. Remember, however, that these experienced people are in great demand and might not always be willing or able to perform according to your timetable.

Although you occasionally will need to hire attorneys with special skills in areas such as zoning or property tax appeals, your relationship with your prime attorney is well worth cultivating. Besides, like a good family doctor, your prime attorney will know what specialists to send you to. In my own case, in almost 50 years of practice, I have had four prime real estate attorneys. The only reason I ever changed attorneys was because that individual 1) got seriously ill, 2) became a judge, or 3) moved out of town.

As a sidebar, one of the major roles of your attorney is to keep you from needing the court system to resolve disputes. Even when I've been proven right by the legal system, I have generally found the process to be very expensive and unpleasant, both in terms of money and lost time.

I've talked at some length about real estate attorneys, in part because they're inherently valuable to your real estate career, but also because if you understand how to think about them, you'll know how to deal with a host of other professionals who can be similarly helpful. You probably can't afford the overhead of having your own in-house architects, contractors, mortgage brokers, or leasing agents. You will have to go through a similar selection process to find them as you did selecting a lawyer. Don't hesitate to ask for references and, if applicable, to see examples of their work. You'll pay more for experience, and sometimes it's well worth that premium. Keep in mind that the right person for your last project might not be the right person for the next one.

Finding the Money

Money has several aspects.

First, be prepared to *save and reinvest the money you make.* You need to deny yourself in the short term to make good in the long term.

But deferred gratification alone is almost never enough. Much of your wealth accumulation will be illiquid. (In other words, it can't easily be converted into cash.) You need to find other ways to make the money equation work. You want to maximize the value of not only your time and energy, but also of your own limited pocket book.

In most cases, you'll need to get a bank or some other lender to buy into your plan. Real estate is increasingly a numbers game, but some banks still bet on individuals. Similarly, individuals whom you approach to put up equity money are more apt to be betting on *you* personally. Behind the numbers, in other words, it's still a people game. As a Huntsville, Alabama-based developer recently put it, "When you are starting out with little money, trust is your currency." That holds at all stages of your career. Lose trust, and you are in trouble.

Once you get hold of someone else's money, you have to dole it out like hen's teeth. Why? First, it's embarrassing and problematic to run out of money. In addition, every time you go back to the well, you will 1) decrease your own control over the project, and 2) underscore in the minds of your partners that your projections weren't accurate. (No matter how good the excuse, there is no substitute for success.) You also may have to considerably reduce your equity stake to bring in new money, which means that you're going in exactly the wrong direction.

Basically, you have to have *adequate financing at an acceptable cost.* Without it, you can't get started. Most likely, you have only limited cash of your own, and you need other people's money. But this isn't always possible. There are times when capital is readily available, and other times when—no matter how good your idea might be—the financial spigot is turned off.

Despite overall consolidation in the financial services industry, there are still multiple sources of capital out there. Mortgage brokers can help you figure out which lenders are most active in the market at this particular time, and for your particular type of property. Keep in mind that the cheapest money is not always the best. The timing of the repayment, the security you have to put up, or the amount of the loan may be more important to you than the interest rate. Also, if you get in trouble, having a relationship with an experienced lender—who may give you time to work out your problems—may pay off in a big way.[4]

Managing the liability side of your balance sheet is a theme we return to repeatedly as we consider the arc of a career in real estate. After all, this is a capital-intensive industry, in which most of the cost is borrowed. As a result, more than half of your rental income is apt to go to your lender. The amount you borrow, the interest rate, and the terms for repayment (that is, the principal payments) are the major determinants of your cash flow. It's all too easy to focus primarily on the *asset* side: that is, the price we pay for the property. But almost equally important is the *liability* side: that is, how we finance it, and at what cost.

Risk and Reward

I don't want to conclude this chapter without mentioning *risk.*

Risk in real estate is real. However, you can learn to manage many of the risks you will face. As a matter of fact, if you ask entrepreneurs in any industry, most will say they are risk averse. They are able to get others to share the risks and thus minimize their own exposure. We examine how they do so in more detail in later chapters.

So the risks are real, but so are the rewards. Real estate can be a great field—the best of all fields, as almost any real estate entrepreneur will tell you. (Today, you won't hear many doctors or lawyers saying the same thing about *their* fields.) Real estate can be rewarding not just from a creative or financial standpoint, but also from a personal standpoint: You will meet and interact with many fascinating people.

It can also be rewarding from a social, even societal, standpoint: You can reshape the physical fabric of a community. Not all entrepreneurs are motivated primarily by the prospect of financial gain— many like *building*, and later, *seeing what they've built*.

With this picture of risk and reward in mind, you have to decide if this is the field for *you*. Think about what you've read so far. This is a field with a lot of moving parts. To balance and manage all these parts requires a great deal of patience, persistence, and skill. You never know for sure when to pull the trigger and actually commit to go ahead on your first deal. If it works, you'll never really know whether you were smart or just lucky—in the right place at the right time.

If your first deal turns out to be something other than the great success you had hoped for, do you change course and focus on your day job? Or, do you regroup and decide that you have learned from your first real estate experience and have made contacts and relationships that will help you get it right the second time? (Most entrepreneurs don't get it right the first time.) When do you jump out of your day job nest and start your own business? Have you built a reputation where people trust you and are willing to do business with you? Again, there are no easy or right or wrong answers.

Maybe the bottom-line question is this: *Have you caught the bug?* Has real estate gotten under your skin and made any other career choice look dull and unappealing? If so, it's highly unlikely that you'll stop now. Instead, you're likely to start thinking about scaling up: The subject of Part II of this book.

But first, let's meet some people who are just starting out. Let's see how they gain experience, establish good work habits, take the plunge, and do their first deal.

Endnotes

[1] The *capitalization* or *"cap rate"* is the ratio of the projected annual cash return to the estimated project cost or valuation. The cash return is calculated before deductions for financing costs, capital expenditures and income taxes. It may be based on a current, prior, or stabilized year.

[2] As an example of how leverage works, if you buy a property for $1 million that throws off an operating cash flow of $100,000, your return on assets or cap rate is

10 percent. As long as the interest rate is less than 10 percent, you have positive leverage, and the more you borrow, the higher the return on your equity. Conversely, if the interest rate is more than 10 percent, you have negative leverage, and your return is reduced by the differential. The repayment schedule also enters into the equation. If the combination of interest and principal payments exceeds 10 percent, your cash flow will be reduced. It might be more important to you to pay down the principal on your mortgage quickly, or you might prefer the greater cash flow with a longer amortization period.

[3] To limit your personal liability, you may want to set up a corporation to serve as the general partner of the new entity.

[4] You may not have that opportunity, given that so many mortgages today are packaged and resold as part of a larger portfolio. If a problem occurs, the trustee may have limited authority to make a special arrangement for an individual borrower. We have seen that in the recent collapse of the subprime loan market.

2

Finding a Focus

These real-life stories illustrate a variety of paths that people use to break into real estate. Our characters are all self-made. They come from many backgrounds. They train for a career in real estate in many different ways. There is no one personality type or background that leads to their success. What they all have in common, however, is an enthusiasm for the field, and an excitement about doing their own first deals—a deal in which they can share in the profits.

It may well be that one or a number of their stories will speak to you personally. If so, figure out why. After all, real estate is an entrepreneurial field—one in which you can play a role in determining your own success.

Pete and Sara Caron: Capitalizing on the Differential

For most Americans, their equity in their house is their biggest asset, and the purchase of that house, one of their most traumatic adventures. Although writing big checks for the upkeep and repairs for their house may make them think they are in the real estate business, they are not. At least as I define it, to be "in the real estate business" generally requires buying a property with the intention you will be leasing or selling to others.

Names: Pete and Sara Caron

Place: A Boston, Massachusetts suburb

Point of entry: Personal research (web, open houses)

Initial project: Two-family house

Type of project: Simple purchase

Initial funding: "Nest egg," residential mortgages

A hybrid arrangement is one where you buy a two- or three-family house and live in one unit while you rent out the others. This arrangement may motivate you to get in deeper—that is, to buy more investment properties in the future. Or it might simply enable you to live in a better house earlier in your life.

The latter was the case for Pete and Sara Caron. Pete was a computer whiz, and his wife Sara worked as a manager at a Target store in suburban Boston. They had started saving three years earlier for a down payment on a house. Being financially conservative, they also were paying off their college loans ahead of schedule, trying to get out from under that debt load.

The Learning Curve

As their nest egg slowly grew, Pete spent hours on the Internet, scanning advertisements for, literally, hundreds of homes. He paid special attention to situations in which the sellers were selling direct (that is, not through an agent). He and Sara also attended as many open houses as possible, trying to get a feel for the market. But the houses they liked were selling for close to $500,000, and their $50,000 in cash was far short of the $100,000 they would need for a down payment on a $500,000 dollar home. (Lenders were reluctant to give a mortgage of more than 80 percent of the purchase price.) For their part, Pete and Sara were wary of having to pay carrying charges on too much debt. Not only were they worried about their cash flow, they also were aware of how much the housing market is affected by the cost and availability of money. Rising interest rates could cost them more month to month, and also hurt the appreciation potential of whatever property they wound up buying.

Execution: Becoming a Player

One day, they came across a two-family house selling for $500,000, recently reduced from $525,000. The 1,700-square-foot main house was comparable to one they had seen up the street for $480,000. For the "extra" $20,000, the buyer would get an attached legal studio apartment that rented for about $10,000 per year. The home was in a nice suburban neighborhood, not far from the store where Sara worked. Because the other unit was attached, they wouldn't have to worry about having someone living above or below them. The home inspector whom they hired reported that the property was in good condition, with a new roof.

Through a mortgage broker, they found that they could get a $400,000 loan at a favorable rate, and then another $50,000 at a slightly higher rate. The $10,000 income from the rental unit would more than cover the extra cost of carrying the higher mortgage. Based in part on the favorable report of the home inspector, Pete and Sara decided that they were willing to manage the second unit themselves.

In essence, they were capitalizing on the price differential between a single-family and two-family house. The rental unit only cost them $20,000 more than it would cost them to buy the house up the street. The extra income it generated enabled them to borrow more money so they could live at a higher standard than would have been possible otherwise. In their own way, they had entered the real estate business.

Note that Pete and Sara decided not to use a broker—once a rare phenomenon, but increasingly common in recent years. There are obvious pros and cons to hiring an agent, but because of Pete's skill with computer-based research, the Carons' lack of time, pressure to buy, and their willingness to spend a lot of time going to open houses, they took the do-it-yourself route. You have to decide what's right for you.

My suggestion is to start where Pete started: surfing the web. See how much is available online. If you are sure you know the location you want and feel comfortable assessing value, stay with the computer.

If not, use a broker. A good one will help you discover other possibly appropriate neighborhoods or houses, think through options that may be personal to you, and help you negotiate a better price. Remember also, when you buy the house, that you should take into account any repairs you might want to make, as well as any furniture, furnishings, and decorations you might need to buy.

Where do you find two- and three-family dwellings? They normally are found in older areas of cities or close-in suburbs. The best buys are often found in neighborhoods that are in transition (preferably, *improving*). Some of these neighborhoods are conducive to families with children, whereas others are more appropriate for young professionals. You might need to do some work on these houses, but if the price is right to begin with, that may not be a problem. Just make sure you do your due-diligence investigating both the condition of the house and its neighborhood.

Finding Value in Urban Neighborhoods

The careers of Susan and Ed—our next two protagonists—began in similar ways. Although they come from very different backgrounds and their paths have never crossed, Susan and Ed have many traits in common. Both are bright, persistent, people oriented, and love *doing deals*.

They both started out working in residential, transitional urban neighborhoods—Susan in Providence, then New York, and Ed in Boston. Unlike Pete, they both looked at real estate as a full-time career opportunity. With neither capital nor experience, they started working for others—Susan as a project manager, Ed as a leasing broker. They both became adept at adapting to the physical, legal, and market realities of the neighborhoods in which they worked.

Susan Hewitt: Finding a Niche in New York

Susan Hewitt served a ten-year apprenticeship working as a project manager for a New York City renovator of residential buildings. She then took advantage of a weak market to buy (and subsequently sell) a vacant cooperative apartment acquired as an investment at an auction—her first deal on her own.

Name: Susan Hewitt

Place: New York, New York

Point of entry: Project manager, residential renovations

Initial project: Co-op apartment

Type of project: Purchase for resale

Initial funding: Savings

Back in her college days, she had started out as an economics major, but quickly decided that the field of economics was too divorced from reality for her tastes. Far more stimulating were the courses she took in the urban planning department, which initially sparked her fascination with real estate. She greatly enjoyed exploring the needs of the environment—natural and built—while creating something concrete.

After college, she moved to Houston, mainly because she thought it would be an interesting place to live after Providence, and a place where she could get a toehold in a booming real estate market. She was able to set up a number of job-related meetings, but quickly became discouraged. Everyone told her to start by working in a bank, rather than trying to work on actual projects.

She next moved to San Francisco, where she came close to getting a job with a firm that was in the process of converting a ferry building on the waterfront to commercial uses. Unfortunately, the job wouldn't start for several months, and she was running out of money. Somewhat reluctantly, she returned home to Providence. Already, she had learned an important lesson about landing a first job in real estate: *You are bound to have more contacts in the place where you grow up, and people are more likely to take a chance on someone whom they know, or whose family they know.*

In a relatively small city like Providence, this proved especially true. One strong contact led to another, and as a result, Susan found her first mentor: a local entrepreneur who was in several businesses, including real estate. He was a pioneer in converting a number of historic buildings into offices in the downtown commercial area. As an assistant project manager—one of the best ways to learn the business—Susan became involved in construction, leasing, and politics. She liked the directness of dealing with local contractors. She greatly enjoyed the *variety* in her daily routine: No two days were ever exactly alike. And being an outgoing woman in an industry mostly dominated by men, she quickly established her presence and began carving out a niche for herself.

After two years on the job, she decided to go to business school to pick up some understanding of the money side. Then, needing a job at graduation to pay off her debts, she considered taking a job with a large, institutionally oriented real estate company that paid a good salary. But her advisor (who happened to be me) told her she would never be happy in that kind of environment. She was too much of a free spirit.

That led her to try to find a more entrepreneurial job in New York City. This time, she used her Providence contacts to make a connection with two men who were doing loft renovations there. Her background—with both on-the-job experience and an MBA—made her an attractive candidate to join them. She became the third (and most junior) person on a small team.

Although the firm was very small, it did a number of incredibly complex projects in Lower Manhattan—projects that were greatly complicated by the difficulties (legal and otherwise) of doing business in New York City. Not only did the buildings need substantial physical work, but in many cases there were existing tenants, whose tenancies were governed by a variety of rental laws. On the plus side, several of the properties were entitled to historic tax credits, which could be sold to pay for some of the needed improvements. The tax credits were generally bought by large corporations who could write off the credits against their other tax obligations.

Susan and her two bosses worked in close quarters in a basement office, often eating lunch together and talking business as they ate. She was exposed to all parts of the business, including the management of their completed buildings. Susan realized that being involved on the management side of the business was a great learning experience for her, but she personally didn't enjoy spending all her time dealing with a steady stream of tenant inquiries, demands, and complaints.

Although Susan was given a very small equity stake in some of the projects that came along later in her tenure at the firm, her economic returns were insignificant. The projects took longer than expected, and an economic downturn in her last few years there affected results, which in turn impacted her returns. Some of the projects in which she was slated to have a larger equity interest were cancelled when the economy turned down.

Despite the financial disappointments, Susan knew that she had learned much that could be useful to her in the future. She had learned, for example, about

- The conversion-to-condominium process
- Rent regulations
- How to talk with contractors and workmen
- How to deal with lenders (especially in adverse times)
- How to handle distressed properties in a weak market

As a sideline to her regular job, at an auction she bought a cooperative unit at 3 Sheridan Square for $50,000, thinking of the purchase as an investment. She soon discovered, however, that buying a cooperative unit was much more complicated than buying a condominium unit.[1]

Susan had to do considerable research not only on the individual unit, but also on the financial structure of the entire building— including the odds that the other shareholders would meet their obligations. She also had to make sure that the unit was vacant, and that she would not have to worry about evicting an existing tenant who might be entitled to continued occupancy under one regulation or another.

It also required her to be a patient owner, able to support the unit until the market improved enough for a sale to be attractive. In this case, it took nine months. Through a broker, Susan eventually sold the unit at a good profit. After a long apprenticeship, she finally had done a deal on her own—and she had her first real cash.

Ed Mank: A Leasing Broker's First Deal

Ed Mank's entry into real estate was a little more deliberate. He chose Boston's Beacon Hill as the area he wanted to focus on. But before taking the plunge to buy his first building, he worked for a year as a leasing broker, which is one of the many ways to learn the business.

Name: Ed Mank

Place: Boston's Beacon Hill

Point of entry: Leasing broker

Initial project: Small unit apartment building

Type of project: Rehab

Initial funding: Silent partner, bank mortgage

While in law school, Ed Mank decided he did not want to practice law. He thought he would do better in sales. As he looked at the world, he quickly realized that most of his friends in sales sold either cars or real estate. Not seeing himself as a car salesman, he opted for real estate. He started networking and talking to friends in the business about potential employers. Two of those friends were then working for a small, well-regarded leasing and brokerage firm with excellent contacts in the upscale Beacon Hill and Back Bay sections of Boston. One of those friends, Peter, recently had bought several rather run-down income-producing buildings in another part of Boston, and was leaving to concentrate entirely on those properties.

Over lunch, Peter said candidly that some people in the industry questioned whether he as a broker should represent clients while being in the business of buying for himself. But this was fairly common, Peter pointed out, especially in markets with a sizable number of potential properties for sale. He also made the point that because brokers rarely had the financial resources to acquire more than one or two properties at a time, they weren't likely to affect pricing in a major way. The key to him was to decide up front which role he would play at the time he first heard about the property.

After a number of interviews with the rather conservative owner of the business and his wife, Ed was offered the job—on the condition that he tone down his brash demeanor a bit. Ed would be paid a low starting salary, the owner explained, while he was learning the ropes. In his first two weeks, however, Ed brought in enough commissions for the firm to convince the owner to change their arrangement. Henceforth, he would draw no salary, but would get 50 percent of any commissions he brought into the firm. Over the course of his year with the agency, he made four times as much in commissions as he would have made in salary.

The Learning Curve

Why did Ed do so well? Besides his winning personality and his talent for negotiation, Ed understood that the key to effective selling is *understanding the product*. Whenever there was a lull in traffic at the office, he visited apartments that were for rent and buildings that were for sale. In short order, he developed a near-encyclopedic knowledge of Beacon Hill and the adjacent residential area of Back Bay.

During his time at the agency, Ed lived as frugally as possible, occupying a basement apartment in one of his colleague's buildings. He knew that to become a player, he would need capital, which meant that he would have to save some cash from his commission income. Meanwhile, he got to know many of the suppliers and contractors in the area, so that someday he would be prepared to operate his own properties. Because he had minimal technical expertise, he knew he had to build relationships with contractors he could trust.

Becoming a Player

Ed's break came one day when he was taking his laundry to the local dry cleaner. Harry, the owner of the dry-cleaning store, told Ed that he heard there was a building for sale that needed upgrading. After some conversation, they agreed they would each put up $500 as a deposit to tie up the property if Ed liked the deal. Ed went to see the owner, who quoted what Ed recognized instantly to be a low price. As Ed started to negotiate—which he always did, out of sheer habit—Ed saw a look of consternation come over the owner's face. Realizing his error, Ed immediately backpedaled and accepted the price.

The purchase and sales agreement, signed in April, gave them 60 days to perform their due diligence and close the deal. Ed took the lead in this and subsequent steps, with Harry acting only as a silent partner. Financing was Ed's most immediate problem: He had limited cash, no track record, and no established banking relationship. Luckily, he found a local banker who recognized that Ed knew the market and who also understood that the building was undervalued. On that basis, the banker was able to justify a high enough mortgage to cover most of their costs. Toward the end of June, before the 60 days expired, Ed and Harry closed the deal.

Ed soon acquired additional properties, all of which he managed in similar ways. His ideal deal would be to make an acquisition at the end of June. He then would give 60 days' notice to the tenants that he was going to upgrade the apartments and raise their rents as of September 1. The timing was important because leases in that area normally expired on August 31 to coincide with the academic year, and notice had to be given by the end of June.

Ed would quickly redo the entrance lobby and stairs. If he could gain early access to units that were to be vacated, he would also upgrade the kitchens and baths. He persuaded a hardware dealer to provide him with appliances on six months' credit, and located contractors who agreed to do the work in a compressed summer schedule.

By September, he hoped to have signed leases at higher rents. This enabled him to do a revised pro forma income and expense statement justifying a higher selling price. In October—that is, a little more than four months after purchasing the property—Ed would hope to sell it at a big profit, with a closing scheduled for early January. January was not an arbitrary choice: This date meant that he would have owned the building for just over 6 months, which was then the holding period necessary to qualify for capital gains tax treatment (today it would be 12 months). By selling in January, he also avoided owning the building during the most expensive months of the heating season and pushed the gain into the next tax year.

Ed continued to work as a broker. Although few of his deals conformed to this exact timetable, he kept learning the ropes, and building capital for future deals.

Executing Against the Plan

What have we learned about Ed and about the process of breaking into the real estate business? First, Ed had all the character traits of an entrepreneur. He was optimistic, hardworking, persistent, and—although somewhat aggressive—great with people. He was also shrewd. He had a game plan and executed it. He spent the time to learn the market, understood the advantage of leverage in a rising market, and started by buying a small property where he could own much of the equity. He found that bankers, contractors, and others are often willing to do favors for a bright young person starting out, if that young person can show them how he or she can add value. Trust was his currency.

He was also willing in his first deal to share the ownership with Harry, who—in return for finding the deal and putting up his share of the cash—got half the profit. Ed felt that making money for his local partner would help him in finding investors for future deals, whether it was Harry or someone else. (Word would get around.) Buying wholesale, adding value through renovation and re-leasing, and then selling quickly at retail put him in a position to once again start looking for his next opportunity.

Two Players, Two Teams

Our next stories involve two football players who have taken very different paths in real estate. Rich Erenberg, a former running back, looks for holes in the line to run through, taking advantage of his blockers. He discovered undervalued properties in Houston at a time when that city's economy was in trouble. John Dewberry, a former quarterback, is more strategic. His game plan is eventually to redevelop much of Midtown Atlanta with new high-rise, mixed-use projects. Rich keeps his team small. John eventually builds an organization. They exhibit two more approaches to becoming successful in real estate.

Rich Erenberg: An Unexpected Opportunity

Rich Erenberg never wanted to be anything other than a football player. After graduating from Colgate in 1984, he spent three years playing for the Pittsburgh Steelers as a running back until his ninth knee operation ended his professional career. Eventually, he discovered that real estate called upon many of the same talents that had made him successful in the sports world.

Name: Rich Erenberg

Place: Houston, Texas

Point of entry: No background

Initial project: Residential condos

Type of project: Rehabs for rent and resale

Initial funding: Self-financed RTC "distress" sales

Rich's path into real estate wasn't direct. He started by enrolling in a financial training program in Pittsburgh, learning how to analyze and sell investment products to wealthy individuals. For a variety of reasons, this didn't work out. For one thing, he wasn't comfortable using his reputation as an athlete to get potential clients for financial firms. Just as important, he discovered that he preferred to work for himself.

The Learning Curve

It wasn't long before Rich got a call from his friend Steve Morse, another ex-Steeler. Steve had moved to Houston to take a position at Dow Chemical as a chemical engineer. While looking for a condo for himself, Steve had become friendly with the real estate broker who was showing him around. Houston, at the time, was in dire economic straits—low oil prices had ravaged what was then a one-industry town—and Steve found himself intrigued by the amount of cheap but high-quality real estate that was then on the market. He encouraged Rich to come down and look around for himself.

Becoming a Player

Together, Steve and Rich discovered the Resolution Trust Company (RTC), a federally chartered entity that had been tasked with disposing of all the assets taken over by the federal government when the local commercial bankers and savings and loan companies went under. They found they could buy apartment units for between $5,000 and $6,000, which only a few years earlier had cost between $20,000 and $30,000 to build new.

Rich began to spend half his time in Houston. He and Steve started by buying single units, which they renovated for $2,000 to $2,500. They did most of the demolition, drywall, painting, and "fixturing" on their own, bringing in electricians and plumbers when needed.

When the units were completed, they would approach tenants in the same complex, ask them how much they were paying in rent, and offer to lease to them a similar or better unit at $200 to $300 per month less. (At the time, few leases in Houston contained any stipulations that prevented tenants from moving.) They would then physically help their new tenants move to their new apartment.

The formula worked, and Rich and Steve repeated the process several times. Being young, inexperienced, and non-native Texans, they had no access to bank financing. But after they had remodeled and rented an existing unit, they could often sell the condo to the renter or a new investor for $15,000, effectively doubling their money in a few months. The resale of the units provided the cash for the next deal. Eventually, through hard work and determination, they were able to purchase a block of ten units. They felt like they had finally arrived.

Right Place, Right Time

Rich and Steve were in the right place at the right time. They bought at distressed prices when the supply of properties for sale drastically exceeded the number of buyers. They took advantage of a situation where they could offer customers the same product in the same location, but at a lower price. They were also capitalizing on their discipline, versatility, and work ethic—holdovers from their football days.

The fact that they could buy, fix up, and sell a unit in such a short time frame was crucial. It enabled them to take their limited capital and turn it over several times in the course of the year, compounding it with each subsequent sale.

In spite of the success of their real estate ventures, both Rich and Steve kept their day jobs. Steve held on to his job at Dow Chemical, and Rich continued to live in Pittsburgh, where he had capitalized on a favor he had done for a rabid Steelers fan to establish another business. Neither Steve nor Rich was yet making as much money as he had while playing professional football, but their real estate venture was giving them a way to earn extra income and begin building up some equity, which they used to buy more apartments.

Rich also appreciated the valuable hands-on experience he was obtaining. He found real estate a great fit for him, and looked forward to doing more of his own projects.

John Dewberry: From Finance to Development

Our second football player took a very different approach. John was a two-time Atlantic Coast Conference star quarterback and academic All-American at Georgia Tech. He was also ambitious. He knew that one day he wanted to run his own business. While pursuing an industrial management degree, he took most of his electives at Georgia Tech's school of architecture, focusing on courses in design and construction management. Based on that exposure, he knew that real estate was the field for him. He was turned on by the idea of developing buildings in an urban environment.

Name: John Dewberry

Place: Atlanta, Georgia

Point of entry: Development "gofer"; lender; mortgage broker

Initial project: Small shopping center

Type of project: New construction

Initial funding: Insurance company, contractor/partner

The Learning Curve

After college, he signed with a professional team in the Canadian Football League, but a torn hamstring cut short his football career, and John returned to Atlanta. Kim King, a former quarterback at Georgia Tech and then announcer of the team's games, offered him a gofer job in his small real estate development firm. For six months, John did everything from putting land under contract to taking Kim's car to get washed.

Kim advised him that if he wanted to become a developer, he should start by learning finance, which he could do by working at a bank. He would learn about a business that he knew very little about, but which provides an essential service to the industry. John got a job at a small savings and loan, where the CEO had graduated from Georgia Tech. Because the bank was limited in terms of the size of the loans they could make, John got involved in the "syndication" of loans over \$3 million.[2] This job put John in contact with Marine Midland Bank—a larger institution, with its headquarters in New York state—and ultimately landed him a sales job in Marine Midland's Atlanta office.

This job, too, proved a great learning experience. As a construction lender, John was exposed to all aspects of the development business, seeing a number of property types of various sizes. He also encountered a wide range of borrowers, with very different personalities and approaches. Some were very professional; others weren't. John found himself put off by some developers, who had a disorganized approach to projections and planning. He didn't see how they could keep all the moving parts of the projects in line without a game plan. Like football, John was coming to believe development was all about *attending to details,* and taking care of the little things.

Starting His Own Business

John's first year at Midland, 1988, was a good one, in part because the Atlanta area was experiencing the tail end of a boom. But by 1989, there was a severe pullback in the market. Despite the downturn, John thought that it was time for him to start his own company. At Marine Midland, he served as an intermediary: a mortgage broker between borrowers and lenders. He thought that with his good contacts, he could do the same on his own. All the borrower cared about was whether John could deliver the money. Even if he did less business, he would not have to split the fee. And while running his mortgage business, he could begin to look for his own first deal.

This was how Dewberry Capital, initially a mortgage brokerage company, was born. At the end of his football career, John had $5,000 in cash. Now, three years later, he had accumulated $50,000 by saving most of what he earned working at the S&L and Marine Midland. If worse came to worst, the $50,000 in the bank gave him two years of living expenses.

John began arranging mortgages, while looking for deals on his own. He focused on small, grocery-anchored retail centers. With no real cash equity to put into the deal and almost no experience, he had to find projects where he could get financing *based on the credit of his tenants*—a common tactic for many in real estate.

On one business trip to Charleston, South Carolina, to service a mortgage client, he met the division head of the BI-LO stores in the area. BI-LO was a subsidiary of the giant Dutch food conglomerate Royal Ahold. The manager was furious at the landlord of one of his stores, who stubbornly refused to replace a leaking roof. The frustrated manager told John to find him a new site. After John optioned what they agreed would be an acceptable site, Hurricane Hugo arrived and blew off the roof of the existing store, which resulted in the owner being able to get the insurance company to pay for a new roof. As the result of an act of God, the leaks got fixed, and John lost his deal.

Execution: Building on a Relationship

The division head liked John and offered him the chance to find a store site in an adjacent town. John discovered his lack of experience was proving an asset. Because of the downturn in the industry, most of his more established competitors were in trouble—owing money to the banks on their old deals, and unable to finance new ones.

John put together a 65,000-square-foot project, including a 30,000 square foot BI-LO. He signed up additional tenants, a drug store, hardware store, and clothing shop. Based on their credit and the projected cash flow, an Alabama-based insurance company offered John a $3.75 million loan on a $4 million cost. Normally the bank would have loaned $3.5 million, but they gave an extra $250,000, taking as security some adjacent land—"outparcels" that could be sold separately.

This still left John $250,000 short. He made a deal with his contractor, who put up the money personally as a side investment separate from his construction company. John would first pay him back his loan with interest, and then share 25 percent of any upside with his investor. John also believed that having the contractor as a partner would result in better cost control and less difficulty in sticking to schedules.

The first deal, happily, was a winner. In a couple of years, John was able to refinance the mortgage and repay his investor with the proceeds. John's persistence had paid off, and he could now give up his mortgage brokerage business and focus full time on real estate development. He also found that although he came from a financial background and was skillful at funding his projects, his real kicks came from putting together and creating a physical project. He was excited and ready to do and learn more.

The Cardons: Finding Extra Value in the Land

The Cardon family in Phoenix provides us with an interesting example of a family business—one that we carry through three generations in this book. There are 6 siblings in the second generation, and 39 first cousins in the third.

Name: Cardon family

Place: Phoenix, Arizona

Point of entry: Family gas-station chain

Initial project: Gas-station "plus"

Type of project: New construction, land speculation

Initial funding: Self-funded

No, this isn't a typical family. But the Cardons' experiences highlight many of the issues particular to managing family businesses. We can also see how each generation added value—going from simply operating gas stations to becoming players in the booming Phoenix real estate market.

Pat Cardon, representing the first generation in our story, was born in Mexico, but moved in 1912 at an early age to Arizona with his large Mormon family. (Upon arriving in Arizona, the family lived in a tent with a dirt floor.) Pat, the second oldest of the family's 10 children, started working at age 12 in a local dairy. Eventually, the 10 siblings devised a plan to get themselves out of poverty, which involved putting every Cardon through college. The oldest would go first, with the rest working to pay for his tuition and books. The others would follow in turn, with the graduates increasingly picking up the costs. The result: All the Cardons earned Bachelor's degrees, and five earned advanced degrees.

During the Great Depression of the 1930s, Pat worked at a gas station while attending law school. He soon became the lessee of the station. Not particularly excited about practicing law—even though he passed the bar—he became a gasoline distributor for Shell Oil. He then began building full-service gas stations for his own account. He convinced sellers to finance most of the purchase price of the land by taking back notes. His three sons helped with the construction and running of the stations from the time they were teenagers. A strong work ethic was part of their life.

It was Wilford, the oldest of Pat's six children, who ultimately got the family into the real estate business. Wilford was attending law school in Washington, D.C. in the mid 1960s when he got a call from his father. His father said, "I have an offer to sell the business. Either you come home and run it, or I'm going to sell it."

Wilford returned home and worked with his father and brother Elijah for four years, until his father suffered a fatal heart attack. Wilford then succeeded him as leader of the family business. Earlier he had encouraged his father to buy larger parcels than they absolutely needed to build a gas station on a particular site. He reasoned that because these stations were often located at well-traveled intersections, the extra land could eventually be sold off later to developers for other uses.

Shortly after he started working with his father, for example, Wilford convinced him to purchase a 20-acre corner parcel for $200,000, put the gas station on one acre in the front, and stockpile the remaining land. Three years later, they sold that back acreage for $1 million, while retaining ownership of the station in front. Wilford had proved his point. The family was now in the real estate business.

Making Their Own Luck

Family businesses abound in the real estate world, for a number of good reasons. Real estate companies are often started by entrepreneurs, who in many cases can name their successor. Ownership of assets can be divided to benefit younger family members disproportionately, to pass assets on to future generations—and when the relationships work out right, the psychic benefits, too, can be enormous. (In Part IV, "Taking Stock," we look at families in business together in some depth.)

Although Phoenix then was by no means the size it is today, its growth rate was rapid. There also was a frontier mentality, which made it easier for people to be upwardly mobile. Like so many of our protagonists, the Cardons had the good fortune to be in the right place at the right time.

The Cardons also made their own luck. Because they were retailers, they could leverage the purchase of land on strategic corners for gas stations to buy excess land cheaply. Although the back land was unlikely to have value for years, the income from the gas station allowed them to borrow virtually all the money they needed. Having an interim income-producing use for the land while it appreciated was a real plus. Whether your use is as a gas station, a parking lot, a trailer park, or a warehouse—or some combination—depends on the site, its location, and its market.

The Cardons got into the real estate business in an unusual but logical way, playing off both their strength as a retailer and the values they inherited from their father. Hard work, ambition, vision, and a commitment to family and religious values helped them travel a long way from that tent in the desert.

Endnotes

[1] In a condominium, you buy the physical unit directly, and can place your own mortgage on your unit. Your unit has its own real estate tax bill that you pay directly. In a cooperative, you own shares in the overall property, which has a master mortgage and tax assessment for which all the shareholders are responsible. A default by one has to be made up by the others to avoid foreclosure. As a result, most newer buildings have been built as condominiums rather than cooperatives.

[2] Syndication, in our context, simply means a group of investors joining together to buy or make a loan on one or a group of properties. The syndicator facilitates this process for fees based on a percentage of the equity raised, the management of the property, and/or the success of the venture.

3

Moguls in the Making

In this chapter, our stories have protagonists who are more recognizable to those in the industry. In later stages of their careers—as you'll see in subsequent chapters—these players grow at a faster rate than those in Chapter 2, "Finding a Focus." But remember, at this stage, their careers were just beginning. They had not achieved legendary status—and there was no guarantee that they would!

Hersha and Hasu Shah: The Immigrants' Dream

Our next story concerns the Shahs, who started and still head up a successful hotel company that owns dozens of small to medium-sized motels in the eastern part of the United States. Their story is one that we examine at various points in this book. As we look at their entry into this business, keep an eye out for the values and skills that led to their early success.

Name: Hasu and Hersha Shah

Place: Harrisburg, Pennsylvania

Point of entry: Personal drive

Initial project: Small motel

Type of project: Rehab

Initial funding: Equity from earlier house deals, bank loan

Hasu Shah came to this country from India to finish a college degree in chemical engineering—first at New Mexico State, and then, when New Mexico raised its tuition, at a small college in Tennessee. After graduation, he went back to Bombay (today's Mumbai) to marry his childhood sweetheart, Hersha, when he heard that her parents were pushing her, at age 18, into an arranged marriage. Neither Hasu nor Hersha wanted that to happen.

After their marriage, they relocated to Trenton, New Jersey where Hasu had a job with the New Jersey State Police as a chemist in their State Bureau of Identification. Hersha—with two years of college in general science and microbiology—was able to get a job there, too. She did blood tests in a laboratory for rape and alcohol cases: a far cry from her sheltered life in an upper-middle-class family back home.

The Learning Curve

After a year in Trenton, Hasu transferred to a job in Harrisburg, Pennsylvania, to work in the State Department of Environmental Resources, a position that called upon his engineering background. He worked there for ten years, while at the same time accumulating single-family houses at foreclosure sales.

With minimum cash down and a willingness to manage the houses, he rented the houses out, and slowly built up equity. He finally reached his goal of accumulating $50,000 in equity, an amount he believed would be adequate to enable him to move his family back to Bombay, buy a business and an apartment there, and still have some money left over for a savings account.

But he was in for a surprise. After liquidating his housing portfolio and making the long-planned move back to India, he found that he and his family had become more Americanized than he realized—and that economic opportunities were better in the United States. He returned to the United States and was able to get his job back in Harrisburg.

Execution: A Hands-On Experience

The good news was that most of his $50,000 was still intact. He decided that he had enough capital to enter the motel business, which was (and still is) a traditional industry for entrepreneurs from India. He soon discovered, however, that his capital didn't take him very far. He finally found a motel he could afford: an 11-room property that was cheap for several unhappy reasons. It was close to Three Mile Island (site of the notorious near-meltdown of a nuclear plant), it backed up on a cemetery, and it was falling apart.

Hasu and Hersha decided—she with some hesitation—that she could manage the motel while he held on to his day job. By then, their two sons were in elementary school. They hired a young couple to run the place, and Hersha—who was there every day—was able to make a number of physical improvements to the motel. She also went around to various local companies to drum up business. They named it the Starlight Motel.

She came upon a truck-driving school in the area, and convinced the CEO to send his students there. Soon the Starlight was filled with truck drivers in training, and after six months, the Shahs were encouraged to add six more rooms. It wasn't a close call: They were then earning a 40 percent cash return on their investment. Before long, Hasu decided he was ready for a larger motel. He sold the Starlight, and bought one with 30 units—the Red Rose Motel—in the small farming community of Elizabethtown. This time they would live in and manage the motel themselves.

More Than "Location, Location, Location"

There were many reasons for the Shahs' initial success. Obviously, it wasn't "location, location, location"—the old real estate axiom. (Three Mile Island was *not* a good location, although there's something to be said for taking advantage of depressed property values.) They worked hard as a team. They had good people skills, and a customer orientation that stemmed from their Hindu tradition of hospitality. They added value through their ability to operate their properties more efficiently than other potential buyers. They lived frugally, reinvesting their earnings. They were persistent, shrugged off rejection, and were flexible enough to adapt to changes.

Walter Shorenstein: Building a Reputation

Walter Shorenstein learned the real estate business from the ground up. He was born and raised in Glen Cove, Long Island. After serving in World War II, Walter found himself on the West Coast, where he was offered a job as a junior salesman with Milton Meyer and Company, a commercial real estate brokerage located in downtown San Francisco.

Name: Walter Shorenstein

Place: San Francisco, California

Point of entry: Commercial real estate brokerage

Initial project: Office building

Type of project: Existing building

Initial funding: Seller, several bank loans

Walter didn't want to return to the East Coast, and he couldn't see himself in the corporate world. Instead, he chose to focus his energies on real estate—in part because it didn't require a lot of capital, and in part because he believed there was no limit to what an ambitious and energetic young man could accomplish. He was right: Over the next half century, he became one of the major figures in the commercial development of San Francisco. But this took time. He spent years as a leasing broker before becoming a principal in a major deal.

Combing a Market

In the postwar era, much of the real estate brokerage business in San Francisco was controlled by established old-line firms. Because many of these companies had been in business since the 1800s, they had close relationships with the city's property owners and biggest tenants. This longevity, however, eventually proved to be a shortcoming: The devastating depression of the 1930s had made them extremely conservative, and they were slow to recognize the extraordinary growth potential in their own backyards.

Knowing he would have to find new investors, Walter combed the potential market from all angles. He noticed that the automobile dealers were doing the most advertising in city newspapers, and surmised (correctly) that this meant they must be making money— money that they could profitably invest in real estate, with the right guidance. He also approached the industry from the supplier side, tracking down potential buyers who were selling product to builders.

As Walter saw it, the entire city of San Francisco, with all of its buildings—existing and prospective—was *his product.* He felt he had gotten the equivalent of an MBA in his military stint in the Quartermaster Corps, where he learned to improvise and organize. He didn't hesitate to ring doorbells when he found an interesting property, and more often than not, he was invited in to meet and speak with the occupants. He looked at the classified help wanted ads in the newspapers to see who was adding employees, and thus might need new space. In no time at all, Walter became one of the more productive brokers in his office, quickly working his way up to becoming Milton Meyer's partner.

But Walter didn't stop there; he also wanted to buy properties himself. His first sizeable ownership deal occurred some ten years into his career. (*As we will see in many of our stories, it takes time to build a reputation.*) Walter had been approached by an insurance company that was looking for rental space for its growing operations. Normally, the company would have used an established real estate firm, but Walter's wife knew the secretary to the president. She put in a good word for him, and he got the assignment.

Walter located a building that he thought would be right for the company, and set up a meeting with the owner. The owner wasn't interested in a rental deal; instead, he wanted to sell the property. Walter saw an opportunity for himself. The two agreed on a purchase price, and the papers were drawn up with 120 days to close. A few weeks later, Walter was asked whether he would close earlier. After doing a little digging, he discovered that the seller had a buyer who would pay more, but who wouldn't wait the full 120 days.

Meanwhile, Walter's prospective tenant had decided the building wouldn't be a good fit for them. So, Walter went directly to the owner of the building and told him he knew about the higher offer. But rather than sell his agreement at a profit, he would relinquish his rights to the property. As a relative newcomer to the city, Walter believed it was important to maintain high ethical standards. He wouldn't risk damaging his reputation for one commission. He asked only that he be considered when the next deal came along.

Doing It Walter's Way

His gamble paid off. Soon after this conversation, the owner of the property offered him the Merchant Exchange Building, on California Street off Montgomery—a prime location. The price was $3 million, with the owner agreeing to take back a $2 million mortgage. Walter paid a visit to Ben Swig, one of the newest, smartest, and most active players in the market. Ben thought he could have purchased the property at a lower cost several months earlier, but Walter—convinced that the building was renting under market value—was able to persuade Ben that it was still a good deal.

Ben suggested a 50-50 partnership, in which each player would put up $500,000. Walter would put in his commission, and Ben would lend him the balance. Although flattered, Walter wasn't interested in being subordinate on the management of the property. If he was to be an owner, he wanted this to be *his* deal. So, he went to a banker with whom he had an established relationship, explained the situation, and asked him to loan him his share.

"Don't worry," he told his banker friend. "If Ben Swig thinks it's worth the price, it's worth the price." The banker agreed, but was required by institutional policies to cap the loan at $250,000.

Walter's glass was half full. Making his way up Montgomery Street past a cluster of banking institutions, he ran into the chairman of another bank. He casually mentioned the deal, with an emphasis on Ben's interest, and that of the "astute" lender who was lending him $250,000. The second banker agreed to loan the rest, and the deal was done.

No Longer "Just a Broker"

With the deal closed, Walter had attained a new level in San Francisco's real estate scene. He had accomplished this through a combination of patience, perseverance, reputation building, and—most important—relationships. Ben Swig's involvement gave Walter the credibility to finance his share of the equity.

As a footnote to our story, Walter's first ownership deal continued to pay dividends: Soon after taking possession of the building, Walter increased the rents to create a $500,000 operating income on the $3 million investment. Because of his access to information on the market, he had been able to anticipate that he could add value. After a year or two, he convinced Equitable Life to give him a $3 million loan to pay back all the existing loans. Walter was no longer perceived as "just a broker."

It is worth noting that if Walter had been wrong in his judgment, he would have been on the hook to the banks for his $500,000. He was most definitely leveraged. When we're just starting out, however, we often worry a lot less about the risk of betting the ranch.

The Bucksbaums: Retailers Becoming Developers

You may have noticed that our stories are getting a little more complex, and are starting to hint at bigger things. So let's make the leap to a company that has become orders of magnitude larger than those we've looked at so far.

Name: The Bucksbaum family

Place: Cedar Rapids, Iowa

Point of entry: The family grocery business

Initial project: Small retail center

Type of project: New construction

Initial funding: Insurance company loan based on tenant credit, family equity

General Growth Properties is now a public Real Estate Investment Trust (REIT). The company is the second-largest owner of regional shopping malls in the United States.

It was founded by the Bucksbaum brothers of Iowa. Originally, they had no intention of getting into the mall business—in fact, far from it. They backed into being real estate developers as a result of their efforts to expand the small grocery store that was started by their father. Their entry illustrates another way of getting into real estate: They capitalized on their own grocery store tenancy as a catalyst for development and for attracting other retail tenants.

But their story also points out, as many of our other stories do, that real estate—especially the development side—is a *distinct business*, requiring special skills and experiences. It's different from the grocery store trade (and everything else). So, using your grocery store as a way to add value is only the starting point.

The brothers joined the grocery business full time after completing their World War II service. It was not easy for this small store to compete with chains such as A&P, which had enormous purchasing power. Because they couldn't compete on price, they stayed open six and a half days per week and offered free delivery. Thriving against the odds, the brothers opened two additional small grocery stores in Eldora and Vinton—Iowa farming communities of about 10,000 people each.

Learning on the Job

Their first major expansion came with the opportunity to be the supermarket anchor in a new 150,000-square-foot shopping center on a 17-acre site in Cedar Rapids, which a developer from California was putting together. When the developer couldn't finance the project, he offered to sell it to the brothers. They knew nothing about the shopping center business, but because they wanted the site for their store, they agreed to go ahead with the deal.

Martin, the eldest brother, went to Chicago to figure out their next move. They found an experienced architect, who explained the steps they needed to take. He would first prepare a design. Then they would get leases from national chains, which would enable them to secure financing.

Problem number 1: No one would give a loan on a center anchored by such a small local grocery chain. As a result, they were forced to associate their stores with a larger group—Nash-Finck in Minneapolis—which ran a chain called Sun Marts. Ultimately, their reluctant father went along. With the Sun Marts name behind them, they were able to get leases from national chains, and a $1 million mortgage commitment from Mass Mutual.

Problem number 2: The architect had overdesigned the project, putting basements under the whole center, and an extra level of office space above some of the stores. The costs came in at $1.3 million, requiring $300,000 in cash that the brothers did not have. They scrambled, hocked everything, did some redesign, moved Matthew to Cedar Rapids to oversee the contractor, and finally managed to get the center opened.

Problem number 3: The center, which still had some space vacant, was not profitable. The brothers decided to open a toy store in one of the spaces, buying from vendors who would sell to them on consignment. With a rent based on a percentage of sales and no upfront cost for inventory, they greatly minimized their need for cash. The middle brother, Maurice, was installed to run the operation. He was so successful that they soon began to open other toy stores. Their background as retailers gave them another leg up.

Managing Both Sides of the Balance Sheet

As Matthew later commented, the brothers were able to look back many years after the fact and laugh at all the mistakes they made. But at the time, these were no laughing matters. Their inexperience and naiveté worked against their economic survival. Still, their hard work, resourcefulness, and willingness to take risks served as a firm foundation.

Their prime motivation was to build what to them was an exciting new venture: a shopping center. They would not have been successful, however, if they had not been able to redesign the center, thereby reducing their overall cost to fit the limited financing available to them. They were able to manage both sides of their balance sheet.

The Bucksbaums' story also tells us how important *family* can be when you're starting out. We often hear horror stories about family businesses in which vengeful family members destroy one another, but it doesn't have to be that way. Who better to involve and trust than siblings—especially at the outset of an enterprise, when there isn't much to fight over? Besides, at this stage, siblings often come cheap. It is later, when there may be differences as to who is adding what value to the enterprise, that quarrels may become more heated.

Starting at the Bottom in Texas: Trammell Crow and Gerry Hines

Trammell Crow and Gerald Hines eventually ran two of the largest real estate development companies in the United States. They served as examples of companies that tried to do business the *right* way: caring for their tenants, their employees, and their communities. Curiously, although both were headquartered in Texas—Crow in Dallas and Hines in Houston—they personally never met or did business together.

Names: Trammell Crow, Gerald Hines

Places: Dallas and Houston, Texas

Points of entry: Accounting and banking (Crow); mechanical engineering (Hines)

Initial projects: Warehouses

Type of project: New construction

Initial funding: Bank financing based on pre-leasing

Why Warehouses?

Although their backgrounds and approaches to real estate differed, they both started by building small warehouses. Why was this? For many people, warehouses are a good place to start. They are a pretty simple form of construction. The land doesn't have to be in a prime location, although it must be near good transportation. Because warehouses have relatively few employees, they don't require much in the way of parking, and therefore aren't as land intensive. Ongoing property management is simpler because the landlord doesn't have to provide much in the way of services. Because the time required to construct a new warehouse is only three to six months, there is rarely much overbuilding in a market. Little speculative space is built, and—given the short-term construction process—shortages don't last long. This translates to better control over supply and demand, which means that rents are reasonably stable.

On the flip side, the lower level of risk results in less upside, as purchase prices rarely rise over reproduction cost.

Trammell Crow: The Learning Curve

How did Trammell Crow get into this business? Because he had taken some accounting courses, he got a job in a bank, starting as a runner. He took evening classes in auditing—at the bank's expense—at the American Institute of Banking. At the age of 24, five years after starting with the bank, he finally earned his CPA. His subsequent experiences in the military as an auditor further expanded his financial scope.

After completing his military tour of duty, he decided to join his late father-in-law's grain business, Doggett Grain. While there, he got experience helping to design and build a grain elevator. He also took responsibility for trying to lease some vacant space in the Doggett Building, which their firm owned and where they had an office. He signed leases with some floor-covering companies based on improvements he proposed to make to the building.

He found that he was good at the leasing and people aspects of the business and that he enjoyed those activities. This encouraged him, while he was still at Doggett, to try some side deals on his own. Although he had never built a warehouse building before, he thought it would be a good way to start.

The Magic of Pre-Leasing

Ray-O-Vac, one of the tenants in the Doggett Building, needed more space than was then available. Crow convinced them to let him build and lease to them a warehouse building that would meet their needs. Given his accounting background, before starting, he ran numerous projections covering a multitude of scenarios. He worked up estimates with the contractors who had done the work in the Doggett Building for him. He also developed a relationship with John Stemmons, who controlled vast acreage zoned for industrial use in the desirable Trinity Industrial District. He was able to secure a 99-year lease on the land he needed, which reduced the amount of up-front cash required. Feeling optimistic, he decided to build 4,500 square feet of extra or "speculative" space, on the assumption that he could find a tenant.

When this 11,250-square-foot building was leased, he was able to arrange financing to cover virtually all of his costs. As with most people starting out, his ability to obtain a mortgage was dependent on the valuation a lender would put on his particular project—a valuation dependent on the cash flow of the property. If he waited to build until *after* he had signed up a tenant, he could obtain his financing based on a retail valuation of the property.

Contrary to the common practice at the time, he wrote short-term leases, figuring that upon renewal, he could charge higher rents. With that expectation, he initially charged slightly below-market rents and was able to fill up the building quickly.

With Texas (and Dallas, in particular) on a growth binge, Crow was rewarded for his optimism. Dallas—blessed with a good rail and road system—became a central distribution hub for its region. Trammell had developed a model for success that he was soon able to replicate.

Gerald Hines: From Mechanical Engineering to Development

Gerald Hines's background was substantially different. He grew up in Gary, Indiana, during the Depression. In college at Purdue University, Gerry studied mechanical engineering. After graduation, one month in a local engineering lab convinced him that he needed a job with more people contact. He relocated to Houston, mainly because several of his fraternity brothers were also moving there. Landing where the growth was about to be was luck rather than foresight.

But Gerry made his own luck, too. He landed a job with one of Houston's first mechanical engineering consulting firms, and made his way up through the ranks, first becoming a junior partner, then a senior partner. The emerging technology of air conditioning, combined with Houston's hot and humid climate, served as major catalysts to the firm's growth.

Learning While Doing

On the side, Hines found himself bitten by the real estate bug. He liked designing and constructing buildings. His next-door neighbor needed a 5,000-square-foot warehouse, and Hines set out to provide it for him. Even then, his interest in design led him to give this building more architectural detailing than the typical warehouse. He worried about things that many developers did not: the quality of the brickwork, for example, and the placing of the fascia so that sunlight would reflect properly off the structure.

Like Trammell Crow, he found a builder who would both work with him and educate him at the same time. A mortgage broker taught him about appraisal and loan evaluation, and how to maximize the loan and minimize the need for cash. As an engineer, he found the math needed to understand real estate finance fairly simple. The broker introduced him to a lender who financed not only his first project, but also many of his later buildings.

Also like Crow, Hines didn't try to charge the highest rents. He believed that if you could demonstrate that you had the best interest of the tenant at heart and also provide outstanding service, you could build a reputation for fair dealing and integrity. He was right. He was able to pre-lease and construct a number of similar—but even-larger—structures over the next five years.

Starting Small

Both Crow and Hines understood the importance of a number of activities and attitudes, including the following:

- Pre-leasing
- Paying attention to detail
- Finding mentors
- Having the patience needed to learn the business, and
- Having the willingness to *start small*, building your equity and your reputation over a period of years

It's important to note that although they controlled and substantially owned their early projects, they *didn't give up their day jobs.* They were able to do real estate on the side until they had the equity, the contacts, and experience to go out on their own full time. They also were fortunate to be starting at a time when lenders were willing to back new entrants to the field and provide most of the capital they needed.

All of our stories in this chapter and in Chapter 2 show many of these characteristics. In each case, the protagonists found ways to use their training to add value to an initial project that got them started. Next, you'll see the steps they took to *scale up* their businesses.

Part II

Scaling Up

As I emphasized in Part I "Starting Out," you can get started in real estate in a multitude of ways. The same is true of the next phase of your real estate career, which I call *scaling up*—the process by which you take on new projects and build a business.

In this part of the book, I again start by discussing the main issues you have to face as you decide whether and how to scale up your operations. Then, in two separate chapters, I continue the stories of our protagonists as they go on to the next stage in their careers. Those in the first of these two chapters look opportunistically for projects where they can add value. Those in the second chapter focus, in addition, on developing a sustainable business.

4

Five Good Questions

It is exciting to scale up—to build a viable business from scratch, making something out of nothing.

It is also a time of great uncertainty. For most entrepreneurs, both in and out of real estate, it is the period we remember best for the rest of our lives. It's a time of taking chances, forging new relationships, and testing ourselves. It is nerve-wracking and exhilarating. The path is rarely one laid out in advance. Our decisions tend to be incremental, based on the opportunities that are presented to us. With little to lose, we bet the store.

One way to think about the scaling-up challenge is to consider the following five questions, which pertain to most real estate players:

- Do you *want* to scale up?
- How do you scale up?
- What kind of organization should you build?
- Where do you get the money?
- What kind of investor are you?

Do You *Want* to Scale Up?

If your first deal was a winner, why not try another?

There are lots of reasons why you might not stay in, or get back in. You may be like Pete and Sara in Chapter 2, "Finding a Focus"—the couple whose goal was to own a home rather than to be in real estate as a business. You might have a job unrelated to real estate that requires extensive travel or other commitments, leaving you little time for outside investments. You may lack the money to do another deal, or you might need what money you *do* have for other purposes. You may have found that your last project took too much time or effort. Maybe you didn't much relish the risks you were incurring. Maybe you feel that the market is no longer as favorable for doing what you did before.

Most of our protagonists made it successfully through their first deal, got the bug, and wanted more. They played off their training as project managers, rental brokers, engineers, retailers, mortgage brokers, or accountants. Many still hedged their bets by keeping their day jobs. They did deals on the side for years, until they felt they had accumulated adequate assets or fee income to set up their own shop. For some, "adequate assets" meant one or two small shopping centers; for others, it meant bigger motels; for still others, it meant owning not just one but a number of warehouses.

What they all had in common were many of the traits that we talked about in previous chapters: vision, persistence, good work and people skills, an optimism about what the future might bring, and a degree of confidence in their ability to surmount whatever obstacles were put in their way. They were opportunistic.

How Do You Scale Up?

Here are five primary approaches to consider:

- Sizing up
- Increasing the number of projects
- Taking on other property types
- Growing geographically
- Expanding the functions you perform

You might take one of these routes, or multiple routes. Let's examine each in turn.

Sizing Up

Have you ever wondered why so many New York City property owners are so wealthy? One simple answer is that *their buildings are bigger,* reflecting the larger market size.

For most of us, size is relative. Remember how, when you were 10 years old, the 11-year-olds looked mighty tall? Size is relative. For me, it was a *big deal* to build a 68,000-square-foot office building on a site that previously was occupied by a 15,000-square-foot structure— more than four times as big!

It is certainly tempting to have visions of larger sugarplums dancing in your head. But, with increased size comes increased risk. *You can do five or six smaller projects successfully, and then a single large failure can destroy you.*

Certainly, there are advantages to size. A larger building attracts more attention in the marketplace. It can offer more services and amenities. You have more flexibility in subdividing space to accommodate the needs of specific tenants. With more diversity of tenants, you are less vulnerable to the loss of one. You might be able to spread the cost of replacing a roof or boiler over more square footage. The project may be large enough to justify its own on-site management, allowing you to better monitor your investment. It often justifies spending more of your own time on the project. Assuming the same rent per square foot or per unit, simple mathematics tells you that there is greater potential profitability in the larger project.

The flip side is that you might not be able to perform as many functions yourself in the larger building. Its size or height, moreover, may require a more expensive style of construction, or require underground versus surface parking. When a building reaches a certain size, code requirements—such as for fire-suppression systems or handicapped accessibility—may kick in. You have to be careful to consider whether the market will allow you to charge rents adequate to cover the added costs. New construction may become uneconomical, compared with the price of purchasing existing buildings.

A larger project often takes longer to build, making you more susceptible to downturns in the market. Because the dollars are greater, you might have to rely more on money from others to fund your project initially, and perhaps again later if you have to deal with cost overruns or delays in leasing. Remember that the worst time to be out raising money is when times are bad and the sharks are circling.

Up until now, we have been looking at "size" in terms of an individual building. Size can also be defined by other aspects. You could build an industrial park with multiple sites for buildings, each of which could be developed individually. A residential project might involve a series of townhouses or lower-rise structures built in phases. A small shopping center anchored by a grocery store is a far cry from a regional mall with multiple anchors, common courts, and hundreds of specialty shops. Parking can be on-grade or in multilevel garages.

The more complex the project—the more difficult it is to execute, finance, and manage—the more experience you need, the more of an organization you have to build. You have to weigh the advantages of size against the inherent risks in scaling up (risks that could lead to losing control of your project, or losing it altogether).

Increasing the Number of Projects

It is important to distinguish between the *size* and the *number* of projects that you are undertaking. Most projects are owned in separate legal entities, often with different sets of partners, with mortgage financing that is secured by that specific property. That's both the good news and the bad news. Each of these entities must be operated independently, no matter what the size of the project. You cannot use one project to benefit another. You have fiduciary obligations to each set of partners.

The risk level of the project also makes a difference. It may be easier to handle a number of fully rented apartment buildings than one that is vacant and requires substantial rehabilitation. A large developer I know limited the amount of new square footage he would build at any time to a percentage of the size of his overall portfolio, which included many completed projects. I don't know whether he was disciplined enough to stick to his plan, but it's certainly useful to have a broader context within which you try to make your major decisions.

Time also governs the number of projects you can take on. There are only so many places you can be at one time, and there are only so many crises you can handle at once.

Taking On Other Product Types

In Part I, "Starting Out," we saw our protagonists find many niches where they could add value: small apartment buildings, basic warehouses, grocery-anchored shopping centers, small motels, and so on.

As they grow, many are tempted to expand into new product types. They view the real estate industry as one in which their skills are transferable. The process for acquiring and developing properties is similar enough that they believe they can play in multiple arenas.

But sooner or later, almost everybody runs up against limits on their ability to handle other product types. Sometimes, it is a matter of capital availability. As we saw in Part I, a warehouse pre-leased to a single tenant or a grocery-anchored shopping center may be easier to finance than a residential complex with no up-front tenants and leases that rarely extend for more than a year. Undeveloped land requiring a zoning change will require an even higher percentage of equity capital. Because most of us are short of capital starting out, that can be an important factor.

Don't underestimate the operating skills that may be required to run a business at a particular location. If your tenant leaves, it might not be easy to find a replacement who will succeed at that location.

In determining how much and what you can take on, the stage where a project is at the moment is important. Obviously, the further along the project is in the process, and the more stable its cash flow, the less risk it presents.

Multiuse projects that involve—for example—a hotel, an office building, apartments, and some retail may maximize the use of a site. Each of these uses, however, may require separate financing. Lenders are often leery of properties where the cash flows for the different uses are interdependent. It is more difficult to predict outcomes and to determine how much can be safely loaned.

Joint venturing with others who have skills in that area is an option, but has its problems if you and your partner turn out to be incompatible. It is difficult to anticipate all the problems that might arise, but a carefully crafted joint venture agreement can help you articulate and deal with many of these issues.

Growing Geographically

Location, location, location! This is probably the first rule of thumb you ever heard put forward as the key variable in determining the value of a property. To a certain extent, it is valid—but you should also recognize that locations do not always hold their value. You have to look not only at the characteristics of a specific site, but also at its underlying market. We saw that in condominiums in Houston after an oil crisis, in research space in Silicon Valley after the dotcom bubble burst, and in numerous community shopping centers throughout the United States after Wal-Mart entered their market.

There is much you cannot control. It is easy to get lost when you start wandering far from home. I have a distinct advantage when it comes to keeping my buildings in Harvard Square occupied: I know most of the potential players. But I'd have no such advantage a couple of miles down the Charles River, in the faster-growing Kendall Square area, which is dominated by a different world-class university (MIT) and an entirely different cast of characters and building types.

I found this out many years ago, to my dismay, when I made land purchases on Moriches Bay in Long Island and the Reston area of Virginia. In neither case did I have the right contacts to get the necessary zoning changes—something that the broker in both cases had told me would be a cinch. And how could I know that the river bottom alongside the Moriches Bay land was covered by several feet of manure, left over from an abandoned duck farm on the other side of the river?

Of course, developers *have* expanded profitably to other locales. Diversification of your assets geographically is often prudent. There may be limited opportunities in your hometown. There might be room for only one mall, or a small number of motels. If you do find reasons to go farther in a field, remember that there are ways to minimize the risk. For example, *go where your existing tenants want to go.* Many retailers are anxious to expand geographically. They often have done detailed market research to see where they want to locate. Most prefer to do business with experienced developers who know what the retailers want; know how to size, design, and construct their centers; and have the financial resources to complete the projects. National retailers do not want their expansion plans thwarted—or even slowed down—by developers who can't deliver. Maybe you have a relationship with a financial institution or corporation that is expanding geographically, where its tenancy can anchor a new office building you lease to them. If so, take full advantage of that relationship.

Another approach is to capitalize on any particular operating skills you may have. Motels, self-storage facilities, and parking garages are examples of product types where knowing how to run the business is as important as local knowledge.

You also may expand geographically to areas where you can take advantage of close relationships you have there. No matter what your reason for geographic expansion, it is crucial to have good local partners who understand the permitting, construction, and leasing patterns in that market. The more foreign that market is to you, the more it is important to involve others. Take your time in picking your partners. I know of one case where a so-called reputable local partner moved many of the "shared" tenants he had with his partner to a building he was constructing by himself. Too often, people take the first recommendation of someone they know without investigating other options. There is nothing wrong with interviewing several—and besides, you can't help but learn more from their comments about the market, as well as about your particular deal. Here, as always, *checking references* is important.

Last but not least, travel time and distance are important. After I got my driver's license, I used to drive an older cousin to his various construction sites, always within a two- or three-hour drive from Boston. He had me pick him up at ungodly early hours. It was not until I was older that I realized that there was method to my torment: He wanted to arrive at his site before his construction supervisors got there. It was amazing how early they showed up!

Very few of us have private jets, or even drivers willing to pick us up at 5 A.M. We have to balance what we can take on with our ability to be available to handle the crises that come up in development projects. We can handle only so many from afar. That's one of the reasons I concentrated on doing projects in the Boston region. Even though I taught there three days a week, I could always find time to meet at the site any day that it was necessary.

On the other hand, telecommunications have shrunk the world, and the advent of the airplane and high-speed trains has expanded where we can be involved. Just remember, however, distance remains a factor. Phone lines go dead. Airlines drop scheduled flights, and bad weather happens. Don't spread yourself too thin!

In short, there are advantages and disadvantages both to geographic concentration and diversification. It is up to you to achieve the right balance for yourself.

Expanding the Functions You Perform

To be successful in real estate involves more than just having a vision of what can be done to add value to a property. It also involves *execution.* It involves assembling the resources and managing the many disciplines required to make your vision a reality. It involves, for example, land acquisition, design, approvals, financing, land development, construction, marketing, leasing, operations, and management. As a rule, *the more functions you perform, the more opportunity you have to add value or charge fees.*

Starting out, you might have the time to do more yourself, if you have the necessary skill sets. If you don't have both time and skills, it's better to outsource. In many cases, the value of the learning experience is outweighed by its cost.

As you scale up, you and your organization might take on more functions and be active in more steps of the process to protect your vision, control the design, speed the approval process, and ensure smooth (major) lease negotiations. You might also want to try to move the job forward at a faster pace.

Some people choose to get more involved for financial reasons. They hope to either reduce the costs of paying outsiders or to justify fees for themselves for performing construction supervision, placing the financing, finding tenants, or doing property or asset management.

Others look to fee income to cover the cost of adding personnel. They hope to expand their ability to scale up. They may believe they can attract potential tenants, lenders, and financial partners if they have more in-house capabilities. Be careful, however, that hiring a number of ambitious young people anxious to do deals doesn't affect your decision-making process. You don't want to be pushed into unprofitable projects just to satisfy their needs. This is also true for your outside brokers, suppliers, lenders, and investors, who likewise are apt to encourage you to do deals so that they can be part of the action.

What Kind of Organization Should You Build?

The stories of our protagonists in this book are separated into two chapters. The first focuses on players in the field who stay relatively small, while the second is about those whose businesses grow substantially larger. It's not obvious why people end up in one group rather than the other. Both groups include people who are successful and others who are not so successful. Few start out with a clear vision of where they expect to end up. It's safe to say, though, that multiple factors are at work: personality, opportunity, timing, luck, and inclination.

It is up to you to decide where you want to go with your business. What personnel are needed? What will be your role, and how does it fit you personally?

The vast majority of real estate firms not only start small, they *stay* small. The staff generally consists of an owner, a bookkeeper, a property manager, and perhaps a project manager hired on a temporary basis to carry out a specific development. The owner tends to be involved not only in major decisions, but also most minor ones.

If you do not know how many or what type of deals will be done in your shop in a given year, or who will have what responsibilities, *the fewer personnel commitments you make, the better.* Flexibility is key, especially if you are short on cash. As I said earlier, joint venturing— that is, finding partners appropriate for a specific deal, who have local knowledge or a specific skill—is very common. The trade-off, of course, is shared ownership and control.

If you do not have fee income to cover added staff, it comes out of your pocket. If your goal is to build your capabilities to access and carry out deals, however, you might have to bite the bullet. Good people may cost more, but they generally more than pay for themselves. Don't try to buy people on the cheap. Most have families to support, and cash today has to be their priority. Otherwise, they will not be happy campers for very long, and someone will steal them away.

Often individual entrepreneurs will hire a junior associate who is willing to trade cash for experience. The challenge is to find someone who is adaptable and who will be a quick learner, not just someone who will work for a pittance. The ability to recognize the potential in young people can be a real plus at all stages of your career.

There's no one right way to grow your organization as you scale up. Most entrepreneurs I speak to talk a good game about their willingness to delegate. (Almost everyone claims to be the exception to the rule that entrepreneurs are biologically incapable of delegation.) But successful delegation is not just letting go of the reins. It involves allocating time to hire great people, giving them good guidance, and then leaving them alone to do their jobs. It involves being optimistic enough to assume that others follow your lead, but also realistic enough to *follow up* on those people.

The bottom line is this: *Do you really care for people and how they grow?* If you only see them as a means to an end, or a way of serving your purposes, it won't work. Stay with the small organization. If you decide to accept partners, understand that they will want to be partners in more than name only. They will want to build their own name and reputation, as well as their personal balance sheet.

This can be a serious problem as you grow your organization, especially if you want to hire good people who are capable of taking on responsibility. Management of others is time-consuming, requiring more meetings and more willingness to understand the professional and personal needs of your associates. It is even more complicated if you open field offices in other cities. You will want to maintain control of acquisition, disposition, and financing decisions, but the rules about which other decisions need prior approval from you or your central office tend to get fuzzy. Talk it through in advance with those affected. Misunderstandings lead to not only bad decisions, but also to resentments that can tear apart organizations.

Over time, as your younger people develop, or as their relative value to your business increases, you may want and need to make adjustments to each person's percentage interest. On paper, this is easy to do if you rework the percentages on new deals, grandfathering interests in prior ones. But sitting down and explaining your decision to someone whose shares are being cut back is rarely easy. The reallocated shares may have to come from you—the founder—with or without help from your other senior officials. Transparency and good communication are crucial. The amount of the compensation is important, but people also want to feel they are being treated fairly.

Sharing ownership is complicated. To attract, motivate, and retain good people, you can give them shares in your management company (the entity that receives fees and promotional shares from all the ventures you undertake). Another option is to give equity shares, or lend them money to make investments in projects that they may work on. One potential problem in giving ownership interests is that the people whom you bring in at the time you start your company may not be the ones you need as your company grows or changes direction. *Times change. Retain flexibility.*

You also have to agree on what happens to the interest of someone who leaves or is fired. You likely do not want that person to continue as a shareholder in your company's new deals or those in process. In completed projects, there might be no compelling reason *not* to let the person continue as a limited partner. But, if you want the person out, you prefer it to be done quickly without litigation.

By establishing vesting periods and buyback arrangements, you can protect yourself somewhat, but such mechanisms have to be in place from the beginning. As an owner, be aware that how you handle such situations impacts how others will think about working with you.

From the other side of the fence, if you're an employee, you want to make sure that you don't lose what you have earned if you are let go without valid cause. Good attorneys can suggest workable options.

Where Do You Get the Money?

As you scale up, one of your key constraints is almost certain to be access to capital, both for debt and equity.

In your first deal, you tend to cobble together funds from friends, relatives, and your own savings. As the deals and associated cash requirements get larger—often with longer time frames and varying levels of risk—you most likely will have to expand your base of investors and find new avenues for raising money.

Most of us who finance our small-sized projects individually will continue to look for wealthier investors who can put up the sums we need to finance our expansion. Others with larger aspirations establish commingled funds that give them the freedom to move more quickly to acquire properties. Others go the public route, establishing Real Estate Investment Trusts (REITs).[1] Even if you are not large enough to take advantage of these options, be aware of them. You may find a new set of well-heeled competitors on your block with the resources to outbid you.

Aligning your priorities with those of your investors is important. If you, as the promoter, are rewarded for success only after your investors get their money back plus a preferred return, will your incentive be to sell more quickly? Are you/your investors willing to wait a long time to achieve your "payday"? If the goal is to hold the property for the longer term, how will you be compensated in the meantime? On the flip side, if your total compensation is based on your assets under management rather than profits, will you take advantage of timely sales or hold to collect your fees?

Refinancing is one way to return capital to investors earlier, and without immediate tax consequences. The downside for the promoter is that the added carrying charges may reduce the cash flow on which the promoter's share is calculated. It is a complicated but important subject, with no easy answer. Again, though, you should understand the variables. When raising capital, you also have to focus on the debt side. Up until now, we have been discussing raising equity. You have to decide how much leverage is available to you, and at what cost, as well as the level of risks you are willing to take at that particular time.

The overall state of the financial markets is crucial in this regard. With the globalization of markets, there is much more capital wanting to invest in real estate. Hedge funds, commingled funds, and REITs have been formed to accommodate institutional and foreign investors. Interest rates are relatively low. Lenders are making bigger loans, and due to increased competition are advancing higher percentages of value. Even more important, they are generous in their determinations of value—that is, the appraisals upon which they determine how much they will lend. For the same property, a 70 percent loan may be worth $700,000 to one lender, whereas the other may see it as $770,000, depending on whether the property is valued at $1 million or $1.1 million.

The increase in competition to acquire properties drives up prices. Those who have bet on a rising market have been winners in recent years, although the many sellers happy to bank the proceeds may prove to be the eventual winners as capitalization rates return to more normal levels.

Still, it is not just macroeconomics. If you upgrade your property with long-term leases from higher-quality tenants, your property becomes more financeable and valuable. Sometimes you can find corporations that want to liquify their assets, removing what may be an undervalued, illiquid asset on their balance sheet by selling and leasing it back to you. If the credit is good, lenders will often lend you virtually all your purchase price.

The lender in a development project sometimes may lend you the money you need for construction, allowing you to contribute the land at an appreciated value as your equity. This is more likely to occur if you have rezoned the land or pre-leased the property. Normally, however, lenders want you to have some of your own cash in the deal.

As a rule, the *purpose* of your investment should affect the amount of leverage you are willing to take. If your goal is to generate regular cash distributions to distribute to yourself or to your investors, you may want to reduce your leverage, giving you more cash flow to maintain your distributions in a downturn.

On the other hand, if you are short of cash starting out, you may want to borrow as much as possible to maximize your share of the enterprise. This is understandable, but can be risky, especially in development deals where your cash needs are less certain.

If leasing the property takes longer than you expect, or the rents come in below your projections, high financing costs may overwhelm you. If you need additional cash to cover unanticipated expenses, you might not want or be able to go back to your financial partners for more money. As I said earlier, if and when your existing or new investors think they have you over a barrel, they may suddenly demand onerous terms.

As you become successful and build your own (or your company's) balance sheet, you may be able to increase the amount lenders will give you if you guarantee their loan personally, or if you are willing to provide additional security in the form of liens on your other assets. It is easy to advise against doing this, but you might not have a choice. Some lenders require guarantees for at least a portion of the loan, especially during the construction period.

There is another risk you should be aware of. In recent years, lenders are especially wary of potential environmental violations for which some courts have ruled that the lenders might be liable. Lenders may want you to guarantee personally any such exposure. The cost of cleaning up a polluted site can be considerable, and the regulations governing what are considered "acceptable" levels of pollution have gotten stricter. You might consider taking out environmental liability insurance, which covers certain eventualities, albeit at a cost.

Government financing may be available, especially for projects that serve a public purpose. Some of these programs provide interest rate subsidies or other types of subsidies to bring down the cost of housing for lower- and moderate-income families. Loan guarantees from a public authority may allow the developer to borrow more, reducing the amount of equity required. In both cases, this enables otherwise uneconomical projects to be built for an underserved market.

Tax credits have been legislated to encourage the rehabilitation of historic properties, the construction of subsidized housing, and the concentration of commercial and industrial properties in certain urban areas.[2] Tax laws are also written to allow the deferral of capital gains taxes due upon what otherwise would be a sale through the trading of similar (or "like-kind") properties. Congress also sets depreciation schedules that affect the amount of noncash deductions you can take on an annual basis against the other income from your property.

Not all these policies work out as planned. At one point, lenient tax policies with accelerated depreciation schedules for newly constructed projects attracted investors to the field who had little interest in the cash flow from the property itself. Buildings were developed where there was no need, and the subsequent oversupply destroyed property values in many markets.

But this, in turn, created opportunities. Lenders who wound up with distressed properties often sold them at much discounted prices. For patient buyers who had cash, many fortunes were made.

In any case, *watch what is happening in Washington.* The government might actually be helping you; if so, you should know about it. Many real estate–related organizations and accounting firms publish newsletters that can help keep you up-to-date.

The bottom line is that we all know there are risks involved in leverage. On the other hand, the ability to leverage is one of the major benefits to being in real estate. Properly handled, it can be a major factor in creating real estate wealth. Without leverage, many of us would never have been able to scale up. We might still be waiting to do the next deal.

What Kind of Investor Are You?

Some people thrive on taking on new challenges, and taking risks. They are willing to bet on growth in their market, on rising prices, and on higher rents to justify their purchase. They feel the need to be part of the action—part of the *deal flow.*

Others aren't comfortable unless they are value investors, buying at 50 cents on the dollar. At different times, each of these approaches can work.

My preference is to take the value approach—in other words, to buy below replacement cost, where there are market dislocations, or where you have some other clear advantage. It may be difficult to predict the cycles, but if you have bought at the right price, you are bound to be more competitive in *all kinds of markets.*

The downside is that you must have patience and be willing at times to watch your more active peers get the headlines. Your goal should not be just the *accumulation* of assets, but the *keeping* of assets. Being a contrarian can have its benefits.

In conclusion, the possibilities are endless for scaling up. Your challenge is to *determine which approach makes you most comfortable.* How you spend your time and over what time frame are personal as well as business decisions.

Finally, don't fool yourself into thinking that you can change your personality and become a different person. (If you're like most humans, you can't.) Instead, focus on *picking the right path for you, and then hope you make the necessary adjustments as your world changes*—and make them on a timely basis, of course.

Now, back to our stories. Our protagonists all have taken different routes to scaling up. Over the following two chapters, pay attention to how they pick their path—and equally, whether and how they decide to change it.

Endnotes

[1] Shares of the REITs can be tradable on public exchanges, giving the investor liquidity. These public REITs often specialize in one area of real estate: office, residential, hotel, and so on. Some have a regional focus, some national. Some are small with an equity value of $100 million, whereas Equity Office Properties was recently sold at a valuation of almost $40 billion. The income from the REITs flows directly to investors without incurring an intermediary income tax.

[2] The amount of the tax credit that can be taken is determined by the specifics of the legislation. The credit is normally calculated as a percentage of allowable costs, and then amortized and taken over a period of years. Industrial corporations often buy these credits from a developer to use against their other tax obligations.

5

Good Moves

In this chapter and in Chapter 6, "Grand Visions," we look at the next stage of growth for five of our entrepreneurs. Although they all focus on different areas of real estate, they scale up opportunistically taking advantage of projects where they can add value. In expanding, they all face problems of finding new sources of financing and deciding the size and type of organization that best suits their business and their personal style. They worry about how to control what have become more complex operations with new sets of partners.

Susan Hewitt: A Business of Her Own

Susan Hewitt's ten-year apprenticeship with the residential converters in Manhattan was coming to an end. Given the weak local economy, there were few new deals in the small firm's pipeline. Susan, meanwhile, had recently made a good profit buying and selling a cooperative unit she had purchased at auction. For these reasons and others, she thought it was time to move on.

Name: Susan Hewitt

Start-up location: New York City

Scale-up location: New York City

Type of project: Acquire and work out defaulted co-op mortgages

Type of scale up: Size, number of projects

Funding: Capital from two wealthy families, and later, a hedge fund

Organization: Sole practitioner (with backstopping from the family offices)

She put the word out that she was looking for a new job. Through a business school contact, she met the chief investment officer of a family holding company. Real estate was one of the industries where they had made investments. He asked her where she saw opportunities.

She told him about her experiences in buying and selling unsold or foreclosed cooperative units. She talked about the difficulty in determining whether the other cooperative owners—or in many cases, the sponsors who held the unsold units—could meet their obligations.

She explained that she had become convinced that the key to success in such cases was getting to the institutions, primarily the Resolution Trust Company (RTC), that controlled the underlying mortgage. She thought they would accept discounts to get out of what were, in most cases, nonperforming loans. If so, as part of the deal, she thought she could pick up some of the unsold units of the sponsors at favorable prices. She had faith in the scheme, she said, but because she didn't have the cash to do it herself, she was looking to work for someone else.

You don't need a new job, her interviewer told her. *You've had ten years of experience. You should run your own business.*

This caught Susan's attention. The investment officer went on to say that his group might put up half the $5 million he thought she needed, if she could find someone to put up the other half.

Making It Happen

The plan greatly appealed to Susan's entrepreneurial instincts, and she set out to try to make it happen. Not long after, she had a productive conversation with the representatives of another family office—run by someone she knew—who said they might put up the rest of the money she needed. First, however, she had to meet the successful and well-regarded patriarchs of each of these families, and eventually, the two patriarchs had to meet each other. Both placed great stock in relationships, and both wanted to make sure that everyone involved in the proposed deal could pass the "sniff test."

After her own one-on-one meetings, which went very well, Susan scheduled a grand luncheon at which the patriarchs would meet each other for the first time. Throughout the meal, Susan kept looking for clues as to how it was going—and what the fate of her business might be!—but everyone had his poker face on. For Susan, it was a nerve-wracking two hours.

As it turned out, the suspense was well worth it: The two families agreed to put Susan in business for herself. One other important detail remained to be worked out: her compensation. As the result of some tough-but-friendly negotiations, she ended up receiving a salary plus 25 percent of the promoter's profits of the enterprise. For their part, her company's investors got control and a major share of the new business's upside. After all, they were committing the funds she needed to get started.

Susan considered herself lucky. She wasn't worried about having two partners with a controlling interest in the company—in fact, not feeling totally comfortable out on her own, she was pleased to have smart people to consult with and to run ideas by. She was given office space on East 59th Street, in one of the family offices. After ten years of working out of a cramped basement office in Lower Manhattan, she was happy to have a reasonably roomy office with a view of the George Washington and Tappan Zee bridges.

A Slow Ramp-Up

The fledgling business got off to a slow start, in part because the RTC, which held many of the defaulted loans to sponsors, was slow to establish a procedure for sales. Susan began building relationships—not only with the RTC, but also with the relevant banks and with the four lawyers who were handling the largest number of bankruptcies. In time, these relationships with the lawyers proved to be especially fruitful.

Finally, after six months, Susan closed on her first deal: the acquisition of a 70-unit building on West 17th Street. She bought what was originally a $2 million loan for $350,000, or $5,000 per unit. She also had to put up another $500,000 to clear municipal tax liens on the property—liens that had higher priority than the mortgage. In addition to that $850,000, she set aside $100,000 to cover deficits in building operating costs while she sorted out the legal status of the various tenancies.

Last but not least, the building was in tough shape—it had been poorly maintained—and it lacked some basic amenities. (Some of the apartments were walkups, which would be nearly impossible to unload for a good price.) To her astonishment, she discovered that the live-in super had been raising chickens on a patch of ground behind the building. In short, there was a lot of work to be done.

To reduce the carrying cost to the tenants, she rewrote the $2 million loan at $1 million, a number that was still higher than the cash she had in the buildings. This helped clean up the balance sheet of the cooperative and brought the property into conformance with the lending standards of the Federal National Mortgage Association (FNMA). Her expectation was that FNMA or the National Cooperative Bank would eventually take over their loan and return the investors' capital to them.

All of this took well over a year, during which Susan was finally able to sell off many of the vacant units. The key in this process was ensuring that lenders had enough confidence the cooperative would succeed that they would give permanent loans to new buyers of individual units. She gradually dealt with a number of tenants who were illegally taking advantage of the city's rent-stabilization law to qualify for lower rents. She was personally involved in all facets of the operation: hiring contractors, attorneys, brokers, and property managers as needed, and then supervising their work closely.

Meanwhile, because the RTC was selling off additional loans, there were ample opportunities for Susan and her investors to pounce upon. Because she had a first-mover advantage—understanding both the market and the process—Susan was able to bid successfully for a number of properties.

Changing the Money Model

Sooner than anyone had expected, her original capital—plus an additional $3 million subsequently committed by the two families—was fully invested. Susan was convinced that the market still presented great opportunities, especially in the borough of Queens, just across the East

River from Manhattan. Because the two families involved didn't want to unbalance their portfolios by putting still more money into real estate, they suggested that she look for additional capital from new investors.

So Susan explored her options, and eventually approached a large Boston-based multistrategy hedge fund. The fund's operators agreed to back her, but insisted that her existing investments be rolled into a new fund in which they would all share. Susan would still be entitled to a 25 percent share of the promoter's portion of the profits, but only after both sets of investors, her prior and her new, were returned their equity. The new investors also wanted a say in approving new acquisitions. Because Susan found them bright, experienced, and willing to let her take the lead, she didn't see a problem in that demand. After all, their backing would open whole new vistas to her.

Susan felt that after nearly a decade and a half of hard work and attention to detail, she was on the verge of real success. Not only had she scaled up, but now she was ready to go to an even higher level.

Ed Mank: Bigger Projects, and The Need for Patience

We met Ed Mank in Part I, "Starting Out" as he was getting his feet wet in real estate: an energetic, resourceful, persistent entrepreneur who used his entry point as a leasing broker to score a coup with undervalued buildings on Beacon Hill.

Name: Ed Mank

Start-up location: Boston (Beacon Hill)

Scale-up location(s): Boston (waterfront), Lowell, and Cambridge, Massachusetts; New Hampshire

Type of project: Various

Type of scale up: Size, product and geographic diversification

Funding: Self-funding, partners, bank loans

Organization: Minimal

As Ed's scope of activities expanded to other property types and locations around Massachusetts, these same traits served him well. Although venturing into these new areas brought him challenges he had not anticipated, over time he was able to work most of them out. He, like Susan Hewitt, is an example of someone who scaled up acquiring larger projects without building a big organization. In real estate, it is possible to do this.

Expanding in His Current Market

Soon after acquiring his first property, Ed decided with three of his friends to acquire a leasing and brokerage operation on Beacon Hill. They saw no compelling reason to share their commissions with their current employer, who received half their earnings in exchange for an office and use of his name and advertising. They purchased a small operation, which included ownership of a three-story property that served as their office. They bought 100 signs advertising their company and placed them wherever they could around the area. This was a clear case of marketing leading reality: The number of signs implied a much larger operation than was actually there.

In an effort to boost revenue, Ed began to encourage landlords and tenants to sign three-year apartment leases rather than the one-year leases that were the norm at that time. Among other good outcomes, this tripled the commission. (*Commissions are based as a percentage of the total dollars committed in the lease agreement.*) He tipped janitors in the buildings they were leasing so that they would address him as "Mr." when he showed space. (Credibility, as we've seen, is key.) They also let him know whether any problems were cropping up in their building that might affect the tenants.

For Ed, one high point came when his grandfather—who spoke limited English and was quite ill—came up from New York to visit him. Ed showed him the big locked box holding dozens of keys of units they were showing for others, and took him to see some of the units. His grandfather naïvely concluded that Ed owned those buildings, and marveled aloud at the great success his grandson had made of himself. Ed decided not to contradict him.

Ed continued to buy and sell small Beacon Hill and Back Bay apartment buildings. His trading activities allowed him to put aside money for investments. His first larger-scale purchase was a sizable old-line Back Bay apartment building facing the Charles River, which he bought with his partners. They made cosmetic improvements, and they installed new appliances purchased on credit from suppliers. Three years later, the partners faced the dilemma of whether to convert the building to condominium ownership. They decided it was a good idea, but rather than convert the building themselves, they sold it at a profit to a converter to do the job. Some people outside their small organization thought they had sold too cheap—but Ed knew there were several units that, because of their poor design, had never rented easily, and most likely would never sell. In addition, there was more chance that his gains would be taxable at the lower capital gains rate if they sold the entire building, instead of selling the units individually.[1] Time and the market proved Ed and his partners correct.

The lesson for buyers is obvious: *When the sellers are more knowledgeable than you are about the market and the property, be careful. They may well know something you don't know, and can't easily figure out.*

A Different Part of Town

Ed's next major venture came in a completely roundabout way: as the result of a party that he and I threw for 200 of our friends at a six-story former warehouse building on the Boston waterfront. We had purchased the building to convert it to apartments. Along with our spouses, we decorated the top floor—with its old wooden beams and 35-foot-high ceilings—with fishing nets and armfuls of flowers from the wholesale flower market. We served kegs of beer, barrels of gazpacho, dozens of quiches and pastries from a local bakery, and burlap bags full of peanuts that Ed purchased from the vendor who supplied Fenway Park. The local union head found us a pickup band of musicians who had always wanted to play together.

One of our guests was an important architect, the key owner of Lewis Wharf, which was the adjacent and much larger warehouse property that he (like us) hoped to convert. Munching peanuts at our party, and looking out our window at his buildings, he decided on the spot that the two properties should be planned and developed together. He offered us a good price, which much more than covered the cost of the building (and the party). We accepted, mainly because we realized that he controlled the land that we ultimately would need for parking for our units. He had said he would try to work out an arrangement with us, but still, he held a trump card, and it's better not to bargain with someone who holds a trump card.

But here's the interesting part: During the process of the sale, Ed convinced the owner/architect—and even more important, his partners—that they needed his real estate skills to operate and lease the property. Ed traded his management fee for a small equity position in the combined property. He and his original partners liquidated their Beacon Hill rental office, and soon after, Ed moved his office—which included a bookkeeper, receptionist, and a young associate—to the second floor of Lewis Wharf, which was designated for offices while the upper floors were to be converted into apartments.

Over the next several years, the property was cash-flow negative, because there was little tenant interest in locating in what was then a rundown area. The winter months were particularly discouraging. Cold winds blew in off the harbor. Office workers only a few blocks away in the central business district found no good reason to visit the docks, and the lack of foot traffic and other human activity became self-fulfilling.

As a result, there were numerous calls on the partners for additional investment. They—not surprisingly—were unhappy with their investment, and after a while were unwilling to come up with their share of the additional financing. Generally, I don't like to have this kind of negotiation with my partners. Whether things go well or poorly in the future, you often will be accused of having inside knowledge. But Ed didn't have much choice if he wanted the development to proceed. Gradually, little by little, he put up their share of the capital calls and bought out their interests, accumulating just under a 50 percent position, with the architect owning the remainder. Condo sales for the upper-floor residential units were weak, and Ed had to buy several of the units personally just to keep the lenders happy.

Ed kept himself afloat during this period through commission income. He could continue to act as a broker, on some deals, while acting as a principal on others.

The story does have a happy ending for Ed, which suggests that persistence pays off. Almost 20 years after our party, Ed and the architect decided that they had to split. Although the waterfront had then become a hot market, they could not agree on what to spend on renovations or what else to build on the site. They decided on a sealed-bid auction, with the higher bidder forced to buy out the other. The architect found a partner willing to buy out Ed, and the two bid much more than what Ed thought the property was worth. For the first time in his life, Ed had made a multimillion dollar hit. For 20 years, he had made a good living buying and selling smaller properties, making an occasional commission, but now he actually had substantial *cash* to invest in future deals. His original decision to take an equity interest in this waterfront property and help manage it had been validated. *Like many situations in real estate, it takes time and patience.*

Expanding Beyond Boston: New Product Types

As with many real estate entrepreneurs, Ed soon found ways to spend his nest egg. A few years earlier with three other friends, he had bought a complex of factory buildings in Lowell, Massachusetts, a city that had lost thousands of manufacturing jobs in preceding decades. The price was cheap: $500,000, or 33 cents a square foot for about 1.5 million square feet of space.

Although this initial price appeared to be a bargain, the costs of upgrading and meeting codes were not. With plenty of competition from other abandoned factories, the rents were too low to cover the fix-up costs. Moreover, tenants demanded quality space, and building inspectors were loath to relax standards. All in all, it proved difficult to stop the renovations midstream, and there went a good chunk of Ed's cash from his downtown waterfront coup. Eventually, the area began to improve, as some of the fast-growing fledgling start-up computer firms began to take space, and Ed and his partners were able to stop the cash-flow outlays by selling at a price that got them back most of their investment.

Ed had better luck with expanding his interests in a substantial retail/office/movie theater complex in the center of Harvard Square, almost directly opposite the subway stop. The property had been purchased for $950,000 by a group led by a Boston real estate brokerage firm. After the mortgage, Ed had to put up only a few thousand dollars for his 3 percent share. Despite its great location, rents in the square were still surprisingly low, and for five years, there was never any leftover cash to distribute.

As with Lewis Wharf, though, Ed gradually acquired the interests of a number of small investors who became tired of waiting for distributions, slowly bringing his interest up to about 20 percent. He picked up another 20 percent from an investor who also was in the Lowell deal (but wanted out of both). Again, Ed's cash came in handy. Finally, he purchased the share of the original real estate broker.

This gave him about 62 percent of the ownership, and control of the deal. With the sale of his interest in Lewis Wharf, he moved his office to Cambridge. His staff had not grown, but he had a different, talented young associate. Harvard itself was beginning to expand its footprint, leasing a large number of commercial buildings in the area. Retail rents also took off, and Ed, although he had not predicted it, was able to increase the property's operating cash flow sixfold over a period of years.

Not long after, Ed's enthusiasm and competitive spirit led him to buy a major ski resort in New Hampshire. He had lost an auction to acquire a small tennis facility nearby, which was home to the Volvo Tennis Classic. Ed was a serious tennis and squash player, rather than a skier, but he liked the area that the ski resort was in and thought the land itself had potential for second homes. So, he put together a group of friends, with himself as managing partner, and made the purchase.

Ed had scaled up using the funds from the sale of his waterfront property. He still owned interests in several properties in the Boston area. Now, with the acquisition of the ski resort, he had, for the first time, a new type of business to run—one that required operating skills and came with a sizable staff.

Opportunism Is Good . . . Except

But more on that in the next section. For now, I'll simply point out that Ed has again shown that persistence, hard work, and imagination are key. As an opportunist, he followed the maxim of buying when he saw a chance to upgrade a property. What was different now, of course, was that the time lag between when he bought and sold was years or decades rather than months. He also learned that there are many ways to be in the real estate business, and that each one requires a steep and sometimes expensive learning curve. And as he discovered in Lowell, there is often no easy way out after you've made a bad initial purchase.

He found he did not want to be simply a limited partner. He saw that they had *limited control, and when they wanted to exit their position, they had to take a sizeable discount, especially when selling at a low point in the market.* (It is often at such low points that the call for additional capital goes out to cover operating losses.)

Ed was able to turn such periods to his advantage. Whether this opportunistic entrepreneur knew more about the project or was just lucky, or visionary, or simply too stubborn to give up something he was deeply involved in is hard to figure out—even for those of us who know him well. Most likely, it was a combination of all four factors.

Rich Erenberg: New Product, Same Philosophy

Rich's initial success in Houston as a trader—buying foreclosed condos at distressed prices, fixing them up, renting them, and then selling them at a quick profit—got him into the real estate business. He soon found himself spending half of each month in Houston, and half in his home base of Pittsburgh. Although Pittsburgh was the center of his other activities, he saw no reason to invest in a stagnant Pittsburgh market at what he considered high prices when he could invest at bargain prices in Houston, even as its economy was going south.

Name: Rich Erenberg

Start-up location: Houston, Texas

Scale-up location(s): Houston

Type of project: Retail centers

Type of scale up: Size, product diversification

Funding: Bank loans, private investor, "blind pool" fund

Organization: Lean in Pittsburgh; back-office merger in Houston

He found, however, that others were beginning to recognize the opportunities that he and his partner Steve Morse had found in Houston in the late 1980s. The market was becoming more competitive. Prices were going up, and his profit margins were going down. In addition, Steve was spending more time on his day job at Dow Chemical, while Rich was doing most of the work.

A Different Product Type

Rich decided to shift gears and see whether he could find underpriced retail centers in the Houston area he could reposition and fix up, in more or less the same way he had been doing with the condominiums. But now the deals were bigger, and he needed to bring in outside investors. (Scaling up, as we've seen, often requires a new set of financial partners.) As an outsider, however, he didn't have a ready set of local Houston investors who knew him and were willing to bankroll him.

Eventually, he found a retail center that was for sale for $1.3 million. This was a neighborhood retail center that met his criteria: only 50 percent leased, in need of a facelift, with no landscaping, and with a poorly laid-out parking lot. What to a seller was a bad deal that he wanted to get out of was to Rich an opportunity. He thought he could turn the property around.

Financing was his next challenge. It took him 25 calls, but he finally found a lender who agreed to advance $950,000.

This meant that he still had to raise $350,000 in equity. Wangling an introduction to a wealthy New York family, he flew up to meet the matriarch. She asked, bluntly, why she should do business with him. He told her about his plan for the center. He said he didn't know a lot, but he was a good listener and would work hard if she gave him the opportunity. To his surprise, she bet on him, putting in a sizable chunk of the $350,000. He was able to cobble together a number of friends for the balance.

The project was successful. In fact, it became the best retail property in the area. Because his total cost basis was low, he was able to fill up the property quickly by charging rents at 70 percent of market— the same strategy he had employed with his condominiums.

Organizational Challenges

Over the next few years, he was able to do a few more retail projects. But, he realized that to grow further, he would have to make some changes in the way he did business. First, Steve, his initial partner, was traveling extensively for his "day job" and simply wasn't able to participate meaningfully. Steve would not be part of Rich's new deals.

Let's look at this split from Steve's perspective. Steve was able to be a partner in the early stage of the business, make some money from the joint projects that he and Rich did, and then pull back. *Because the value was in the properties, rather than the business, there were no sizable break-up costs.* Steve could continue to own or sell his shares in the properties. In other words, real estate is a field of easy entrance, and it is also a field of easy exit, assuming that you have the power to cause a sale. At a certain stage, Steve had to make a choice. He decided that he saw his future in a career at Dow, where he had been promoted at a rapid rate.

Rich, meanwhile, had to think through what kind of organization he wanted if he hoped to grow. At the time, his staff in Pittsburgh was a bookkeeper plus a young person who helped with analysis and oversight. He was considering adding a supervisor to handle the management of existing properties. All his other services were outsourced.

Financing Growth

But Rich also had another problem. As opportunities came more rapidly, he found he was going back to the same people for money for each deal. Explaining the deals in detail, finding out whether they had money to invest at that time, setting up new legal partnership agreements, and calling down the money as he needed it was not only time-consuming and cumbersome, but kept him from acting quickly in tying up deals.

He decided to try to put together a "blind pool fund" that would allow him to do multiple deals. This meant that each investor would agree to put up a certain amount of money, which Rich could call upon as needed. The selection of the actual projects was up to Rich, and would not be specified in advance. Given his relative inexperience, he knew it would not be an easy sell.

At about this time, he was approached by Doug Engel, who owned Clarion, a boutique firm doing leasing and property management in Houston. Rich was one of Clarion's larger customers. Doug suggested merging their operations, with Rich handling development and Doug's firm handling its traditional Houston work plus the back-office accounting for all the partnerships. Rich and Doug would set up a separate holding company to own their interest in Clarion and individual projects.

Rich saw the merger as a logical way for him to grow, and as a way to give him extra credibility in raising money for his new fund. He had worked with Doug for years, and believed he would be a compatible partner and a good sounding board for his new ideas.

With the new holding company in place, he raised his first fund of $10 million of equity, which he expected to leverage with $30 to $40 million of debt. Again, he maintained his strategy of only doing one-off, opportunistic deals where he could add value: deals with vacancies, deferred maintenance, the need for cash, better market positioning, and so on. In this fund, 50 percent of his investors were new, and 50 percent were existing—including the New York matriarch, who continued to stay with him. Over a six-year period, he bought and successfully liquidated eight properties for this fund. He was still basically a trader, doing much of the acquisitions and sales himself, although the deals were becoming larger and the holding period longer. Gradually, he was building up his own capital to invest in his next fund.

After three years, when the first fund was substantially invested, he raised a new $15 million fund. He was beginning to acquire properties in Pittsburgh, as well as Georgia, Tennessee, and Florida. The properties were primarily a mix of what he considered undervalued retail and office. Given the favorable prices, he was willing to risk operating in other less-familiar geographic markets. He capped his next fund, three years later, at $5 million. Some of his private investors felt they had enough exposure to real estate. Besides, he was seeing fewer new deals he liked.

By this time, he had acquired 60 properties for about $180 million—an average of $3 million per property, many of which he had sold at a profit. He had found a niche in properties that were too big for small players, but beneath the radar of larger players. From an organizational standpoint, this considerable volume didn't involve much change. Rich had added only one assistant in Pittsburgh (although Doug had added some back-office personnel in Houston). Most of the leasing, management, and construction for projects outside of Houston continued to be outsourced. Rich continued to take the lead in investigating and acquiring new deals (and in their subsequent sales.)

The Value of Persistence

With the earlier funds substantially invested, Rich was getting ready to start his fourth fund. He thought he had come a long way. He was an established player who had made money for himself and his investors. Although he had scaled up geographically and expanded into other product types, he had maintained his opportunistic approach to investing. He added value through buying existing properties. He did not develop any properties from scratch. He kept his staff and overhead small. His persistence had paid off, although he realized that the future of his enterprise depended almost entirely on his own entrepreneurial talents. He was comfortable with the way he was running his business. And in a sense, he still was a running back—flexible enough to follow his blockers while looking for opportunities where he could break through.

John Dewberry: Adapting Your Organization to Your Game Plan

With the successful completion of Dorchester Square—the 65,000-square-foot, grocery store–anchored shopping center in Charleston, South Carolina, described in Part I—John Dewberry was able to focus full time on becoming a real estate developer. The former Georgia Tech quarterback no longer needed to be a mortgage broker to pay the rent. Dewberry Capital, the firm he started a few years earlier, could now be used to provide development services for his new projects. Because his living expenses were minimal, he could reinvest whatever profits he made.

Name: John Dewberry

Start-up location: Charleston, South Carolina

Scale-up location(s): Atlanta, Georgia; Jacksonville, Florida

Type of project: Retail centers, multifamily residential, downtown office building, mixed use

Type of scale up: Size, product and geographic diversification

Funding: Insurance company with equity position, overseas investors with "preference," wealthy investors

Organization: Selective upgrading of key functions, but still small

As opposed to Rich Erenberg, John had a long-term game plan of redeveloping Midtown Atlanta. His other projects were meant to prepare himself for that. Also, unlike Rich's situation in Pittsburgh, he saw Atlanta, his home base, as a rapidly growing market, with no shortage of opportunities.

Same Product, Different Markets

As you'll recall from Part I, John had started with a grocery-anchored retail development because with no real capital of his own, he could obtain financing for most of the costs based on the credit of his tenants. The retail project could stand on its own, legally and financially. His own personal balance sheet (still pretty modest) was not an issue.

He followed that model and developed two similar centers in Charleston, South Carolina, then two in Atlanta, and finally one in Jacksonville, Florida. He financed these centers primarily with an insurance company that was willing to advance nearly all the debt and equity for 50 percent of the profit. The company understood that with leases in place, there was minimal risk that the end product would not be worth substantially more than its original cost. The remaining risk was in construction, but these centers were not complicated to build, because the landlord only provided a shell for the tenants to do their own interior fit-ups. *This was a corner of the business in which geographic expansion was a workable strategy.*

John had brought his 18-month-older brother, Douglas, in to help him. Douglas had worked for a commercial bank; the plan was for Douglas to assist John with project financing and other areas in which John needed a trusted hand. Douglas accepted a minimal salary with the promise of a bonus and a small share of equity in the deals.

Continuing the Learning Curve

John's goal was to do mixed-use urban developments. He was especially drawn to Midtown Atlanta, an area that he knew well, and which was then run-down and neglected, but which he thought had tremendous potential. First, he thought, he had to get more experience in other property types—and continue to build up his own capital.

With this downtown development goal in the back of his mind, John believed that the next useful learning experience for him would be to develop a multifamily residential property. This kind of development has more potential risk attached to it, because leasing typically doesn't begin until construction is substantially completed. Also, leases tend to be short term, so there's more volatility in occupancy—and, as a result, in cash flow. Because he had no experience in this area, John outsourced much of the leasing and management services to an established firm.

Through a friend who was a mortgage broker, he was able to get equity financing from a group of Saudi investors who had been investing in the region. They received a preference—that is, the first distributions from the partnership—until they had received a 9 percent return on their invested cash. They then got back their invested capital. After that, 60 percent of additional distributions were split to the investors and 40 percent to the developer or general partner.[2]

On that basis, John completed two projects in Atlanta—one with 172 units, and another with 212—in the early 1990s.

The Midtown Opportunity

John thought he now had the capital, experience, and reputation to make his move in Midtown. He found a site—near several office buildings that had been constructed for out-of-state tenants such as IBM and ATT—that he was able to buy at a discount from a Pittsburgh oil company that no longer needed a presence there.

Midtown was not far from some desirable residential neighborhoods, and the site was near a historic park. At this location, John contemplated building retail on the ground floor, with apartments above.

At about this time, though—in the late 1990s—a broker sent John a vacancy report showing office occupancy in Midtown at 95 percent and rising. The broker therefore encouraged John to go in that direction. John concurred and designed a 160,000-square-foot, 7-story building that he anticipated would cost about $24 million, or $150 per square foot. He would call it One Peachtree Pointe.

The cash flow after operating costs was estimated to be $2,560,000, or $16 per square foot. Based on this projection, the return on his costs would be slightly more than 10 percent: that is, $16 on a $150 cost. Because he could borrow much of the money at a lower cost than 10 percent, the return on his own capital would be higher.

Note that for simplicity's sake, I'm talking in terms of per-square-foot numbers (and aggregate project numbers). This makes it easier to determine how rents and capital costs compare to other competitive projects.

The problem was that this would be a speculative building, with no leases in place. Still, a financial institution agreed to an $18 million construction loan, which left John with $6 million to raise.

Williams Advisors, an advisor/broker, obtained a commitment for half the required equity from a Dutch group that had been investing in Atlanta for many years. The group insisted that John raise the rest. International investors are often leery of projects with no local support. ("Skin in the game," slang for putting your own money into the deal, often turns out to be very important.) John Dewberry got two friends to put up $1 million each, and he agreed to put up the $1 million balance.

John's gut instinct to go with offices (based on the broker's suggestion) turned out to be a good one. The building opened 25 percent leased, and was 90 percent leased in a year. His costs had escalated, but he was able to get a new permanent mortgage adequate to cover these costs, repay his construction loan, and repay his investors much of their money. The broker who sent John the initial report recommending office use also did well. He found tenants for most of the space in the building, earning substantial commissions for himself. John was encouraged enough to begin acquiring additional sites in the Midtown area.

Building an Organization

He also had to address some organizational issues. To build and operate his retail and residential projects, he hired project managers who were specialists in these product types. He himself was on top of all the details of One Peachtree Pointe.

But now, with bigger, more complex multiuse projects in sight, he needed new organizational skills. He wanted people who could operate across functional lines. In interviewing potential employees who were already in real estate, he found it difficult to find people who could think outside the box, and who had the imagination to handle the different types of projects he now wanted to do.

He decided to take a gamble, by bringing in two key people with no real estate experience. One was his old high school friend, Steve, who had migrated to the West Coast to go into the investment banking business. In fact, for several years now, John had wanted Steve to join him to run the finance side of his operations. Finally, Steve agreed to come on the condition that he and John would also set up an investment banking operation to invest in ventures other than real estate. John agreed. He thought that real estate finance was much simpler than what Steve was primarily interested in, and Steve would be able to do the real estate on the side. There also was the potential of John benefiting financially from Steve's investment deals.

Lara, his other new hire, brought different skills. An MBA and former track star at Georgia Tech, she had experience in non–real estate start-ups and management consulting. She would put some order into the operating side, and she would oversee the transition from a functional to a matrix-style organization, one where the key staff members could form project-based teams wherever John saw opportunities. Together, the three would form an executive management committee, which would have the depth and breadth to carry out John's dream.

There were other changes, too. His brother continued to work with him, but several of the earlier hires were replaced. Both the leasing and management of the residential properties were brought in-house, in part to counter a lack of attention from outside service providers. John continued to buy land, especially in Midtown Atlanta. By 2003, approximately 40 percent of his by now substantial net worth was tied up in land, primarily in Midtown. He also was exploring the possibility of playing on his experience in Atlanta to solicit mixed-use urban-development projects in other cities. If so, he would have to decide whether he should team up with local partners, which most likely would depend upon the project.

The Player-Coach

John had definitely scaled up. He was now in multiple product types. He had focused on an area of Atlanta where he thought he could add value, but he had also expanded geographically. He had a vision of what he wanted to do, and what he thought it would take to succeed. In a very real sense, John was still a quarterback, with a game plan in hand that he intended to stick to. On the other hand, he suspected that as he expanded, he might have to adjust his role from being a pure "player" to being a "player-coach."

The Cardons: No Shortage of Opportunities

Wilford Cardon and his two brothers, Elijah and Craig, inherited a small gas/oil services business from their father. They had evolved into real estate, as the extra land they purchased when building their own gas stations proved to be valuable.

Name: The Cardon family

Start-up location: Phoenix, Arizona

Scale-up location(s): Phoenix

Type of project: Gas stations, convenience stores, single-family residential, commercial

Type of scale up: Volume, product diversification

Funding: Internal, S&Ls

Organization: Increasingly complex partnerships

There were plenty of opportunities to expand their gas stations holdings as Phoenix expanded physically. Wilford also saw that the gas station business itself had changed and provided a new set of opportunities. Technology facilitated the rise of self-service stations. (Many of us found that, to our great surprise, we could insert a credit card in the pump and fill our own tanks.) With a lower labor cost, the stations became very profitable.

Meanwhile, automobiles were being made with longer-lasting mechanical systems that required fewer repairs. Extended warranties by the manufacturers shifted the repair burden to the manufacturers and their dealers. Most stations no longer needed to run labor-intensive repair facilities. As a result, self-service gas stations became coupled with convenience stores located in the space or area formerly occupied by the repair facilities. The strategic locations of the Cardons' existing stations often proved excellent sites for convenience stores. They built new stations, and they also remodeled existing stations.

These stations and their adjacent convenience stores turned into cash cows, providing funds that could be invested, at a time when the Phoenix market was exploding, in other real estate businesses such as industrial and commercial real estate, land investment, and a home-building company. The Cardons even started companies that sold building supplies to the industry. They took advantage of their growing capital base and reputation to diversify.

But Wilford knew he had a growing problem: how to *manage* all these fledgling businesses. Because he did not want to build a large internal organization, he partnered in many of these ventures with either family members or others whom he felt he could trust. He was involved in defining the strategic vision of the company and helped to provide or arrange for its financing. He relied on others, however, to make these operations work.

Some Key Externalities

The Cardons' business was aided by three external factors. First, the advent of air conditioning made Arizona a great retirement option. Second, cash was flowing into local savings and loan institutions, so there was no shortage of funds for aspiring developers to borrow. Because land prices continued to rise as the population expanded, the temptation was obvious—scale up through leveraging. Why build 20 houses on 100 acres when you could borrow and build 100 houses on 500 acres? Most of the land he owned had greatly increased in value. Banks were willing to lend based on that appreciation. For his other joint ventures, lenders were willing to accept his guarantee as security. It was a frontier mentality, where everyone seems to be making money.

Third, section 1031 of the U.S. federal tax code permits sellers under certain circumstances to exchange their investment properties and defer payment of any tax on the gain. In other words, the Cardons could transfer the equity from one piece of land to another without immediate tax consequences.

A Personal Vision

Wilford considered it his mission to act as a steward of the family assets. He regarded ownership of his assets as similar to the ownership of fine paintings. *You can possess them for a while,* he would say, *but you can't own them.*

He believed that those who had the talent to manage assets had the responsibility not only to do so effectively, but to do so in a way that would improve the lives of others. He and his family could take out what funds they needed to live comfortably, but they should not overconsume or waste the assets. Although his three sisters did not have an equity interest in the business—the brothers owned it equally—the brothers were responsible for the sisters' financial well-being (on an equal footing).

Wilford also examined the intersection of his business and family lives with his religious obligations as a Mormon. Over the years, the brothers worked together to give each of them the time to take off from the business and undertake church-related missions. Over the years, Wilford engaged in several such missions—some to Europe, and more recently to Brazil. In Brazil, he created an opportunity for young people to obtain an education either in their home country or in the United States. His explanation? He wanted these young people to have the same kinds of opportunities that his family had, in an earlier generation.

Seeing the Broader Picture

The Cardons' value-based approach to business is idiosyncratic, and the particulars obviously wouldn't appeal to everyone. What should resonate for all of us, however, is the explicit goal of *seeing our careers in a broader perspective.* Why do we want to create wealth, and what will we do with it if we succeed? How will we balance our career, our family, our religion, and our responsibilities to others?

A final perspective: I had lunch recently with a friend who is a *success* by most definitions of the word. He confessed to me that he wished that his world were simpler. We talked some more, and wound up agreeing that although scaling up may have its rewards, "making your life simpler" isn't one of them.

Endnotes

[1] Selling a number of individual units raises the risk that the IRS will treat you as a dealer in property rather than as an investor, making you taxable at short-term rather than long-term capital gains rates.

[2] This approach to splitting profits is fairly common. The preference gives the investors some income protection. The developer is motivated to repay the investors' capital as soon as possible to be able to share in the cash flow. Whether the amount of the preference should be 6 percent or 9 percent or 10 percent, and whether the investors' share of profits should be 20 percent or 50 percent or 80 percent, are subject for negotiation. Beside the reputation and the track record of the developer, the prime determinants are financial market conditions, the nature of the project, who controls what, the risks involved, and the projected time frame.

6

Grand Visions

We continue with our scaling-up stories, this time refocusing (as in Part I, "Starting Out") on five people who went on to become major players in their corner of the real estate industry. Their challenges go beyond doing individual deals. Each is trying to establish an operating business capable of doing multiple projects in a wider geographic range. They each have their own approach to crafting an organization that will help them achieve their goals.

Hersha and Hasu Shah: Building a Chain, Slowly but Surely

Ten years after coming to America and after a short interlude back in India, Hasu Shah and his wife, Hersha, had made a small success out of the Starlight Motel, located on the periphery of Three Mile Island—the site of a near-meltdown of a nuclear plant.

Name: Hasu and Hersha Shah
Start-up location: Harrisburg, Pennsylvania
Scale-up location(s): Central and Western Pennsylvania
Type of project: Motels (rehabbed and new construction)
Type of scale up: Volume
Funding: Partners, bank loans, public capital markets
Organization: Organic growth through involvement of family members, friends, and coreligionists

Trading Up

As noted in Part I, Hasu soon sold that property and purchased another larger motel eight miles away in Elizabethtown, Pennsylvania: the Red Rose Motel, with some 30 rooms. The family decided to live at the Red Rose and manage their new investment. It was not easy for Hersha to combine the role of manager with her responsibilities to her two young sons. Her elder son Jay found himself in the sixth grade at a new middle school, where he was the only student from India and— initially, until he proved himself—the object of some discrimination. After school, the boys did chores at the motel while doing their home-work in the motel office. Family dinners were often interrupted by calls from guests and prospective guests.

And yet, they accepted the challenge. As Hersha later recalled:

A guest is just like God in our country. So we did everything to please our guests. So that is the same business here; hospi-tality is the same thing, it's the same principle here. So I took care of all the guests. I had 30 guests. That's what I thought: 30 rooms and 30 guests.

After the 30-room motel became profitable, it was sold to buy a 52-room motel, which then was sold to buy a 125-room motel in Harrisburg. The price in Harrisburg was cheap, but for a reason: The motel had a reputation as a locale for drug dealing. Because traditional lenders did not want to finance such a place, Hasu was forced to find a private lender who charged an interest rate that was 6 percent over the going rate.

The Shahs fired all the help except two front-desk people and two housekeepers. Because there wasn't much business, there was no need for more help, and they were afraid some of the help might have facilitated the drug dealing. Hersha again made the rounds, slowly convincing local businesses that the place was now "clean"—in all senses of the word. They reopened the motel's long-defunct restau-rant, and began to attract local meetings. As revenue increased, the money was reinvested in new carpeting, beds, furniture, and equip-ment. Hersha secured a large contract from Conrail. Given the rail workers' hours, this turned the hotel into a 24-hour business. With occupancy up from 27 percent when they took the motel over to almost 90 percent, they obtained a Holiday Inn franchise for their operation. Hasu now thought it was time to quit his day job and spend full time in their motel business.

Expansion: Bringing in New Partners

The next purchase came as the result of a casual conversation Hasu had with a man who also came from India. That individual was unhappy working as a troubleshooter for Lever Brothers because the company kept moving him every two years. Hasu suggested that his friend buy, live in, and run a motel. If he did well—Hasu told him—he could make more than he did at Lever Brothers. Hasu would do the deal together with him. He thought they could get a mortgage for 80 percent of the cost and put up the rest of the cash from their savings. They agreed to try it, and they bought a Sheraton motel near State College, which turned out to be a great decision for both of them.

What Hasu found was that by recruiting people whom he could trust, and who were well motivated to both be his partner and live in and run the motel, he could expand the family business effectively. He tried to invest conservatively, financing only with first mortgages and avoiding the kind of overleverage involved in incurring the second and third mortgages that so often proved the downfall for motel owners when the economy or market turned against them.

Stepping Up the Growth Curve: Building a Company

A few years later, after accumulating a few more motels, Hasu felt ready to build one or two small new motels. He believed the industry was coming out of its recession. Even as he was plunging into new construction, he found that he could acquire two existing motels from the Resolution Trust Company (RTC) at favorable prices. (As noted in Part I, the RTC was a federal entity set up to liquidate properties foreclosed from a variety of developers and banks.)

So far, virtually all his properties were located in Central or Western Pennsylvania. He had found a market niche for well-run, price-sensitive motels located in smaller cities. People stopping in these cities did not want to pay for four- or five-star hotels. At the same time, the motel had to have a welcoming atmosphere, with clean and attractively furnished rooms. This was best accomplished by owner/managers who would not only set the tone in their establishments, but also keep an eagle eye on expenditures.

As Hasu's operations grew, so did the need for more central administrative services, including purchasing supplies, marketing, and financing the properties. Many of his competitors were part of chains, with all kinds of back-office support, and Hasu knew he had to compete. Gradually, he added people in each of these areas.

Financing Growth: Access to Public Capital

Although he only had ten motels at the time, he considered going public to improve his access to capital for further expansion. With his older son, Jay, now in the business and his younger son, Neil, soon to join them, he knew that growth of the business was on their minds as well as his. They were encouraging him to consider slightly larger projects in more urban areas. There was another incentive: With each of his ten motels under separate ownership, and often with different partners, it was difficult for lenders to evaluate the overall operation. He had seen many in the real estate field establish Real Estate Investment Trusts (REITs) to hold their properties and wondered whether he could play in that game.

But REITs, by law, could not engage in operating businesses, such as running hotels. So Hasu decided on a structure in which the public company would own the properties, but the motels would be leased to an operating company, which he and his associates would also control. The operating company would pay each year a fixed percentage of the price—between 11.5 and 12.5 percent—to the REIT, plus a percentage of revenues over a certain amount. That way, he could continue to run and provide services to the hotels, and at the same time create an entity with capital that he could use to acquire new properties.

Personal Fit: A Commitment to Values

Hasu was confident that if he retained overall control of operations, the culture of the company would not change. This was important to him. He felt his sons would want to carry on his traditions. Although the company now was much larger than it was when he and Hersha had started it 15 years earlier, with approximately 20 people in the central office, it had to maintain its commitment to service, its strong work ethic, and its concern for its employees. For Hersha and Hasu, this would be an important challenge.

Walter Shorenstein: Expanding the Universe

Walter Shorenstein sharpened and elevated his profile in the San Francisco market through his acquisition (in partnership with Ben Swig) of the Merchant Exchange Building.

Name: Walter Shorenstein

Start-up location: San Francisco, California

Scale-up location(s): San Francisco

Type of project: Office towers

Type of scale up: Project size, volume

Funding: Corporate partners, bank loans

Organization: Increasingly complex

As the "new guy on the block," he continued to work hard at building relationships. He also capitalized on up-to-date market information assembled by the many brokers at the Milton Meyer Company, where he had achieved remarkable success. He had become a partner with Meyer when one of Walter's (and the firm's) biggest clients made it clear that if Walter were not made a partner, that client would take his business away. A few years after that, Milton Meyer died, and in accordance with an agreement he and Walter had made, Walter was able to buy out his partner's interest and become sole owner of the business.

Walter had mixed feelings about owning the firm. The brokers were a tough group to manage, in part because many of them were aggressive types whom the old-line outfits would not hire. They were successful—many making more from the business than he did. Yet, it was difficult to control them. As a result, Walter believed that he was taking all the risk, and that one crazy lawsuit could wipe out his profit for the year or even wipe him out altogether.

But there were upsides. The firm gave him rare access to market information about which tenants were expanding or contracting, what the rent levels were, what type of space was in demand, and what the overall vacancy levels were. It also was a stepping-stone to deals in which he could be a principal. Up until that time, his equity interests were primarily small percentages of deals he had brought as a broker to others. Now, he was ready to take the next steps. After a few years of watching the demand for space in existing office buildings, he concluded that the market was ripe for a new office tower. His rule was this: When you have to pay a price for existing buildings which is comparable to what it costs to produce a new building, *start building.*

The Next Step: New Construction

Toward that end, he went to Ben Swig and suggested they co-develop a site downtown at the corner of Pine and Battery. Ben and his partner in New York agreed, but insisted they bring in New York architects who were experienced in this type of construction. They hoped to maximize their return in what they saw as a speculative venture. Accordingly, as rents after operating costs were estimated to be $4 per square foot, they set a limit of $21 per square foot on construction costs.

As a result, the building cut some corners. It was under-elevatored, and the ceiling height was a little low. Tinted glass—not considered desirable by many tenants—allowed them to cut down the size of the mechanical systems needed to heat and cool the space. Still, they were able to quickly pre-lease 40 percent of the space, which was a prerequisite for them to qualify for an insurance company permanent loan. With Walter and the contractor contributing their fees for equity, the loan covered almost all their costs.

The success of this project led Mutual Benefit Life, a relative newcomer to the area, to approach Walter to joint venture a headquarters building for them. Walter was chosen because Mutual Life was afraid the established San Francisco firms would give preference to their longer-term clients in finding the best locations, and because the national developers did not adequately know the San Francisco market.

Extending Downtown: The "South of Market Street" Story

Meanwhile, there was still plenty to do in San Francisco. Walter had been doing some of Bechtel Corporation's smaller deals in the area. When Bechtel decided to build a new headquarters, they asked for suggestions from a number of prominent real estate players. Walter said they should consider the area south of Market Street, an area that then had a negative image. The so-called good space was all north of Market Street. Walter thought he could put together a land assemblage south of Market for less than $30 a square foot, as compared with $200 north of Market.

Bechtel was intrigued, and told him to go ahead. Secretly, setting up a number of separate corporations to make acquisitions, Walter assembled 30 sites without affecting the market prices. No one realized that this was part of an overall assembly, which might have encouraged some sellers to hold out for higher prices. In the process, he convinced Bechtel to buy extra land to take advantage of what their building would do to surrounding land values. Three blocks were assembled, on which Bechtel would build its 400,000-square-foot headquarters.

Then, at a cocktail party, Walter met an executive from Metropolitan Life (Met Life) who said he had been looking for space, but—when quizzed by Walter—said he had not contacted Walter because he "didn't deal with brokers." Walter told the Met Life executive that he wasn't only a broker, but also a principal—and that Met Life should build together with Bechtel south of Market. They could share land and site development costs, and they could save on architectural and construction fees. Bechtel would build a larger project to accommodate Met Life's need for 200,000 square feet.

Met Life agreed, but said that they had to own their own building. The Bechtel lawyers imaginatively came up with the idea of condominium ownership—an unusual concept then for office buildings. Bechtel, Met Life, and Walter would each own a third.

Then along came IBM in need of 300,000 square feet. This was added to the equation, and IBM became the fourth partner. Walter had not only put together the biggest deal of the year, but he had transformed and expanded the commercial district of San Francisco. This was real estate entrepreneurship in its broadest sense.

Two Key Lessons from San Francisco

But what made it work for Walter was not a lucky strike, or a one-time coup. Instead, it was the result of years of knowing the market, of establishing relationships, and building a reputation for himself that made people willing to take a chance on him. It reflected Walter's desire to execute projects where he could shape the plan, and it also embodied two key lessons that Walter had learned:

- Real estate is capital intensive. Therefore, he needed financial partners who not only had their own resources, but who would also instill confidence in lenders (those putting up most of the money). It helped if his partner was also willing to lease space in the building.
- In real estate, each project had to stand on its own and be treated as a separate business.

Walter had come a long way from stepping off the boat at the end of World War II. So had San Francisco. The city had become more than just a point of embarkation for, and arrival from, the Far East. It had become the major financial, educational, and business center for northern California, and one of the fastest growing and most desirable areas in the country in which to live. Walter not only shared in its growth, he also helped to shape it. His vision to expand the commercial district of the city was a grand one, and he pulled it off.

The Bucksbaums: More and Bigger Centers—A Retail Revolution

The Bucksbaum brothers' development of their first shopping center did not go exactly as planned. In fact, it took them out of the grocery store business and into the retail-development business.

Name: The Bucksbaum family

Start-up location: Cedar Rapids, Iowa

Scale-up location(s): Iowa suburbs, downtown Des Moines

Type of project: Local and regional shopping centers

Type of scale up: Volume, size, geographic

Funding: Self-funding, federal funds, intrastate REIT

Organization: Family-based, incremental growth

But as it turned out, their timing was right. With the postwar dispersion of the growing middle-class population to the rapidly expanding suburbs, retailers were anxious to follow their customers. Land was readily available, and favorable zoning was relatively easy to obtain. Desirable locations were being created at the intersections of the road transportation networks—including the national interstate highway system—that were being constructed throughout the country. These sites were often located on formerly out-of-the-way farmland, where there were few existing buildings. As a result, the price per acre was low. Construction of these early local centers, moreover, was relatively simple: Put up the shell, pave the parking lot, and let the tenants finish out their own units. Finally, there were few established competitors in this new game.

It turned out to be a good proposition for both the developers and their tenants. With the expansion to the suburbs, there was no shortage of buildable sites. As a result of having choices, anchor tenants could negotiate favorable rents. This enabled them to expand rapidly and efficiently, using other people's capital to obtain first-mover advantage in a specific geographic area. Unlike owning the property itself, a lease obligation showed up only as a footnote on their balance sheet. The developers made their money charging higher rents to the smaller tenants, who were dependent on being near the anchors, who drew the potential shoppers to the center. Long-term leases from established retail chains enabled developers to obtain financing for almost all their costs.

The Bucksbaums built and leased several stores in their area to Woolworth's, which was then a major retail chain. These chains preferred to do business with local developers with whom they had worked before because it simplified negotiations and reduced uncertainties. So, the key for the developer was to get a foot in the door—in other words, to get started with the retailer. The Bucksbaums had gotten to know the local Woolworth's real estate manager in doing their earlier deal, and he gave them their chance. There wasn't a lot of money to be made on these deals, but the Woolworth relationship helped pay the Bucksbaums' living expenses.

Next, they opened a second small shopping center—a process that went more smoothly than the first. This led, in turn, to a larger center in Bettendorf, Iowa, which included not only an Eagle Food Center, but also a Younkers Department Store. This led to the Bucksbaums establishing a good business and personal relationship with Joe Rosenfield, the owner of Younkers, who helped mentor the brothers.

The relationship soon took an unexpected turn. Rosenfield invited the Bucksbaums to co-develop a center in downtown Des Moines. Although he was expanding the Younkers chain to the suburbs, he was worried about their flagship downtown Des Moines store. Therefore, he created an urban investment trust to help finance such new projects. Matthew Bucksbaum—who had moved to Bettendorf to manage the building of their center there—again packed up his family and moved there. As always, the brothers were opportunistic, willing to follow their tenants downtown, as well as to the suburbs.

A Financial Revolution

In short, there was a great deal of activity going on. And even though the Bucksbaums were building equity in the various projects they had completed, they found that they were always running short of cash. To make matters worse, if they were going to continue to grow, they would need even *more* cash: to tie up sites, go through the design and approval processes, and have the credibility needed to sign up lead tenants. Even though land options were still inexpensive, by and large, the developers had to carry the projects themselves, with their own cash, until construction financing kicked in. Even construction financing was not generally as favorable as permanent, longer-term financing, which became available only when the construction was completed and the project was substantially leased.

In 1970, the Bucksbaums' answer was to package their properties—as well as a few from Joe Rosenfield and another local family—into what initially was an intrastate REIT, whose shares could not be sold out of state. (The regulations for selling shares in an intrastate REIT were less restrictive.) They named their company General Growth Management. The tax advantage of REITs, which permitted income to flow directly through to shareholders, made this format more desirable than the traditional corporate structure that incurred double taxation (that is, at both the corporate and individual levels).

Still, the format was a new one, and required a lot of explanation to potential investors. Their problem was compounded by the need to also explain in those early years what exactly a "regional shopping center" was. Also, while shopping center leases carried fixed rates and normally covered base operating and financing costs, much of the potential upside came from "percentage rents"—that is, rents tied to a level of the retailer's sales. There was little precedent as to how such rents (or the potential for such rents) should be evaluated by investors.

As a result, at the same time that retailing was going through a major revolution, so was the financial industry, in its efforts to keep up with supplying the capital needed to sustain this revolution. The Bucksbaums therefore pioneered in two arenas more or less concurrently: development and finance. Eventually, they changed their REIT from being intrastate to interstate, which opened the REIT up to a broader range of investors and helped them get listed on the New York Stock Exchange. Goldman Sachs was able to underwrite a large stock offering for them, and—to the Bucksbaums' delight—their old friends, Joe Rosenfield, subscribed for a million more shares.

Building on Values

Although the Bucksbaums now owned only 30 percent of their company, the total value of their stock holdings had increased many-fold. Most of their activities continued to be in Iowa and adjacent states. The headquarters was still in Des Moines, where the brothers made their homes. Because their growth was incremental, they were able to primarily manage it themselves. Martin, the older brother, ran the financial and corporate side, while Matthew remained more involved in operations and the third brother concentrated on their chain of toy stores. Their father had since died, but the brothers continued to attribute their strong work ethic, their humility, and their carefully considered approach to decision making to him. They believed that even as they had scaled up, they had maintained the strong values they had inherited. They also enjoyed working with one another—not always a given in family businesses!

Trammell Crow: Trying to Do It All

The success of Trammell Crow's first speculative warehouse in Dallas set the stage for a remarkable phase of growth—one that lasted more than 20 years. Trammell continued to work with John Stemmons, who had leased him land in the Trinity Industrial District for his first warehouses. He used the same builder, the same lawyer, and—for the most part—the same two investors (who provided much of the small amount of cash equity he needed).

Name: Trammell Crow

Start-up location: Dallas, Texas

Scale-up location(s): Major cities across the U.S. and Europe

Type of project: Multiple

Type of scale up: Volume, size, geographic

Funding: Equity and debt from others

Organization: Decentralized, partner-focused; minimal bureaucracy

He had created a niche for himself, which—when combined with his optimistic attitude, drive, and tenacity—paid off. Dallas continued to grow. Lenders were anxious to be part of that market, and therefore were eager to provide him with low-cost financing. He built dozens of warehouses: some pre-leased, some speculative, some in the Trinity Industrial District, some in Brookhollow (one of the first large preplanned industrial districts), and some in other parts of Dallas. He kept betting, successfully, that interest rates would stay low, that rising inflation would allow him to raise rents over time, and that being highly leveraged would pay off.

The Dallas Merchandise Mart: An Innovative New Business

After several years, Trammell's energy, curiosity, and competitive drive led him to take on new challenges. His biggest win in the long run—although not an immediate success—was the development of the Dallas Merchandise Mart. This was something new for Dallas: a development aimed at factory representatives. Leasing was not easy, in part because retailers fought his efforts to bring these representatives together in one location, fearing that having all the wholesalers in the same place would reduce the retailers' ability to negotiate with them. Trammell argued exactly the opposite, although he didn't win too many retailers over, at first.

Finally, determined to prove that he could build a better mousetrap, he started construction on his first building with only limited leases in place. He picked a large site with good road access. Again, Stemmons leased him the land, which cut down his up-front cash-equity needs. He created a facility with ample free parking, air conditioning (not common then in the older buildings with which he hoped to compete), plenty of escalators and elevators, and a giant atrium in the center that would serve as an architectural focal point and meeting place.

He began with a decorators' center, and then created additional centers for the furniture, gift, and apparel industries. Although the gestation period for each of these centers was long and arduous, once they were up, virtually all the wholesalers found that they had to be there. Meanwhile, to their surprise, both the buyers and their suppliers found that their lives were greatly simplified. He eventually built 7 million square feet on 135 acres with parking spaces for 9,000 cars.

The center soon had its own development and operating staffs. Trammell continued to provide the vision, drive, and financing. The Dallas Market Center became the largest such center in the country. He also had created a new industry for Dallas, with thousands of new jobs, and a highly profitable venture for himself and his associates.

Expanding Everywhere

Trammell's vision was not confined to any particular property type. He established co-ventures to build apartments, office buildings, parking garages, and even a few shopping centers. He soon took on geographic expansion—first in Houston, and then in dozens of other markets across the United States. He sent younger partners to markets such as Atlanta, New York, St. Louis, and San Francisco. Eventually, these partners expanded their own regions of operations to other cities. Within each territory, there often were product specialists for warehouse, office, and retail, each with its own reporting hierarchy. Residential development was done in separate companies, with their own officers and partners.

An Organizational Challenge: Finding the Right Partners

But Trammell was not satisfied just being the single largest U.S. developer. He took his creativity to Europe: first constructing a merchandise mart in Brussels, and then launching projects in Britain, Spain, France, and Italy. He took on hotel projects in Asia and developments in Mexico.

How did one man hold all this together? For one thing, he kept his central staff small. He despised bureaucracy, believing that it thwarted creativity. He had the ability to define the essence of a project, both quantitatively and qualitatively, in a very short period of time. He operated by instinct, making fast decisions. His secretary and one or two financial types had to bring into some semblance of order the myriad of agreements, notes, and phone instructions that he left for them. Their workweeks were long, to say the least.

One of the ways that Trammell stayed on top of all his projects was by empowering and incentivizing others to implement them. He knew this was necessary if he wanted to grow. Although he paid low salaries, early on he gave those who earned his trust equity interests in projects in which they were involved. They became his partners, and he treated them as such. He felt their commitment would make a difference.

To find such people, he paid considerable attention to the hiring process, interviewing almost everyone himself. He wanted overqualified, driven, organized people who would be hell-bent to make their projects succeed. Why? Because although his warehouses were highly functional, there was nothing all that special about them, either physically or from a location standpoint. Trammell hoped that the quality of his sales staff would make the difference. Everyone started in leasing, cold-calling customers who may not even have thought of moving. His people were trained to learn about their customers' needs and to convince them that a Crow building was part of the solution.

On the surface, his people were overqualified to be leasing agents. Yet, he knew that the ability to attract tenants to his buildings was central. He believed that the Dallas Merchandise Mart would never have succeeded without his own personal efforts to convince potential tenants to make the change. Every new project, he believed, needed the same hands-on, high-quality sales effort.

The Power of Personality

With hundreds of projects underway, each with its own ownership and operating structure, and with little communication across his various enterprises, Crow depended heavily on his own personal magnetism to keep the sprawling empire together. He focused on creating a culture and incentive structure that would attract exceptional people to work for him and to remain loyal to him. That would enable him to expand both geographically and by product type. He not only succeeded in the warehouse and office areas, but, through regional joint ventures, he also became one of the largest apartment builders in the country.

Each of his ventures, with its own set of partners, was financed in a separate entity with its own mortgages. He encouraged the local partner to not only run the project, but to find the capital for it, too.

As I was fortunate to be with him on numerous occasions over the years, I can provide a few illustrations of his people skills. First, he never surrounded himself with trappings. His desk was in the center of a large open room crowded with other desks and coworkers. He declared that he had no secrets from those who worked for him; and in fact, his office mates could hear his side of all his telephone conversations and see all his visitors. His car was usually one of the smallest and oldest in the garage. During business dinner parties at his rather grand house in Turtle Creek, Dallas's most prestigious address, he always made sure that the least secure person sat next to him, so that he could make an extra effort to make that person feel comfortable.

He encouraged the same behavior from his associates. After a dinner that included spouses, my wife, Lia, told me all about the nice young person whom she had been sitting next to. She predicted that he would have a great future with the company. I could only agree: The nice young man, Joel Peterson, already was the president of the largest of the Crow companies.

For a few years, I was an outside (or nonmanagement) director of a REIT sponsored by Trammell Crow. Before one of our board meetings, Trammell called at the very last minute to say that he couldn't attend. I found out later that one of the junior salespeople in his Dallas office had been involved in a car accident that injured someone else when the car in front of him stopped suddenly. The trial was starting that day. Trammell attended the entire proceeding. He sat near the front, conveying to all present in the courtroom that he was there in support of this young person who worked for him.

Given the extent and diversity of his activities, he recognized how important it was that he be able to trust others to carry out his projects. He knew there was no way he could supervise everyone. He understood that in a field such as real estate, with so many "moving parts," a person's reputation is crucial, and a company's reputation is no better than the reputations of those who work for it. This was a special concern for him because he was hiring talented, but aggressive, highly motivated young people, who needed a clear message as to what behavior was or was not acceptable.

The Power of Culture

Few of us can expect to run operations on the scale and scope that Trammell Crow did. (In fact, it's a little exhausting just to *think* of all that he was attempting to do.) But the personal attributes that he brought to the scene, and which made him successful, are ones that we can certainly emulate. People trusted him. They believed he *kept his word.* He made others want to partner with him. With each project owned in a separate entity and financed with its own mortgage, he needed their help.

When in the 1970s his firm hit a rough patch during one of real estate's periodic downturns, his partners shared their resources to help keep the enterprise afloat. The positive culture he created in his vast enterprises may even be easier for us to establish, in our own smaller firms. In any case, it is something to aspire to.

We will examine later how this philosophy played out for Trammell in the long run. It is not easy to scale up to the extent he did, delegate so much to the people in the field, and still maintain one big happy family. For now, my focus is on how he scaled up. Whether the problems his organization eventually encountered were inevitable is the subject of another chapter.

Gerry Hines: The Road from Houston

Our other Texas Titan—Gerry Hines, in Houston—followed the building of his first 5,000-square-foot warehouse with several others. At the same time, he continued his mechanical engineering practice. In 1957, however, after five years of trying to do both, he decided his opportunities in real estate had grown to the point where he should take the plunge and set up, with a secretary, his own real estate office.

Name: Gerald Hines

Start-up location: Houston, Texas

Scale-up location(s): Multiple

Type of project: Multiple

Type of scale up: Size; product and geographic diversification

Funding: Limited partners, bank loans

Organization: Increasingly complex geographically oriented divisional structure

He was in the right place at the right time. In the three decades between 1950 and 1980, Houston's population almost tripled: from 600,000 to 1.6 million. This increase was double the number of people added in Dallas. Metropolitan New York's population, meanwhile, went *down* by 900,000 people.

In Gerry's first decade on his own, he grew his business incrementally and steadily. He completed 97 projects, 85 of which were office or warehouse buildings. His staff grew from one to ten. He experimented with one high-rise, upper-income residential tower, but vowed that he would never do so again. Unlike his warehouse tenants, who weren't very demanding, his residents made his life miserable with complaints and suggestions for improvements.

New Challenges: Innovative Projects

Like so many entrepreneurs, though, Gerry was rarely discouraged. He kept looking for new opportunities, and he was not content to just do warehouses. He had a good relationship with the Shell Oil regional office, and made a deal to construct a new high-rise office building with a separate parking structure for them in downtown Houston. What came next was a real coup for Gerry, and made his reputation as a prestige office builder. He was able to convince Shell that he could build them a 50-story office tower on the site where the smaller regional office was going—and that he *would* do so if they agreed to move their headquarters from New York to Houston. (The regional office could be built over the garage.)

In a sense, Gerry was only carrying forward the same philosophy he had espoused when he tried to attract tenants for his much smaller warehouses:

> You have to have the best interests of the tenants at heart. You have to provide outstanding service and integrity, and fairness to them in the way you treat them, because many occasions come up where you have the upper hand, and you could gouge somebody. I think it's about being fair, and then having your reputation flow on from there.

For Shell, however, this move was major. It must not have been easy to entrust its execution to a developer without experience in

50-story construction. But thanks to Gerry's superb salesmanship and track record, Shell bought into both Houston and Gerry. The success of the Shell Tower also confirmed another lesson that Gerry had learned: the importance of pre-leasing major blocks of space to quality tenants. With a Shell lease in hand, financing followed. It was no different from leasing a small warehouse to a credit tenant, except that there were just a few more zeros on every number.

During this period, Gerry was working on another innovative project: the Houston Galleria. Normally, regional malls are anchored by two or three major department stores, with the developer making money by leasing at higher rents the stores in between the anchors. These smaller stores relied on the anchors to advertise and bring in shoppers. In this case, Gerry only had one anchor—Neiman Marcus—and that had been a tough sell. Neiman had been planning to construct a freestanding store, as was their custom. Gerry came up with the concept of an ice-skating rink that would serve as a focal point for the center and draw customers to the lower level. In effect, it would be his second anchor.

Experts told him this would not work. He decided to go ahead, but financing was not easy. He finally was able to find investors who had just sold their business to Coca-Cola in exchange for stock. Gerry was able to convince these investors to let him use their stock as additional collateral for a loan from a bank. Their stock would, in effect, qualify as equity. Unless the loan went into default and the stock was called and sold by the bank, the investors would be able to defer any capital gains tax. Luckily, when the Coca-Cola stock that was being held in escrow went up in value, Gerry was able to get the investors to allow him to increase the loan to meet the need for additional equity. *The ability to improvise, to find the resources to carry out new ideas, is a trademark of the successful entrepreneur,* and Gerry had this quality in spades.

But Gerry had staked his entire net worth (about $5 million at the time) to bankroll these two projects. Although it paid off, he knew he did not want to put himself that much at risk again. He would prefer to bring in other investors and to take a lower equity interest for himself. At this point, he had been in real estate for almost 25 years, and hoped to be in it for many more.

Still, he was not one to sit back. Up until that point, his activities had almost exclusively been in Houston. He had developed in various parts of Houston, both downtown and farther out in the Post Oak area. He was one of the first to recognize what the new highways being built would do for the area, and he assembled a large amount of acreage to develop over time.

He financed his projects individually, maintaining much of the equity for himself. Given the success ratio of his ventures, he had little difficulty attracting capital. From time to time, he would have to provide his company's or his personal guarantee until a project was stabilized.

Organizational Challenges: Going National

He realized, however, that opportunities in Houston were not unlimited. He had brought in a number of talented young entrepreneurs to work with him, and they needed new challenges. His staff had grown to several hundred people by that time. If he did not give his key associates opportunities to run their own projects and earn equity, they would likely leave. Up until that time, Gerry had been taking most of the developer's share of the equity for himself; now, he knew, he had to share more.

Gerry wasn't just being pragmatic; he was also excited about the potential of going national. To test the waters, he went in two directions. First, he established a banking division. *By partnering with strong local financial institutions that would also become his lead tenants, he could overcome his lack of experience in those local markets.* This was a period when many of the financial institutions were looking to have their name on high-visibility signature buildings, and Gerry was happy to play to that impulse. Although each building was financed individually, he had little trouble obtaining loans, especially given the quality of his tenants.

In some locales, he established his own office, sending out one of the partners with whom he had worked in Houston to run it. He believed they would know his expectations—quality design and construction (often using "name" or recognizable architects), concern for tenants, and high integrity in the way they did business. For many of his lead tenants, costs were important, but not the prime criterion. These key tenants were concerned that their developers be solid, and able to deliver and manage a quality project. This was an environment in which Hines thrived.

Gerry understood that to succeed, he would have to change some of his own ways and begin to delegate. This was hard for him because he was accustomed to knowing in detail what was going on in every project. It became even more difficult when he went national. His new challenge was thus an internal one: how to give up more of the ownership interest and operating control in projects to his senior staff, while retaining certain controls for himself, especially in financial matters. This proved to be a complicated balancing act, but without it, he knew he could not go forward nationally.

We will return to Gerry's story in Part III, "Hedging Your Bets." But I include Gerry's dilemma—about *whether* and *how* to delegate— here because it's not unique to big players. Far from it! In fact, a friend recently called me an obsessive/compulsive—which I took to be both an overstatement and a compliment. For most of us in this field, trying to keep all the moving parts together in our projects, we can't afford to take our hands off the reins.

And we can't afford *not* to.

In some ways, Gerry Hines and Trammell's stories are similar: both Texans, both expanding their companies gradually as they gained experience, both eventually growing to be mammoth yet privately-owned undertakings. The differences in the way they ran their enterprises reflect two distinct approaches that are typical of many small companies, as well as these large ones—a subject we return to in Part III.

Part III

Hedging Your Bets

If you were to plot your real estate career on a timeline, the longest stretch most likely would be dedicated to what I call "dealing with the cycles." The cycles are absolutely key. I've often referred to this industry as one with ten-year cycles and five-year memories. You have to stay out of that trap! You have to hedge your bets.

You've jumped in, scaled up, and settled upon a business model that works for you and your colleagues. You've gradually built your personal wealth, cutting down on those sleepless nights. You've arrived.

Or have you?

In fact, almost nothing about real estate is forever. Sooner or later, your successful model is going to be challenged by some factor, either outside or inside your organization. The question at that point will be whether you have prepared yourself for the inevitable challenges. Do you know where the levers are, and how to pull them to turn such times to your advantage?

These are your challenges.

7

X Factors

Real estate is subject to all kinds of externalities that can do you in if you're not careful—and sometimes even if you *are* careful.

You can get really good at doing one particular thing, and then all of a sudden, that particular thing may go from being profitable to unprofitable. You can pour your heart, time, and money into a specific project over months or years, only to discover that the world has changed in ways that you couldn't have anticipated, and which are poisonous to your pet project.

There are X factors over which you have little, if any, control. People use the phrase *X factor* to mean lots of different things. I use it to describe an outside influence that you don't control, but which has the ability to change the rules of your game. True, you might be able to anticipate some of these events, but most likely you won't be able to predict their timing, location, degree of damage, or duration.

Some of these factors—for example, natural disasters, civil wars, elections, stock market perturbations, and interest rate fluctuations—are macro level. They affect the entire economy, and by extension, they impact your project. Others are micro, like layoffs at a local plant that depress the real estate market in your area, and hurt your project.

It's easy to say that the disaster that befell you was beyond your control, and in fact, some things *are* beyond your control. (If a meteor crashes into your building, you can't be accused of poor planning.) On the other hand, you can take steps to protect yourself and your business from adversity. You can anticipate that there will be an X factor that will disrupt your operations, and may even scuttle your best-laid plans. And although you may not be able to fully protect yourself against the most extreme potential disaster, you can go a long way toward mitigating the damage that will result. *Preventive medicine is always the best kind.*

I recently learned about a network of personal-services boutiques in California that contact surfers when the waves are just right. The local wave riders, who keep their boards close at hand, simply drop what they're doing and dash down to the beach.

In real estate, unfortunately, there's no one to call you and tell you when and where the surf's up (that is, when the cycle is turning positive). In real estate, the waves may be invisible. But if I can switch to another water-based analogy: Just as an experienced sailor can make an educated guess as to what's below the surface or just beyond the horizon, an experienced real estate practitioner has a feel for the underlying currents driving this field. He or she understands the cyclical rhythms of the industry and takes steps to counter them.

The best sailors stay well away from the reefs. They expect problems and—when appropriate—make major course adjustments. The same thing holds true in real estate. I remember very well a day in 1997 when someone asked the legendary Sam Zell, a guest in my class at Harvard Business School, whether it made sense to own real estate in a public vehicle. "Definitely not," Zell replied, thumping the table with his fist for emphasis. "Real estate shouldn't be owned in public vehicles."

Just a few months later, however, Sam Zell announced the initial public offering of Equity Office Properties (EOP). For the next decade, EOP served as one of the premier public vehicles for real estate investment. Then, in late 2006, Equity Office announced that it had signed an agreement to be purchased by Blackstone Real Estate Partners for approximately $39 billion—one of the largest private buyouts in corporate history. In both cases, Sam Zell decided that it was time for a decisive and dramatic shift in strategy, based in large part on his assessment of market valuations: low (1997), then high (2006).

Most of us are not as smart (or lucky) as Sam Zell. "Dealing with the cycles," for most of us, means that a certain amount of time goes by, and the model that you used to scale up gets tested. Sometimes the first wave you catch takes you for a long and successful ride. Sometimes you get knocked off the surfboard, regroup, and try a different wave, in a different way. But sooner or later, just like in the stock market and the casino, you hit hard times. What matters then is how well you've prepared yourself to *deal* with those hard times.

X Factors: Natural and Man-Made

There are all kinds of threats, or X factors, that can come at you. For the purposes of this chapter, I consider them in two broad categories:

- Natural crises
- Man-made crises

Keep in mind, however, that these categories can overlap, and they can also be related in subtle but significant ways. "Natural" disasters often turn out to be largely man-made, with huge and unintended consequences for real estate professionals. One generation's prime location may become the next generation's ghost town.

Imagine, for example, a vast tract of land somewhere in central Oklahoma. For a millennium or more, it was grassland, traversed mainly by herds of buffalo and the bands of Indians who hunted them. Ranchers, arriving in the 1800s with herds of cattle, might have enclosed some of this wide-open acreage, but their imprint on the land was still fairly light, and their notion of "land value" was hazy at best.

Then, beginning in the later decades of the nineteenth century, the federal government used homesteading programs to encourage farmers to put down roots and work the land here (and all across the sparsely settled Midwest). Now the land was acquiring value, due both to increasing populations and the higher-value uses to which it was being put. Then, during World War I, a global shortage pushed the price of wheat and other staples up dramatically. The federal government encouraged farmers to grow more wheat—and then continued to encourage high levels of production even after demand had peaked and receded. Even as prices plummeted, the farmers—now committed to paying back not only their mortgages, but also the loans on the mechanized farm equipment that was needed to work all those acres—plowed up even more land to make ends meets, accelerating the downward price spiral. Sensible soil-conservation practices were abandoned in the rush to exploit the land.

The next chapter, of course, was the Dust Bowl. Terrible droughts plagued the region. Great windstorms blew the topsoil westward. Millions of acres became untillable, even uninhabitable, and hundreds of thousands of families were forced to leave their farms. Cities that had grown rapidly in the first two decades of the twentieth century became ghost towns. In the cities and the countryside alike, real estate values plummeted.

What went wrong? Lots of things. Certainly, the farmers of Oklahoma can't be blamed for droughts—almost the definition of a natural disaster. And yet, they shared some of the blame (along with the federal government and unscrupulous land salesmen) for the land-use patterns and farming practices that ruined the soil and exposed it to intensive erosion. Certainly, decisions made in Washington artificially manipulated the price of wheat (as had earlier decisions on the part of European nations about going to war).

As you read the following sections, remember that the more widespread the real estate disaster, the greater the chances that natural and man-made X factors have converged, and the more likely that the actors involved have favored the short-term view over the long-term view. Don't get carried away by "location, location, location." Diamonds may not be forever.

X Factors in the Natural Realm

Using the previous definition, there can be both good and bad X factors. The same X factor can be good for one party and bad for another. The late humorist and columnist Art Buchwald had a house on Martha's Vineyard, off the coast of Massachusetts. He used to talk about the time that a hurricane knocked down all the trees on his neighbor's property. The neighbor got a large clean-up bill, and Buchwald got a brand-new water view, which greatly increased the value of his house. Here, I focus on the bad side of X factors, but keep in mind that when the rules of a game change, there is usually someone (either inside or outside the game) who benefits, even as other players are getting hurt.

Obviously, a hurricane, tornado, or earthquake can wreck your short-term plans. Hurricane Katrina destroyed real estate values in large swaths of New Orleans. At the same time, much of the rest of the city became uninsurable, except at exorbitant rates. But a hurricane smashing into the Gulf Coast—like catastrophic slippage along the San Andreas Fault in California—is "predictable," in the sense that it is bound to happen sooner or later.

X factors can come at you in combination, or in sequence. George Martin, the Beatles' producer, invested a lot of money in a very successful recording studio on the Caribbean island of Montserrat, only to see that island flattened by Hurricane Hugo in 1989. Six years later, even before the island had recovered from Hugo, it was again devastated by the eruption of the Soufrière Hills volcano. "Needless to say," as the website of one Montserrat developer recently stated, "The fact that we have a volcano has affected real estate prices and there are a number of desirable properties . . . available at competitive prices."

But would you want to take the chance?

Man-Made X Factors

Let's move on to man-made crises, which include things such as the following:

- Macroeconomic perturbations (for instance, technological advances, financial upheavals, economic upturns and downturns, industrial shifts of fortune, oil spikes and crashes, demographic trends)
- Global warming
- Supply and demand imbalances
- Trends in your niche
- Geographic changes
- Organizational and personal calamities

In real estate, we make bets about the future—and in particular, about future cash flows, because it's the long-term cash flow from a property that establishes much of its value. Most of the time, we assume that the world will remain more or less constant, and we're going to aim our development efforts at a single changing variable. For example, if you foresaw a large and growing elderly population in a certain region of the United States such as Florida or Arizona, you might decide to build for that market. (*Demographics* often play a part in the bets made by real estate entrepreneurs.) Some developers have focused on the boom in Hispanic migration to this country. It's almost always good to put yourself in the path of growth.

Unfortunately, the direction and timing of that growth aren't sure bets. Immigration laws could become more restrictive, for example. A dramatic spike in oil prices—which makes your plan for building cluster housing on relatively cheap land in exurbia impractical—may benefit your competitor, who has land that's closer in and is near a rapid-transit stop. The *need* for housing is still there, but the context has changed. Developers and operators of commercial properties in Silicon Valley have been through multiple boom and bust cycles, mirroring the fortunes of the high-tech sector.

Almost every significant development project requires exceptions, exemptions, variances, and exclusions. You work with the local, state, and federal authorities to get your necessary permits and licenses. That's the cost of doing business. But sometimes a policy change takes you by surprise. A change in the political climate, for example, led to Congress taking away many of the tax benefits of second-home owner-ship. At the local level, even people who would otherwise be inclined to support growth can fall into the NIMBY (not in my backyard) mind-set. Some even can be categorized as BANANAs (build absolutely nothing anywhere near anybody).

You can't escape the consequences of large-scale shifts such as climate change. But again, even an adverse change may have its silver lining for a creative real estate entrepreneur. You might predict that prices of luxury ski villas in the Alps will plunge if global warming continues to reduce the snowfall. Or, conversely, you might predict that prices will *rise,* as the Alps become an increasingly attractive summer resort. (Remember: X factors can create, as well as destroy, opportunities.)

Along with the death and misery they create, civil wars and other conflicts set up strange real estate dynamics. Ethnic and religious groups who lived together peacefully might become enemies, and this might lead members of the various factions to gravitate toward areas of relative safety where their "own kind" live. These newcomers might have little choice but to buy at whatever price is offered to them. As a result, while some land values in the conflict zone are plunging, others are soaring.

It is not easy to predict what is happening to your property. Often you are too close to the situation. Still, you have to try to hedge your bets, and *connect the dots*, in the context of this multifunctional, multidisciplinary, dynamic field. As I stressed in Part I ("Starting Out") and Part II ("Scaling Up"), there is almost an infinite number of ways to succeed—and fail—in this business over time. The people who succeed learn to think more broadly, connect the dots differently, and remain resilient over time. They learn to manage both the liability and asset sides of their balance sheets, with the full understanding that the balance sheet is *always* a work in progress. Creative adaptation is the name of their game. Even though you can't control many of the factors that will affect your project, you can prepare to respond to them.

The struggle to deal with the cycles may prove too much—or, it might bring out the best in you and prepare you to take on future challenges. You often *learn more from your mistakes* than your victories, because the "lessons" of victories can be confusing. (Was I smart or just lucky?) That said, it's still much better to *avoid mistakes in the first place*. In the following section, I make suggestions in six basic categories, all aimed at encouraging you to hedge your bets, to adjust to the cycles. Although general in nature, they have special application to the world of real estate:

- Maintain an appropriate product focus.
- Balance your commitments against the risk curve.
- Follow the cash and build reserves.
- Manage the key operational issues.
- Attend to the key organizational issues.
- Have the flexibility to meet new realities.

Maintain an Appropriate Product Focus

There are several aspects to maintaining an appropriate product focus. Although the stages of funding, planning, acquiring, financing, constructing, leasing, and managing all types of properties are similar, the skill sets and experiences required to succeed in different types of properties do not necessarily overlap.

As an example, over the course of my career, I have successfully rehabilitated several older industrial buildings for office and research uses. When the opportunity arose, I figured I could be equally successful at converting an old factory building into 220 housing units for senior citizens. I would then sell the completed project at a previously agreed-upon price to the Boston Housing Authority, and all would be well. Sounds simple—but as it turned out, I never worked so hard to break even.

I teamed up with a reputable contractor who had done similar projects. I received enthusiastic support from the local community. My attorneys were knowledgeable about the regulatory process. I priced my units 20 percent below the maximum permitted under this particular federal program.

Still, everything took forever. I wasn't part of the club that did such projects, and I ran into unanticipated roadblocks in getting zoning and mortgage approvals. Because of the depth of the building (that is, front to back), my units were too large for the program guidelines, despite my lower per-unit cost. The building and fire departments fought over how my smoke-exhaust system should be designed. There was no provision in this particular law for community facilities, even though I wanted to include them at no extra cost. Despite the fact that the property was in a city where it can get very hot in the summer, I was turned down when I proposed to install air-conditioning units (which were also not covered by the program).

Within almost every product type, there are numerous subcategories which *appear* to be similar, but which in fact are inherently different. Retailing is a good example. I have a friend who firmly believed that his sole expertise lay in building regional malls of 1 million square feet or larger. By his own estimation, he didn't understand the design and tenant mix of smaller centers, so he stayed away from them.

Your niche might depend upon your local knowledge and contacts. You might have a geographical focus. To give an extreme example, I asked a successful former student who is a native of Hong Kong whether I should invest in China. "No," he said. "*I can, you can't.*"

These examples aren't meant to imply that you should spend your career in one specific project niche. In Part II, I encouraged you to think strategically about the ways you can grow your business. The key is *to understand the inherent limits in the particular game you are playing.* Although diversifying your product line might be a worthwhile goal, it brings with it numerous issues of control and competence, especially when X factors make your job even tougher.

Balance Your Commitments Against the Risks

This is good advice under any circumstance. It takes on special importance in thinking about how vulnerable you are in times of downturns. The longer and the more complex the project, the greater the risks. For 20 years, I have been teaching a case about the Fan Pier, a proposed 3-million-square-foot, multiuse project on the waterfront in an up-and-coming area of Boston. As of this writing, after all those years, the first commercial building is only just starting construction. Each time final public approvals were about to be given, a new mayor or governor came in and changed the ground rules. There have been a few times when the developer could have gone ahead, but in each of those times the rental market was not favorable. Luckily, the various owners have had deep pockets, and have been able to carry the project through uncertain times.

Geographic diversification does not always protect you. Owning office buildings in Houston and Denver at the time that oil prices plummeted illustrates how interconnected local economies may actually be, despite 1,100 miles of geographic separation. The same holds true for high-tech corridors such as Silicon Valley in California and Route 128 in Massachusetts, or for various Midwestern cities dependent upon manufacturing. So simply hedging your bets geographically may not be enough.

On the other hand, concentrating all your investments in one locale across multiple property types—for example, owning retail, residential, and office buildings—may not give you enough protection, either. A local disaster would affect all three of these property types.

There also is the balance you establish between the number of risky development projects that you have in process versus your more stabilized, income-producing properties with long-term leases. Development projects are especially vulnerable to downturns, while well-leased properties may continue to generate income despite the onset of hard times.

It's helpful to make comparisons with investing in other fields. If all of your investments are in venture capital, you could be skating on thin ice. The situation is even trickier for the entrepreneurs who are actually running the businesses. They are generally dependent upon sequential rounds of financing to keep their company going. When times get tough, their inflow of invested dollars is likely to dry up. Although real estate is different from venture capital, in that you should have a better idea at the start as to what the end project will look like and what dollars will be needed to get you there, over time markets are likely to change. Unfortunately, unlike venture capital, your investors probably don't expect you to come back to them for more money. They expect you to raise enough money up front.

To make the best of such difficult situations, understand who else might be hurt in the downturn, and who might be your ally. It might be, for example, that your lender does not want to take a loss and is willing to continue to support you.

Take the dramatic case of Larry Silverstein. In his initial purchase of the World Trade Center site in New York just prior to 9/11, he gained control despite putting up personally only half of one percent of the value of the property. After the tragedy, Governor Pataki of New York wanted a quick groundbreaking for a new building. Despite some questions as to Silverstein's status, he was allowed to continue as the developer. The politicians did not want lawsuits aimed at clarifying his position to delay the project.

Although this was an extreme situation, understanding the motivations of others, plus using any good will you may have accumulated, can make it possible to get the other players to give you the time you need to work out your problems.

Follow the Cash and Hold Reserves

The old joke that banks only lend money to people who don't need it is especially relevant in downturns. So, the cash reserves you have built up often make the difference in how you will be treated and what options you have. If most of your wealth is in real estate, you should consider some sales or refinancing to build liquidity in the good times.

It is tempting to wait to put on permanent financing until your project is leased and you can get the maximum mortgage. The risk in this strategy, however, is that in the meantime you will be susceptible to swings in interest rates or in the availability of money, as many holders of adjustable rate residential mortgages have recently found out to their chagrin.

Moreover, because short-term rates are normally lower than long term, it is tempting to resort to short term borrowing as long as possible to keep down your costs. The risks are similar. You can hedge your interest rate exposure, but hedging comes at a cost, and is more common to consider for larger projects.

My natural sympathies are with the entrepreneur who—anxious to retain as much equity as possible—minimizes the cash that he or she raises up front. (We all want to hang on to as much of our "baby" as we possibly can.) But here's where the need to *plan ahead to deal with the cycles* has to take precedence over the ownership impulse. Raise the extra money, even if it reduces your share. When that X factor hits, you'll be better positioned.

I've made the distinction previously between a project-based real estate company and a portfolio-based business model. Some of the big firms in the latter category are publicly owned, often in the Real Estate Investment Trust (REIT) format. Unfortunately, Wall Street's overriding interest in a REIT's short-term earnings doesn't allow for sufficient emphasis on its longer-term growth potential. Short-term underperformance or a reduction in dividends may be severely punished. This makes little sense in an industry where long-term value is what is important, but let's face it: You and I aren't going to change Wall Street's perspective any time soon.

Public companies also have to consider the impact of leveraging. Often, lenders calculate a company's capacity for debt as a percentage of the market capitalization of its stock. If the stock price declines, so might its available credit. The "coverage ratio"—that is, the ratio of the company's cash flow to its interest obligations—is a better measure of safety, but again, you and I probably won't control what measures the lenders use.

One area over which you *do* have some control is the distribution policy of the cash flow generated by your property. Maintaining reserves is not only good operationally, but riding herd on the level of distributions makes it less likely that you will have to reduce distributions in the future, thereby calling investor attention to whatever problems you're facing.

One other factor you might keep in mind is the illiquidity discount associated with a limited partnership interest in a private company. If you try to sell a minority interest, anticipate a minimum of a 20 percent to 30 percent discount to value. (For obvious reasons, noncontrolling interests get marked down.) If you are in a down cycle, that discount is taken off of what may be an already devalued number.

You get the picture: *Plan ahead.* Borrowing the maximum the lenders will give you and then distributing the money out of your partnership may be tempting, but it's usually shortsighted. Put money aside against those rainy days (which almost always arrive). Put more positively, if you have the cash on hand to buy from distressed sellers who weren't as farsighted as you, you will be well rewarded. Many great fortunes in real estate have been made at such times. Building the appropriate cash reserves should be high on your agenda.

Manage Key Operational Issues

When times are good, it's important to be an effective operator of your properties. And when times are tough, it's even *more* important. Much of the work to protect yourself should be done up front, when times are good.

What is involved in good management? Much of it is tending to the day-to-day details involved in keeping your property clean and in good repair; maintaining the heating, ventilating, and air-conditioning systems; responding quickly to problems; and billing accurately and on a timely basis. Satisfied tenants are prized commodities; your job is to satisfy and thereby retain them. At another level, good management means updating your public areas, renovating tenant spaces to accommodate their needs, and making necessary capital expenditures.

Having an effective leasing policy means looking at your leases *as a portfolio*—for example, deciding how each lease's expiration date fits with the needs of that particular tenant (and the needs of the other tenants in the building). Do not wait until a tenant's lease is about to expire to negotiate an extension. You don't want your tenants to sign leases elsewhere because they were not aware you could solve their problem. Smart operators make sure that they stagger their leases so that when they go to a bank to refinance, they can point to a property that is immune to large amounts of space becoming vacant anytime soon.

No matter what you do, however, events occur that are beyond your control, many of which you read about earlier in this chapter. That is why having cash in difficult times is so crucial. If your competitors do not have the cash to make tenant improvements or capital expenditures, if they have fixed financing obligations that make it difficult for them to lower rents without defaulting on their loans, or if they cannot sustain operating losses, you will have a tremendous competitive advantage.

Stay on good terms with rental brokers. Paying them commissions over the years can motivate them to bring tenants to your space when you most need it.

Many of these good practices are not mysterious or arcane; they are more like common sense. There *are* times, however, when specific skills at operating certain types of property can be critically important. Whether it is running a ski resort, a hotel, a regional mall, or a distressed mortgage-acquisition company, it is crucial that somebody with experience is capable of running the business.

Addressing the Key Organizational Issues

During a downturn, you might have to cut back your acquisition and expansion plans, or do less new development. It is tempting to let people go to reduce overhead, and sometimes—for example, if you are in a real cash bind—you have no choice. The danger here, however, is that you may be giving up your capability to take advantage of opportunities either during the correction or the eventual rebound. This often is the time when you need the most help in leasing and maintaining your properties, and keeping your development projects from imploding.

Taking on consulting or management contracts to cover the overhead is often a good strategy. In the depression of the 1930s, my grandfather was able to convince the banks to let him continue to manage properties that he had been forced to give up to them. That work not only paid for his overhead, but even more important, covered his and his family's living expenses. The banks saw that his problems were not unique and viewed him as someone they could trust. A good reputation is a priceless asset.

Handling your organization during a downturn is complicated. As you'll see, the people in our case studies who build larger organizations tend to become dependent upon them. Their businesses are simply too big, and too complicated, to run by themselves.

In the case of geographically dispersed hotel or shopping center groups, services provided by the central office may be essential. You also may need to service your investors. In the case of a publicly listed REIT, you must also consider the federal regulators and Wall Street.

During a downturn, your employees will be nervous about their jobs, and for understandable reasons. They will want more personal attention from you, and more communication with you, even though you most likely would prefer to be out in the field performing triage.

A downturn is a time when the traditional real estate deal structure (that is, with separate legal entities and different sets of investors for each property) can work against you. It is not easy to convince partners in a good deal to let you use their equity to subsidize your losers. They are unlikely to allow you to cross-collateralize loans or shift cash from one entity to another.

If you are outsourcing functions to outside firms, these firms could have their own problems, which could impact you. As an example, your contractor could run into problems on other jobs, which could impact his ability to provide labor and material to *your* job.

Although these outsiders are not your direct employees, in a way they are crucial to the effectiveness of your organization. You can be faced with similar problems with joint venture partners unable to hold up their end of the deal. When you pick your partners, consider their staying power. Find out how they acted in past corrections. Your reputation as well as your money may be at stake. There will not be enough hours in the day for you to do all you want.

Once again, if you have set aside funds, you are certainly in a better position to cope than if you haven't. If you are able to keep your organization intact, that, too, is a plus. You may be in a position to get more from the downturn than "experience."

In smaller companies, by contrast, the owner may be able to make virtually all the important decisions—and also do a considerable amount of the work—himself or herself. This has its obvious pros and cons. Only you can decide which model—local/regional/national; big company/small company/something in between—is the right fit for you.

Have the Flexibility to Meet New Realities

It's not easy to make major adjustments to your business. Having to do so in times of crisis, when the underlying markets may not be coming your way, is especially difficult. However, if you focus on identifying X factors and how to respond to changing times, you might be positioned to take advantage of the downturns.

Traditionally, the time to build is when replacement costs are below market prices. During the downturns, the opposite is often the case. That is the time to *buy existing properties*—a strategy that is followed by many investors. The key is to have the cash on hand to do so.

A disruptive X factor can cause shifts in demand. After Hurricane Katrina, the home-repair business in New Orleans boomed. No one even considered building office towers. If you designed your project to be developed in stages, you might be able to stop in midstream and restart later. You may find your office building is now better suited as a residential conversion or vice versa. Follow the changes in the market.

Be a *scrambler*—that is, someone who is flexible, adaptable, resilient, and (as Gerry Hines put it) blessed with *the ability to take bad news really well*. Such people often run a little scared, expect bad things to happen, and still have the ability to bounce back. They are the ones most likely to do crisis management, hedge their bets, and take advantage of whatever situation may arise.

8

Broken-Field Running

In football—another sport I'm not likely to take up anytime soon—people refer to a technique called "broken-field running." For the ball carrier, this connotes *changing direction suddenly and frequently*, while still taking advantage of those blocking for you. You improvise, either because you want to or you have to. If you execute your cuts just right, you might be able to pile up some big yardage.

The analogy to the real estate game should be obvious. I've already made the point that being flexible, exploring lots of options, and moving deftly when you see an opening are important skills. Working hard, and with concentration, is also essential. This is particularly relevant to smaller, project-oriented real estate entrepreneurs, who (for better or worse) don't have a huge organization to support them. Typically, however, as these entrepreneurs take on more responsibilities, some additional staff is needed. The *desire for control* has to be balanced with the *need to delegate*.

Let's look again at some of our friends from previous sections who have taken the project path, grown, but stayed relatively small.

Susan Hewitt: Riding a Changing Wave

Susan Hewitt enjoyed several successful years of buying defaulted loans from the Resolution Trust Company (RTC) and from traditional lenders. These lenders had also taken title to some of the individual units. Her ability to deal with the regulators in New York City gave her an advantage in a field with few competitors. She purchased a number of loans at favorable discounts. She then had the flexibility to rewrite many of these loans with tenant associations, reducing the face value of their loan by a sizable amount while still maintaining a loan balance in excess of her own cash in the deal. As this improved the association's balance sheet, she could then resell a number of the individual units. (New buyers, as well as their lenders, were reluctant to be part of an entity with excessive debt.)

Name: Susan Hewitt

Start-up location: Manhattan

Scale-up location(s): Queens, Westchester

Hedging-the-risks challenges: Dealing with a changing market and the saturation of her niche through the entry of new competitors, forcing a recasting of her business model

As the supply of defaulted loans in Manhattan began to be absorbed, Susan expanded her operations to other boroughs of New York City, especially Queens. She also began to explore Westchester County, north of New York City, where an oversupply of new and converted units had gotten a number of developers into financial trouble.

The World Changes

On a fundamental level, Susan's business had changed. Instead of being able to buy the underlying loan—a process that gave her control over the property—she was now offered a package of units or shares in cooperatives that were subordinate to existing financing. The lenders on those properties saw enough value that they were not interested in discounting their position. Susan faced a new kind of risk. If the other shareholders failed to make *their* payments, the debt holder could foreclose on everybody. (In the past, *she* had been in that position.) This was a risk that Susan had to evaluate and factor into her acquisition price.

There was another risk. Before she could buy, she now would be personally subject to approval by the co-op board, as would be all of her subsequent buyers. Where she often had been willing to pay up to 40 percent of the initial valuation of the units, she reduced that to 30 percent if board approval was required. On the positive side, the underlying housing market was beginning to improve, and end users were willing to pay more.

What really hurt Susan's business model, however, was that a number of new and less savvy competitors were entering the field. In many cases, they represented institutional money that—at least in Susan's view—didn't adequately take into account the risks inherent in this small but regulated subset of the residential real estate market. These new competitors not only paid more, but began to offer cash incentives to tenants in regulated units to move out—something she had never felt the need to do.

Unfortunately, the Boston-based hedge fund that had financed her most recent round of purchases of discounted mortgages declined to finance her buying units directly. She had to find a new investment partner. She soon found one that not only was willing to support her new company, but also enabled her (in a negotiation with her original partners in the management company) to increase her share of the management company to 40 percent from 25 percent. Over the next few years, backed by her new financial sponsor, Susan acquired about 1,000 condominium and cooperative units in Queens and approximately 2,000 in Westchester. As the residential market continued to improve, she was able to sell almost all of these units at a profit.

Her biggest win came in a property in Queens, where she acquired a block of units in one of the best buildings in the area. The property was 33 stories high and featured large apartments and door-man service. Much of her success came as the result of two unantici-pated events. First, for income tax reasons, the seller did not want to complete the transaction until a year after the initial agreement to purchase was signed. During that period, the real estate market in that area exploded, and she was able to sell the units for almost 40 percent more than she had projected while doing her initial underwriting.

Second, because of the quality of the building and its perceived lower risk, she agreed to pay a higher price. Her financial partner didn't think that the projected lower return was adequate. As a result, Susan had to finance this project separately from the other deals she was then doing. In doing so, she was able to retain 75 percent of the management company's share of the profit. As she later recalled, she wasn't overly concerned about whether she was real smart or just real lucky; in this case, she was happy to take the profits.

The World Changes Again

In spite of this success, she felt that the environment for her business was more competitive. She had picked much of the low-hanging fruit, and would have to figure out how to adapt to new pricing and new competition without dramatically increasing her risk level. She suspected that she would have to find complicated residential projects that were in trouble for reasons other than pure market considerations.

As this hunt began, Susan's people skills turned out to be an important asset. She was accustomed to dealing with all types: regulators, attorneys, boards of co-ops, and tenants. She had the patience to listen, respond with humor, and understand what the other party wanted. Simply put, people liked doing business with her, and that went a long way. She was able to rebound from situations where changes in her business necessitated finding new financial partners.

In searching for deals, Susan discovered that there were many projects that were broken not for economic reasons, but for partnership reasons. The participants not only did not want to have to bother with regulators and tenant boards; they no longer wanted to deal with each other. Often, these partnerships controlled units in good buildings in good locations. (Susan's ultimate definition of a "good building" was one where she would feel comfortable if her parents lived in it.) She found that she was good at getting partners who weren't speaking to one another to agree to sell to her.

One example arose in Westchester County, north of New York City. The original sponsor had died. The financial partner who had backed him was not overjoyed about the sponsor's heir, who now was running the project. Susan was able to make a buyout deal acceptable to all parties, including herself.

Another purchase came about as the result of a bid she put in for 60 units in a desirable 250-apartment, 4-building complex in Riverdale. Both the sponsor and the individual unit purchasers were subject to board approval. The original sponsor had gone under, and after selling some units, the subsequent buyer had decided to dispose of the remainder to take quick advantage of a recent increase in apartment values.

Susan initially bid $7 million, knowing that one potential buyer would probably bid $7.6 million. She didn't think that potential buyer could close the deal, however, and although she was willing to pay somewhat more, she did not want to show all her cards at that time. Sure enough, when the first buyer did not perform, the seller reoffered the package to Susan and one other buyer who had originally bid $7.1 million. The seller wanted to close this deal quickly, and knew that both of these potential purchasers were experienced, had good reputations, and were likely to get board approval.

Susan was willing to go to $7.3 million, but did not want to get into a bidding contest above that level. Her solution was to join forces with the other bidder, a much older man whom she knew and respected. They would share the deal 50/50. There were some questions as to how decisions would be made, and what disagreements might trigger a buyout of one by the other (a buy/sell agreement), but Susan believed that she could handle the relationship.

In fact, she didn't have many other buying alternatives. She was seeing few acceptable deals, even though she had a number of private investors willing to back her. She knew she had lost out by not buying more aggressively in what had been a rising market. Still, she felt comfortable in not stretching. She did not know when the market would correct, but she knew it would.

Defining a Competitive Edge

Meanwhile, she was still in the game, albeit a changed game. She was leveraging her skills in managing in a regulated environment, the contacts she had built up, and the knowledge she had accumulated about local markets in the New York City region. She found her people skills and reputation as a straight shooter to be especially important in a market where there was increased competition. Sellers now had more choices as to whom they could do business with. Her challenge was how to convince sellers to do business with *her*, even if she did not bid the highest price.

Something else had changed. She had accumulated some capital. She had "living money." Her organization and overhead were small, involving only one junior partner. She could be selective, lead a more relaxed existence, and be ready to capitalize on the next cycle or special opportunity. (*The freedom to operate counter-cyclically is often the prerequisite to long-term success in a field where one failure can erase years of winners.*) Whether or not her judgments about the market were correct, she would not feel compelled to do deals to pay her overhead or satisfy either lenders or partners. She did want to stay in business for herself. As she said, "If I have to clean up messes, I prefer them to be my own."

When asked what else she had learned, she responded without hesitation. "I may have to do business with creeps," she said, "but I don't want one as a partner."

Ed Mank: The Perfect Non-Snowstorm

We left Ed Mank at the end of Part II ("Scaling Up") with Ed having just purchased Mt. Cranmore, a ski resort in New Hampshire. Whereas Susan Hewitt stayed focused on one property type, Ed was more adventurous. He did a good deal of due diligence before going ahead. Not understanding much about the ski industry, he consulted a number of experts, visited some of the other ski operations in northern New England, and did projections from many angles.

Name: Ed Mank

Start-up location: Boston (Beacon Hill)

Scale-up location(s): Boston (waterfront); Lowell and Cambridge, Massachusetts; New Hampshire

Hedging-the-risks challenges: Dealing with an operating business with substantial complexity and overhead, and contending with a host of X factors (regulatory, natural, and so on)

His experts encouraged him to buy. Mt. Cranmore was one of the first ski operations in the area, having been founded by legendary Austrian skier Hannes Schneider. The Schneider family had run the place in a low-key manner for decades, with Hannes himself serving as an instructor for many years. Although Cranmore had been celebrated for having one of the first ski lifts, little had been spent on capital improvements in recent years. Ed was told that with a new lift and some upgrades to the base lodge, the operation could be made competitive.

Ed was not naïve. He realized that outside experts—some of whom only earned their commissions if and when the deal went through—might have a "deal bias." But Ed was looking at Mt. Cranmore mainly from a real estate perspective, which was a perspective he thought he understood pretty well. To him, the real value resided in the 475 acres of land. He thought that, over time, he could build 400 vacation homes. When the owners were not in residence, the homes could be rented to other skiers—a standard practice for second homes. The rental income would be shared by the facility manager and the homeowner, benefiting both.

He thought that the total price—$2.5 million to buy, plus another $1.5 million for necessary improvements—was not prohibitive. Amortized over the anticipated 400 units, the $4 million total amounted to only $10,000 per unit. He was able to borrow about $3 million from a bank, and assembled a group of friends to put up the remainder. Like Ed, the friends did not know much about the ski industry—but they were willing to bet on Ed.

Ed himself put up half the group's investment and agreed to guarantee the bank loan personally. Like many real estate entrepreneurs, he was by nature an optimist. In addition, the timing seemed good: This was the early 1980s, a time of expansion for the real estate industry. The U.S. economy had broken out of the stagflation of the 1970s. Ed also had cash on hand; he could draw upon his profitable real estate operations, and also on the profits of an insurance agency he had formed with a partner.

For the first couple of years, Ed made improvements to the lodge and began building his first homes on the property: 66 in all, 30 of which sold quickly, at prices ranging from $125,000 to $200,000. It was an exhilarating initial victory, which Ed took to be a harbinger of great things to come.

In fact, it turned out to be the high point of the venture.

Dealing with Adversity

Now began some of the hardest years of Ed's life, amounting to a decade of reversals. Some were entirely out of his control. The records showed that for a number of years, the average snowfall in the Cranmore area had been 72 inches. For the next decade—that is, during the period of Ed's involvement—total snowfall never exceeded 52 inches in a year. Ed became an early believer in global climate change.

The main slope of the mountain faced south, which gave it a lot of sunshine on cold days—a good thing. The flip side, however, was that not only was there less snow in the area, but on his slopes, it melted faster. His ski season was shorter than that of his competitors. They were able to open their slopes in November, whereas he rarely opened before December.

To counter the potentially ruinous lack of snow, Ed invested in expensive snowmaking equipment. But this system only worked at temperatures below 28 degrees, and temperatures on his sunny mountain often rose to 40 degrees.

Ed certainly understood that the ski industry was weather dependent. What he *didn't* understand, at least at the outset, was the driving patterns of the eastern Massachusetts skiers who made up the bulk of his clientele. If it was snowing in Boston on Friday, potential skiers often did not leave to make the two-and-a-half-hour drive until Saturday, meaning that Ed lost a half-day of lift-ticket sales and ancillary income. Meanwhile, skiing was becoming a family affair, and families with kids (and in more and more cases, working spouses) would leave midday Sunday to beat the rush and get home earlier. For Ed, this translated into another half-day of lost sales.

Another unanticipated blow to his fortunes was the evolution of North Conway, the nearest town to Mt. Cranmore. When Ed bought his mountain, North Conway was a quaint and quiet New England village. Then came an ambitious real estate developer, who in short order transformed North Conway into "Discount City." This transformation was particularly bad news for Ed. Not only did the town lose most of its original charm; the new development was aimed mainly at price-conscious shoppers looking for outlet deals. As a result, there was a shortage of good restaurants, movie theaters, and other attractions that might entice families into the area for more than a day.

By mid-decade, Ed was feeling battered. Then, in 1986, the revised federal tax laws put new restrictions on the ability of the owners of second homes to take depreciation and write off their real estate losses against their non-real estate income. Next came the economic crash of the late 1980s and early 1990s, which further devastated the second-home market, which in bad times is often the first to collapse. New Hampshire, in particular, was hard hit. Banks with large real estate holdings did not survive. Even if there had been homebuyers, there would have been no loans to be had.

Ed had scaled his capital improvements to accommodate 2,800 skiers per day. As it turned out, he rarely had more than 1,500 skiers on peak weekend days, with 250 to 400 being the norm during the week. Unfortunately, few of his operating expenses were volume dependent. He still had to run the equipment to make the missing snow. He had to staff and maintain the lifts and run the lodge. Other expenses over which he had no control escalated. The New Hampshire electric utility that served the North Conway region got into trouble and raised its rates substantially. (Snowmaking is very energy intensive.) As a consequence of several severe injuries and lawsuits at other ski resorts, insurance costs for the industry rose considerably.

Managing the whole operation turned out to be more complicated than Ed had expected, and he found himself having to be at Cranmore four or five days a week. Competitors with more snow days and more off-season attractions were expanding. To retain his people, he had to increase wages.

For most of the ski season, Ed had a regular weekly staff of 50—a number that increased to 90 on weekends. Keeping a group of transient employees happy and productive proved a difficult task. During the off-season, he still had to maintain a core staff, even though little revenue was being generated. Ed personally made up the operating losses on his mountain, which were significant, primarily through increasing the bank loan. He didn't want to ask his partners—his friends—to put up more money.

Ed jumped through all kinds of hoops to build attendance. He built a new lodge. He purchased a new Doppelmeyer ski lift to better distribute skiers around the trails. He bought the same tennis facility he had failed to purchase at auction the first time around, and—with the help of a sports marketing group—set up his own tournaments.

But the hemorrhaging of cash continued, and eventually, even the boundlessly energetic and optimistic Ed was ready to throw in the towel. Now came the biggest problem of all, at least from a personal standpoint: Ed personally had guaranteed his bank loan, which by this point had tripled in size. He knew he would have to negotiate a deal with his bankers, and he knew it would not be easy!

Escaping in One Piece

In a series of marathon sessions over five days, Ed did his best. Finally, in a scene similar to the memorable one in Tom Wolfe's *A Man in Full*, the bank's chief negotiator was reciting from the loan contract the list of horrible penalties that the bank could inflict on him personally. It was bad—*really* bad. "*Stop*," Ed finally interrupted, with a look of feigned terror on his face. "If you'll stop reading, I'll admit to being really intimidated!"

By this time, the vice chairman of the bank had stepped into the conference room to witness Ed's torments. Overhearing Ed's straight-faced plea for mercy, he burst out laughing. Tensions subsided, and the negotiations resumed on a friendlier note. (*An incidental lesson: A little humor at the right time and in the right vein can be a great lubricant for negotiations.*)

Finally, the deal was cut. The bank took over the property, on condition that Ed sign a three-year operating agreement to manage the property on behalf of the bank. Ed got a substantial discount on his personal obligations, and the bank agreed not to foreclose on Ed's other assets. At the end of the three-year period, the bank decided to cut its losses and sold the property for approximately the same price that Ed had paid a decade earlier.

An official at the bank subsequently told Ed that one of the key reasons they went along with him, rather than really put the screws to him, was that during the whole period Ed had been honest with them. He never tried to hide what was happening, or move his other assets to get them out of the bank's reach. (Banks find out about tactics like that.) Over time, Ed made good on most of the losses suffered by his investors, including those of his friends who had acquired Mt. Cranmore homes that had gone down in value. After all, he reasoned, they had bet on him. He never wanted to be seen as a "bad bet."

What did Ed learn from the disaster, beyond the fact that like a farmer, a ski-resort operator is dependent on the weather? The capital and operating costs were too much for the income he could generate. What Ed saw was "real estate," when in fact, what he was buying into was an operating business in which he had no experience or skill. There are limits to what even entrepreneurial optimism can accomplish, especially if the X factors are working against you.

Most of all, Ed discovered much about himself. As an entrepreneur, he had never thought much about what it meant to be a *manager*, trying to get complicated things done through others—especially people whose motivations were very different from his own.

Ed also learned a lot about resiliency—and what's important in life. Despite the economic losses and all the hard work and stress, he had come out the other side with his head up. In fact, he was *proud* of his efforts. He had maintained his integrity. The rest of his real estate portfolio was intact. He could continue to "put his feet up on his desk," as he had when he started in real estate more than 45 years earlier. He had survived the perfect non-snowstorm, and was still in business, on his own terms.

Rich Erenberg: Finding the Home-Field Advantage in Pittsburgh

Rich Erenberg had scaled up by starting a number of investment funds to acquire existing properties where he felt he could add value. The early funds were highly successful. He was having trouble, however, finding properties for his most recent $10 million fund. Prices had escalated, even for less desirable properties, as a result of an influx of institutional and public money into the asset class. Even properties with problems were selling at high prices. Investors, it seemed to Rich, were not being compensated for potential risks.

Name: Rich Erenberg

Start-up location: Houston

Scale-up location(s): Pittsburgh, East Coast

Hedging-the-risks challenges: Finding a new-but-related real estate niche, relocating to a new geographic area, and putting a new funding model in place

Up until now, he had found better opportunities outside of his home base, Pittsburgh. But now with the run-up in prices in other locales, this was no longer true. Pittsburgh had shrunk to less than half its former size: A population that had peaked at 675,000 residents in 1950 had since declined to 325,000 residents. The city was experiencing major financial problems. Corporate and property taxes were high. The manufacturing jobs base continued to erode, and residents were still leaving. Financial problems at US Airways were threatening the number of flights in and out of the Pittsburgh airport. Pittsburgh's weather made it hard to compete with the Sun-belt. The city had become the butt of jokes on late-night talk shows, never a good sign. Although many in the city itself had moved to the suburbs, even the metropolitan area, which includes both the city and the suburbs, was down by more than 12 percent to 2.4 million residents.

And yet, Rich saw some positives. Health care, research, and education were becoming major areas of job growth. Downtown institutions were banding together to tackle the city's financial problems and to take advantage of state and federal economic-development programs. As the local economy adjusted to a changed world, the unemployment rate began to drop. New retail and residential uses were being found for some of the vacant manufacturing complexes. Housing prices in the area were low, attracting some young people to stay—especially after they looked at housing prices on the West and East Coasts.

Buying into Technology Drive

Rich thought that the negative perception of Pittsburgh could prove to be a blessing in disguise: He might be able to find a bargain. Out of the blue, in late 2003, a broker asked him whether he was interested in the former AEG office/warehouse complex. This 200,000-square-foot property on 20 acres had been built about 10 years earlier. It included 115,000 square feet of office space and 85,000 square feet of warehouse. The location was excellent: on a major highway just outside of the Pittsburgh city limits in Washington County, midway between downtown and the airport, and about 20 minutes from each. Parking was tight but adequate, with 550 spaces. The property was adjacent to Southpointe Park, a major office and industrial park on land put together by the county redevelopment authority.

AEG had been purchased a few years earlier by Daimler Chrysler, which shuttered the property and consolidated its activities elsewhere. Not wanting to bother with the headaches and financial exposure of leasing the property, the company put the property up for sale for $14 million—well below the $20 million it cost to build.

Rich did his numbers. Even that price, he realized, was high. If he rented the office space (net of operating costs) at $10 per square foot and the warehouse at $6, and if he built in a reasonable vacancy factor, his cash flow would be about $1.5 million, representing a 10.7 percent return on the asking price.

The problem was that he had to consider not only the initial acquisition cost, but also closing costs, carrying expenses until the building was rented, plus allowances for tenant improvements and leasing commissions. This would add as much as $4 million more to the purchase price. At $18 million, the potential of a $1.5 million annual cash flow did not seem adequate to compensate for the risk of taking on this large and vacant property.

Rich did not give up. He knew that Daimler Chrysler's decision maker was located in New York. His experience was that such companies initially overprice properties, hoping to find an owner-user who may be able to utilize the building as is and pay the higher price. But this strategy rarely works, and when it doesn't, sellers sometimes accept a much lower price just to unload the "nuisance" property. In this case, Rich guessed that Pittsburgh's negative image—at least in the eyes of a New Yorker—might just work in his favor.

The negotiation was not an easy one, but because the seller had no other real option, Rich was able to gradually get the price down from $14 million to $8.8 million. He thought that even with $4 million in extra costs, the potential of a $1.5 million operating cash flow made the project worthwhile. The key for Rich was that he was *local*, and had the time to aggressively work on leasing the property. A non-local couldn't compete on an equal footing.

Finding the Money

Now he had to raise the money. He estimated that if he could raise $5 million of equity, he could borrow the remaining $7.8 million, although most likely he would have to guarantee the loan personally. Because his most recent fund was primarily designed to buy leased, not vacant properties, he was only able to allocate $1 million from it to this deal. He decided to put up $2 million himself, leaving $2 million to be raised from former investors. Based on his track record, he was able to get commitments from his earlier investors and bring in some new ones.

Those investors reasoned that given the rents in the area, at a purchase price that averaged $44 per square foot—or $64, accounting for leasing commissions, tenant improvements, and other projected costs—Rich and they couldn't go too far wrong. And because Rich was making a sizeable commitment of his own money to the deal, they were persuaded that he would spend the time needed to make it a success.

Then, during the due diligence period, while Rich was investigating the legal and physical aspects of the property, he discovered that water had gotten into the ridge on which the building sat as a result of faulty drain pipes installed in the initial construction. On a worst-case basis, the engineers told Rich, this could cost $1.3 million to fix.

Rich saw this not just as a problem, but also as an opportunity. He could now renegotiate the price down. After all, he could walk away from the deal. The company's New York representative was not overjoyed. As a matter of fact, she was furious. The bottom line: Rich got another $1 million off the price, lowering it to $7.8 million. He felt sure he could do the work for less than that number.

He moved his own office to the building to concentrate on rentals. After 18 months, the office space was largely leased, but the warehouses less so. Even though it took longer than he expected, the property now broke even.

Rich also saw positive signs in what was happening around him. More potential tenants were touring his project. A new road to the airport, scheduled to be finished in a year or so, would cut travel time to 10 minutes. The Southpointe Park next door was being expanded, primarily for residential and retail uses.

In a very real sense, the negative of being in Pittsburgh allowed Rich to negotiate a good going-in price. His patience, persistence, and strong negotiating skills were positives. He didn't have to compete with institutional investors, which tend to favor the big coastal markets. So, for a number of reasons, living in Pittsburgh actually gave him an edge.

Looking even further down the road, Rich anticipated a future in which the value of Pittsburgh property would gain (in relative terms) as other high-priced markets declined. Rich still looked for bargains—as he had back in his days in Houston, when he was buying distressed condominiums—but now he rode bigger waves and could afford to look at the world with a longer time horizon.

John Dewberry: Betting on Atlanta

John Dewberry had become a major landowner in Midtown Atlanta—an infill area that he believed would become more and more valuable as that city continued to develop as a major regional service center. Over the past 40 years, Atlanta had more than doubled in size. In recent years, John had contributed to that growth with the successful completion and leasing in 1999 of One Peachtree Pointe, one of the first speculative office buildings in that area. Concurrently, he had grown his organization to the point that he was ready for new opportunities.

Name: John Dewberry

Start-up location(s): Charleston, South Carolina; Jacksonville, Florida

Scale-up location(s): Atlanta, Georgia

Hedging-the-risks challenges: Riding out a down cycle in an "up" market

As is so often the case in real estate, John's next opportunity came totally out of left field, outside of his game plan to expand in Midtown. A broker told him that global travel provider Worldspan—founded in Atlanta by three airlines in the 1990s—was looking for a new headquarters building, in which they would be the primary tenant. Worldspan wasn't interested in Midtown, the broker said, but wanted to be further uptown, near its existing location in northwest Atlanta. John found and optioned an appropriate site, and was able to negotiate the terms of a lease with Worldspan. Based on Worldspan's credit, he was able to obtain a loan for $62 million of the projected $75 million in project costs, and obtained commitments for the remaining $13 million of equity.

But then John hit a major bump in the road: a man-made X factor. In the spring of 2003, after he had put a year of effort into the project, Worldspan was sold to Citibank, which wanted to use the computer-savvy company as a back-office processor. Suddenly, there was no longer any need for a Worldspan world headquarters building. Luckily for John, Worldspan already had reimbursed most of John's up-front predevelopment costs, even though the lease had not been signed.

Back to Midtown

John again refocused on Midtown, with the goal of building a second major office building there. He already owned the land there, he reasoned, and it was costing him money to carry it. He planned a 300,000-square-foot building to be called Two Peachtree Pointe, which he estimated would cost $60 million, or $200 per square foot.

But there was a problem. The overall office market was weak, and vacancies were high. Effective net rents after operating costs had dropped to $10 to $12 per square foot, which would work out to only a 5 percent to 6 percent return on his projected $200-per-square-foot cost.

This was a far cry from the comparable $16 per square foot net rent he commanded at One Peachtree Pointe, on a $150-per-square-foot cost. The increased per-square-foot project cost resulted from higher land costs, a more expensively designed building, and several years of inflation.

John's partners, Lara and Steve, were cautious. Dewberry Capital controlled the site. "Why be in such a hurry to build?" they asked. John countered that a downturn was exactly the right time to get started. When the building came on the rental market in a couple of years, existing vacancies would have been filled, and there would be little new competition. He had *faith* in Atlanta and in Midtown, he explained, rents were *sure* to rise.

There were other compelling reasons to move forward, John asserted. He had added key people to his staff, including a senior construction person from Los Angeles and an experienced leasing person from Chicago. Although John readily admitted that this fact alone shouldn't be a driving force behind a new building, the talented people in the organization needed new projects to keep them engaged and motivated.

Finally, John pointed out, building Two Peachtree Pointe would only increase the value of his other holdings in the area. His longer-term vision was a cluster of high-rise buildings in Midtown, all with ground-floor retail and a pedestrian-friendly environment. The way to make that happen, he argued, was to *make it happen.*

Making It Happen

The lender who had originally agreed to back John on the Worldspan deal agreed to move ahead with the project, even though it was a speculative undertaking. This speculative aspect was underscored by the course of John's negotiations with a potential lead tenant for the building. Those negotiations dragged on for some time, and ultimately fell through. At that point, not liking the way the winds were blowing, John's lender decided to drop out.

In his continuing conversations with Lara and Steve, John reiterated his desire to go ahead. "Well, John, if you're so convinced about the future of this market," Steve finally asked, "why not start using your own cash—especially because the land has no mortgage on it?"

It was the right question, from John's point of view, and he thought it was the right strategy for going forward. Shortly thereafter, in September 2005, ground was broken on Two Peachtree Pointe.

A year later, construction was well under way, but there was still no lead tenant in sight. John was in negotiations with two prospective tenants, but had nothing definite. Nevertheless, John remained optimistic. (*Remember: Optimism abounds in real estate!*) With few new buildings under way, there was a shortage of large blocks of space for major users, and rental rates had crept up. John knew he could compete in price with any new building that might be built, because of the general rise in construction costs. At the same time, there were few new major tenants coming into the market. It became clear that John would have to convince existing tenants to move from someone else's building into his building—and, of course, existing landlords were fully motivated to do whatever they needed to do to retain their key tenants, and keep them out of John's clutches.

On the positive side, by mid 2006, the building was taking shape, and John was pleased with the way it looked. Although naturally nervous about what would happen if he did not find a lead tenant soon, he knew that traditionally Atlantans did not commit to new buildings until those buildings were completed. John had found a new lender, who—because the construction risk was now minimal—offered better terms than the earlier lender. The project was on budget.

The Midtown area had become a much sought-after neighborhood for young professionals, and thousands of mid-priced apartments had been built. Lara had been spearheading an initiative with property owners on the uptown side of Midtown to create a "community-improvement district," aimed at giving the area a focus and identity. Some of Dewberry's properties, including Two Peachtree Pointe, would become part of this district.

Positive Thinking

John continued to think positively. He knew that some people— perhaps even some people in his own company!—thought he was crazy to have started a second office building without any pre-leasing. But, John believed that Atlanta would continue to grow, and that companies would need new space. He believed that at this point in his career, he had the staying power to fulfill his Midtown vision—a vision that went back more than 20 years, to the days when he was taking architectural courses as a student at nearby Georgia Tech.

At this point, we don't know whether John's entrepreneurial decision to go forward will be a winner. This much we can say for certain: If you are going to take a major risk, make sure you have the backup cash to carry you if the building takes longer to construct or lease or costs more. Most foreclosures occur not because the basic idea was faulty, but because the original owner did not have the staying power.

Here's a real estate maxim that's every bit as relevant as "location, location, location": *The second or third owner often takes the prize.*

The Cardons: Never Build Higher Than a Curb

The Cardon family had ridden the waves of growth in Phoenix. In fact, Phoenix was one of the country's fastest-growing areas. Its metropolitan population had steadily increased: from 726,000 in 1960 to 3,252,000 in 2000, with approximately one million people living in the city itself.

Name: The Cardon family

Start-up location: Phoenix, Arizona

Scale-up location(s): Phoenix, Arizona

Hedging-the-risks challenges: Recasting a business and funding model to deal with 1) changing family expectations, 2) overextension into related businesses, and 3) geographic expansion

The Cardons had progressed from running gas stations to developing land to diversifying into virtually every real estate product type. Their typical deal was to contribute land they owned into a 50/50 partnership with a shopping center, residential, industrial, or hotel developer. The developer then would use the land as security to borrow funds to build a project. The two partners would often guarantee the loans personally. The Cardons' game plan, in effect, was to capitalize on all stages of the business, from raw land to the finished product.

Local savings and loan institutions (S&Ls) were pouring money into the Phoenix market. This resulted in a massive amount of overbuilding, which in turn led to *every single S&L* in the state going into bankruptcy. Loans were being foreclosed all over the state, and the Cardon projects were no exception. Having given personal guarantees, and suddenly finding that many of their new partners were insolvent, Wilford had to scramble. For the Cardons, these were scary times, indeed.

In most cases, the Cardons were able to give the land back to the lenders in exchange for relief on their personal guarantee. They gradually unwound their obligations, while still retaining some assets in their own names. They learned a critical lesson: *Diversification of businesses among different real estate asset classes within one market doesn't necessarily protect you in a downturn.*

What else had they learned? First, they learned never to put the "Cardon" name—unblemished, up to this point—on things they did not actually control. Suddenly, their name was in the papers, prominently attached to distressed projects in which they had no operating involvement. As lead investors, they could not sidestep the bad publicity.

Second, each project had to stand on its own. There also had to be enough equity that lenders would not require personal signatures.

Third, they should stick to what they were good at: identifying, buying, and securing permits for appreciating land in the path of growth. In a quote that got widespread circulation in the Phoenix area, they declared that henceforth, they did not want to build anything higher than the curb on the side of the road.

The Keys to Developing Land

Better than most developers, the Cardons understood the keys to successful land development:

- Understand the demographic and physical growth of the area, and the demand for the particular use to which you intend to put your land.

- Know what to pay for land by calculating backward from what the property will eventually sell for to the end user. (*In real estate jargon, this is called the residual land value technique.*) For example, assume you are building a 2,400-square-foot house selling for $400,000. The pro forma might look like this:

Sales Price	$400,000
Construction cost @ $80/sq. ft	($192,000)
Architectural and engineering	($ 20,000)
Permitting fees	($ 20,000)
Other costs (financing, sales, administration)	($ 68,000)
Developer's profit	($ 50,000)
Available for land acquisition	$ 50,000

- Know the zoning constraints that determine what and how much you can build on your land. In Phoenix, for example, you can't build anywhere where the grade has more than a 15 percent slope. With those kinds of constraints in place, how many units can you build per acre? How long will it take, and what will it cost you, to get your permits? What functions will you perform, and what will be the builder's responsibilities?

- Make sure that you will be able to flush your toilets. You will need sewers (or septic systems) and power and water. What will it cost to install these utilities? What roads are required, and to what standards? Do you have to pay for all of this yourself, or will some costs be paid by others? Can you finance some of it by setting up special utility districts, in which case charges can be paid over time by the end user?

- How will you stage your improvements? Can you build in phases, or do you have to incur substantial up-front costs before you can be sure how many units will be sold?

- When you sell to builders, how do you select the most reputable ones, and who are most likely to succeed at selling their product? You probably will be selling your land to them in stages, which means the faster the development, the faster you receive your cash.
- Try not to sell all the best land first, when the prices are lowest. You don't want to be stuck with all the back or less desirable land.
- Make sure you have a margin for error. Almost without exception, your development will cost more and take longer than you think.
- Keep leverage to a minimum. Remember our list of X factors. Any and all of these can affect the timing and profitability of your project.
- Projections are, at best, educated guesses. You have to be able to hedge your risks.

In short, buying land, permitting it, and putting in the necessary infrastructure are complicated undertakings that require considerable skills, local knowledge, and connections. If you're going to go into this tricky business, it certainly helps to pick one of the country's fastest-growing markets.

An Overdue Restructuring

In light of their recent and painful lessons, the Cardons decided to structure their future investment partnerships differently. They sought out a number of high-net-worth investors around the country to whom they could send prospectuses of their new land deals. They would be given the opportunity to invest with the Cardon family, who would put up a sizable portion of the cash themselves. There would be a "promote" for the benefit of the Cardons, but only after all the investors got their money back. Leverage would be kept to a minimum. Return *of* equity was the key—not just return *on* equity. The Cardons were determined to treat every dollar as if it were their own.

Wil Cardon, having completed his MBA in 1998, gradually took over the running of the business from his father, Wilford. This led to some conflicts with Wil's uncles and cousins. The three branches of the family began the difficult task of separating their assets. At the same time, Wil began to worry about the high price of land in Phoenix. Despite the region's fabulous growth, raw land at $30,000 per developable mid-price residential lot seemed high, especially compared to growth areas in Texas, where the price was closer to $10,000 per equivalent lot.

As a result, Wil began to sell Phoenix land using tax-free exchanges to buy acreage outside the Phoenix area—not just in Texas, but also in Colorado, New Mexico, and Southern California. In Denver, the Cardons had a local partner. In most cases, however, they managed their deals through their own project managers, headquartered in Phoenix. Many of these managers were young, but all had some real estate experience before signing up with the Cardons. They were encouraged to invest their own cash in the deals in which they were involved. Wil always thought it a good test of his own investment decisions to see which deals his staff was willing to back with their own money.

The risks in buying land outside the Cardons' home base were obvious. Could Wil and his Phoenix-based staff handle the management and decision-making issues? And would diversification across locations really protect them in a downturn? The answer to that might revolve on whether the downturn was caused by a swing in the national financial markets, or the national economy, or on local supply/demand considerations.

With more than 90 percent of their net worth tied up in land, and 45 percent of that in Phoenix, they knew they were making a bet on their ability to select and process land in the path of growth. They also knew that a number of factors were beyond their control—and probably always would be.

9

Moving the Fleet

Now let's look at our second group: those people who scaled up dramatically and put large sums of money to work transforming urban and suburban landscapes. They built companies whose existence is tied to more than the success or failure of an individual project. They developed large organizations that, like a fleet of ships, were dependent upon their admiral's ability to navigate amid the shoals. But the bigger the fleet, the more difficult it is to adjust its course and to be flexible in a changing world.

The Shahs: A Small Company Goes Public

The decision of the hotel/motel-building Shah family to establish a REIT (Real Estate Investment Trust) appeared to be a logical one. They were now moving their business in a different direction. They would continue to focus on mid-sized, limited-service motels, but henceforth they would focus on larger, more urban East Coast markets. The REIT structure would enable them to obtain the capital needed to fund their ambitious expansion plans. Under the terms of the plan, they would exchange their ten existing motels for a majority share in a new public entity. They hoped they no longer would have to look for new capital every time they wanted to acquire a property. When appropriate, they could later issue new shares to fund further growth—at a higher price, they hoped.

Name: The Shah family

Start-up location: Harrisburg, Pennsylvania

Scale-up location(s): Central and Western Pennsylvania

Hedging-the-risks challenges: Expansion, managing a REIT, redefining role of the founders

So the decision to *become* a REIT appeared to make sense, but *operating* as a REIT was not easy. At that time, hotel REITs had certain structural problems. To preserve their tax advantages, the REITs could not develop, operate, or manage the hotels themselves; they had to outsource these services. Accordingly, the Shahs had to form separate companies to perform these functions. Wall Street found such REITs difficult to value. Who would be making the profits, and at what stage?

Establishing Parameters

Pricing the operations and management agreements turned out to be relatively simple. Fee-based contracts for these services were common in the industry. Development was the trickiest part because the REIT could only buy a completed project. That created the potential for a conflict of interest. If the Shahs' company developed a project from scratch, what should be the price to the REIT? Were the Shahs entitled to a development profit? If so, how much? Their REIT was given the option to buy the completed motel from their development company, but at a price that reflected the market value of the project as completed, and independently appraised. They considered themselves motivated to charge the REIT reasonable fees, because they knew that if the markets perceived them as overly greedy in these transactions, their reputation in the industry could be severely damaged. Accordingly, the family tried to avoid any conflict-of-interest questions.

As a protection for the shareholders, the REIT was required by statute to have a board with a majority of independent directors who reviewed such contracts. The Shahs felt themselves lucky to have found several respected industry leaders who were willing to play that role for their REIT.

Their biggest problem, at the time they were going public in 1999, was that both the capital and hotel markets were deteriorating. Investors were demanding higher returns. As a result, the Shahs had to agree that their operating company would pay at least a fixed 11 percent cash return to the shareholders of the REIT. To protect the shareholders further, the Shahs agreed that the new shareholders would receive their full 11 percent return *before* the Shahs received any return on the shares they received for contributing their ten motels to the REIT. This was a new situation for the Shahs, and it put constraints on how they thought about and used their money.

As it turned out, the Shahs' REIT—Hersha Hospitality Trust—was the last of the hotel REITs to receive funding in that market. The underwriting brought in $12 million of new equity for the trust. The new shares received 35 percent of the ownership of the company; the Shahs (and their partners) got 65 percent, or $25 million in shares, for contributing their motels. This valued the entire company at $37 million.

The Growth Trap

Over the next three years, in keeping with their strategy, the Shahs grew the portfolio from 10 to 20 motels. They accomplished this by selling 8 of their original motels and acquiring 18 new ones. To fund the acquisitions, they used the proceeds from the sold properties, drew on their $12 million in new funds, and in several cases convinced the seller to take "UPREIT" shares in the REIT, in lieu of cash.[1]

Soon, however, the Shahs found themselves caught in a dilemma. The financial markets wanted growth, but they did *not* want the trust to issue new debt or stock until the market price of their stock went up—which wasn't likely to happen until they added new motels. On the positive side, the company's motels in the mid-priced market were less subject to economic cyclicality, and continued to operate at higher margins than did the hotels of many of their competitors. Their trust was one of the few hotel companies that did not cut its dividend during this period. Still, Hersha Hospitality Trust's stock rarely rose above its initial $6 level. The Shahs discovered that during a downturn, it is difficult to raise cash without substantial dilution of the existing shareholders' equity—a course which neither the Shahs nor their shareholders were keen on.

Three more years went by, and slowly, the situation improved. The economy began to strengthen, and the financial markets began to come out of their doldrums. The Shahs again had access to new capital. They raised $25 million in convertible preferred stock with a ten percent coupon. Although the dividend cost was higher than they would have liked, it allowed them to begin acquiring properties that they considered undervalued.

Soon they were able to raise $75 million in a new secondary offering at $8.50 a share, which represented a welcome 40 percent increase over the initial $6 share price. They followed that with more offerings totaling some $150 million. They also raised $125 million in debt, at interest rates that had now dropped to an average of 7¼ percent. The capital markets had opened up to them and other hotel companies.

A Balancing Act

The Shahs were engaged in a challenging balancing act: taking advantage of rising equity prices during good times to issue new shares, and then leveraging that increased equity to take on more debt. They proved very adept at this game, and their resulting growth was phenomenal. Within another three years, the portfolio grew from 20 to 70 motels and hotels. Some were developed from scratch; others acquired. Most of these mid-sized, mid-priced properties were now located in larger urban areas all along the East Coast, with a few in smaller markets. Although considered limited-service, many had their own food operations, meeting rooms, and other retail uses.

With this growth came a whole host of operating issues. The company was no longer able to partner just with friends who would live in the properties and operate them. The four initial co-owner/operators had long since left their motels to help run the centralized operations of the Shahs' various companies, and it was difficult—if not impossible—to re-create that relationship in 60 new properties with 7,696 rooms. Obviously, there was a need to develop an organization to help operate and market them.

A change in the laws governing REITs helped. The law now permitted hotel REITs to operate their own hotels through wholly owned subsidiary corporations. Henceforth, the Shahs could turn over this function to the REIT itself. Development, meanwhile, continued to be performed by a separate entity.

The Shahs' new corporate hires were both more experienced and more functionally oriented. By and large, they came from larger hotel organizations. They were more motivated by salary and bonuses than by equity interests. Whereas most of the Shahs' 2,000 employees in their various companies still worked on site in the motels, there were now 115 employed in corporate activities, 80 of whom were in Harrisburg and 35 in Philadelphia. The company moved its Harrisburg headquarters from space they had constructed many years earlier—in the courtyard of one of their first motels—to a newly renovated building.

The Family Angle

The roles of the two sons, Jay and Neil—who had joined the business after college and graduate schools—continued to grow. The brothers worked well together, taking on more responsibilities from their father, who was increasingly becoming an advisor. He was still involved in new deals, but now his involvement was more selective. Jay supervised the REIT, looked after relations with the capital markets, and monitored the staffing of the various enterprises. Neil was heavily involved in strategic issues facing the company, as well as in acquisitions.

Their mother, Hersha, was proud and supportive of what they were doing, but wondered how big the family business should become. On the personal front, Hasu and Hersha continued to spend time hosting groups from around the world who came to visit Harrisburg, and also joined delegations visiting other parts of the world. They took a lead role in improving their community—for example, by playing a major role in the funding and building of a new temple in Harrisburg to accommodate the growing Hindu population in the area.

Jay and Neil were very conscious of the legacy that their parents had created for them, through their many years of hard work. They believed that it was important to protect and reinforce the culture of the firm, which in part meant making more explicit their core values of honesty, communication, achievement, and community service. They had to do this at the same time that they established institutional standards for hiring, reporting, and underwriting.

The Shahs had taken their business a long way in over a quarter century. They had survived a number of dramatic swings in fortunes, and in the process, had created a platform for continued growth. They now had a reputation, and a legitimacy, in the hotel industry. They also had the experience needed to operate on a broader scale.

Investors had responded positively to this expansion. The Shahs were able to issue 7.2 million new shares at a price of $11.20. The downside for the Shahs was that, over the years, their ownership share of the ever-growing trust had declined from 65 percent to 10 percent. In other words, as the pie had gotten much bigger, and their shares had become more valuable, their ownership percentage had decreased.

What seemed at first to be mainly a way to raise expansion capital proved to have far broader implications, include many more restrictions, and consume much more of their time than they anticipated. Now, they had to navigate not only the real estate and hotel markets, but also the public securities markets—a triple challenge.

So, was a public REIT the only mechanism for them to use going forward? Did they have adequate control of their destiny if the stock market became bearish on hotel REITs? Was the REIT structure best for the younger Shahs, who had to consider its implications for the growth of their own net worth? These were questions worth pondering.

Walter Shorenstein: Changing Horses Midstream

Walter Shorenstein continued to build his position in San Francisco. He acquired the Bank of America Building—San Francisco's most prestigious office tower—in a $600 million deal, one of the largest ever in the United States, up to that time. He financed the purchase almost entirely with a first mortgage from Bank of America and a second mortgage from Wells Fargo.

Name: Walter Shorenstein

Start-up location: San Francisco

Scale-up location(s): San Francisco

Hedging-the-risks challenges: Establishing funds with institutional investors to acquire property nationally

Walter was on top of all aspects of his deals. His organization was a flat one. He managed his deals by walking his buildings and seeing what needed to be done. As his son Doug put it, he had 2 percent knowledge of what his people were doing, but 98 percent knowledge of what they *should* be doing, and he was not hesitant to express his opinions.

He attempted to balance the expiration dates of his tenant leases so that his buildings were full when it was time to roll over his debt obligations. (*Looking for tenants at the same time you're looking for mortgage money can make that money more expensive. Lenders like to see full buildings.*) He also tried to anticipate downturns, renegotiating leases ahead of schedule.

As a result, his buildings performed well, on a relative basis, in the recession that followed the overbuilding of the late 1980s. But he didn't do many new deals in this period, either. The four institutional investors who had partnered with him in his successful South Market Street venture, and who had supported him in other projects, had pulled back from real estate. As a result, when the market began to turn up again, Walter had to search for new partners.

Picking Partners

At that time, Walter's son, Doug, began to play an increasingly important role. Doug had moved back to join the company several years earlier after a stint in a New York law firm. During his early years at Shorenstein, he focused primarily on the leasing and debt sides of the business, rather than in the operational side. His main interest going forward was in doing transactions—both purchases and sales.

In 1991, Doug was introduced to David Swensen, Yale's chief investment officer, by someone with whom David had worked when he was at Salomon Brothers. David had not been happy with the options he had in the real estate asset class. He thought that there were far too many transactional costs. Managers appeared to be motivated by the fees they charged. Even worse, those fees were based on property appraisals in which he had limited faith. He saw that the managers were motivated to grow assets under management and to hold them without selling. Given that system, he was reluctant to give managers *carte blanche* in making acquisitions, although he realized he was not expert enough to make the decisions himself.

David wondered whether the private equity model that was prevalent in the venture capital arena might be applied to real estate. In the scenario he was envisioning, investors would put their money in blind pools and give managers discretion in putting out the money. Fees would be minimized, intended primarily to cover the firm's operating costs. Back-ended sharing of profits would replace transaction fees. Managers would be encouraged to co-invest at a level commensurate with their net worth. They would commit to not raising a new fund until most of the existing fund was invested. *Alignment of interests* would become the mantra.

In an effort to set something like this up for real estate, Yale was willing to help experienced operators start their own funds—even if they had never run their own businesses or worked with institutional investors before. The university was looking to establish close working relationships that could be replicated over time, and over the lifespan of multiple funds.

Doug listened to this vision, and soon decided that it would make sense for the Shorenstein family. He liked the idea of diversifying the family's investments geographically (although he wanted to remain in the office arena, where he felt they had expertise). Blind pools would enable him to buy and sell based on his view of the market.

The fund business presented new challenges. In the case of institutional partners, each potential investor would have to be solicited individually, with presentations to staff, committees, and sometimes even their advisors. Each investor's due diligence on his firm would be extensive. The Shorensteins would have no trouble qualifying, in the eyes of most investors, but this high level of transparency was not something the family was accustomed to.

A New Game

This was not a game for Walter. In the past, Walter would call his investors, explain the deal, and get their commitment on the phone. Walter favored a buy-and-hold strategy, not wanting to feel pressured to put out money. Age was also a factor. Then in his 70s, Walter did not see himself traveling around the country making presentations to people half his age.

Doug, by contrast, enjoyed selling and was good at it. Having Yale as his lead investor gave him both access and credibility. He welcomed the role he would now play, and felt ready to take on the responsibility.

The new fund would continue to focus on high-quality office buildings. Other than a few projects completed with IBM, however, most of the Shorensteins' projects had been done in northern California. To appeal to his target audience, Doug would have to build an organization that could buy and manage on a national basis. Accordingly, he set up a New York office and hired two proven acquisitions specialists to work with those on the West Coast. He felt certain that his West Coast operational people could hire and supervise local property management personnel internally. He did not believe that managing quality office buildings would be dramatically different from city to city. The key was to maintain a high level of customer-oriented service.

Leasing was a different story. Local firms would be hired to do leasing because that was an area in which specialized local knowledge was important.

To improve his firm's administrative capabilities, he convinced Glenn Shannon, a former law partner in New York, to come out to California to head up operations. The organization had to become more structured, professional, and process oriented in certain areas.

It also was now larger, which meant that new ways of doing business would be needed.

Doug was also fortunate that his father was not only considerably older, but also that his father had a great many political and charitable interests in which he could continue to exercise his entrepreneurial talents. For the most part, Walter was willing to become an advisor and to let Doug and Glenn make changes that were quite foreign to his way of doing business. He also committed a sizable portion of the family assets to the funds, in part because he recognized both the changes occurring in the financial markets and in San Francisco itself. He liked the idea of geographic diversification. As a result of his father's flexibility, Doug did not experience many of the tensions that arise when roles change within a family—a larger subject to which we return in Part IV ("Taking Stock").

A Phased Approach to Change

The organizational changes did not happen all at once, but the first fund started in 1992 was a winner. Its biggest acquisition was a portfolio of properties from a financial company that was anxious to dispose of its real estate investments. This package of quality buildings was purchased at well below replacement cost, and proved to be highly competitive when the market turned up.

After each fund became invested, Doug formed a new one, increasing the family's stake as they redeployed proceeds from the sale of some of their San Francisco holdings, eventually including even the Bank of America Building. Yale continued to be their lead investor. Although Doug still had to do considerable traveling and make presentations to past and future investors, the company's reputation grew, and he had little trouble filling what became larger and larger funds. The strong performance of his early funds—with a number of highly profitable sales that quickly returned investors' capital and some initial profits—made his case for him.

Doug was not reluctant to pull back from a market when he thought prices too high. During one 18-month stretch, for example, he didn't make a single investment. But this long hiatus was broken with the purchase of the John Hancock Tower, one of Chicago's most prominent and tallest office buildings, at what many thought to be a high price. In this transaction, Doug discovered the income potential of a roof. By leasing space atop this tall building for communication equipment and towers, his firm added $5 million to the rent roll. Capitalized, that added $60 million to the overall value of the property. Even in an overheated environment, in other words, it was possible to find value.

True, he had to work harder. There was no end of new competitors: new funds, REITs, financial institutions, and wealthy U.S. and foreign investors. The increasing amount of leverage provided by cash-rich lenders, moreover, was cutting back the equity required to do a deal—in other words, more equity money chasing fewer aggregate dollar opportunities.[2]

Thinking About How to Grow

The company considered a number of options to expand its opportunities. One was to expand geographically, increasing the numbers and sizes of cities where they would do business. (Up to this point, they had focused mainly on a few major cities.) Another approach under consideration was to do some mixed-use as well as purely office developments. A third approach would be to partner in deals where the local operator was involved in a complex ownership structure that needed restructuring. The Shorensteins—with ready cash in their funds, the ability to act fast, and a reputation for understanding the real estate implications of a deal—hoped they would be perceived as logical and attractive partners. This third approach appealed to Doug, given his legal and his real estate background.

The fund would have to share ownership and profits, and decision making, with the local operator. In return, however, that local operator might be willing to subordinate its position to a preferred return for the fund. This reduced the risk to the fund, especially as prices commanded by desirable properties continued to rise.

At the same time, Doug was not averse to reducing his company's on-site management responsibilities by outsourcing to others. He saw the company's strengths as doing transactions and performing overall asset management. Given the history of the firm, he was comfortable with development if the opportunity arose. For now, however, the firm would be primarily an investment company, with a portfolio of existing properties that it would be willing to buy or sell when the market dictated.

The nature of the fund business encouraged turnover of properties. Most of their institutional investors looked at a five-to-ten-year time horizon. Their nontaxpaying status made them insensitive to turnover. Their goal was to find managers who would buy, add value, and sell at a profit. They would then reinvest the proceeds in the manager's next fund. The manager would cash out its promotional profits, which enabled it to compensate key employees and acquire new properties where the company could again add value. With this model, both the Shorensteins and Yale were accomplishing their objectives.

The Bucksbaums: A Market-Driven Strategy

During their early years in real estate, Martin and Matthew Bucksbaum worked hard to create some of the first shopping malls. Over the years, these centers grew in size, complexity, and impact. It's not too much to say that the Bucksbaum brothers, along with the Chattanooga-based Lebovitzes and other leaders in the industry, helped shape suburban America, providing a new, convenient, and appealing shopping model for an increasingly consumption-oriented society. The Bucksbaums also innovated on the financial side, forming one of the first public REITs to hold their regional malls and to provide them with the capital to continue to expand.

Name: The Bucksbaum family

Start-up location: Cedar Rapids, Iowa

Scale-up location(s): Iowa suburbs; downtown Des Moines, Iowa; Midwest

Hedging-the-risks challenges: Expansion of company, adapting to changes in financial markets, death of co-founder

The size and experience of the company's development team was becoming more and more critical to a key aspect of the business: persuading retailers to commit to centers that were still in the planning stages. The retailer had to be convinced that the centers—now larger, more complex, and more complicated to build, would be both well tenanted and well managed, once up and running. At that time, the markets accepted that the development and management functions in these centers were performed for a fee by separate companies controlled by the Bucksbaums. The stock price of the REIT rose substantially, and the Bucksbaums became quite wealthy.

Martin, however, saw impending changes in the real estate market. Congress was in the process of passing legislation that would encourage pension funds and other similar institutions to invest in real estate. Martin believed that these new sources of capital would pay more for shopping centers than the value attributed to them in public markets. This conclusion led the brothers to try to take their REIT private—that is, to buy back the stock owned by outsiders—but this only led to other bidders seeing a potential conflict of interest coming in offering to pay even more.

Given this reality, the Bucksbaums determined that their best option was to sell their existing centers directly and liquidate the REIT. They arranged a sale of most of the centers to Equitable Life, while still retaining the management of these centers for themselves. Taking their cash, they began to continue to develop new centers, financing and owning each project separately. They gave ownership interests in each project to their key employees, many of whom subsequently became millionaires in their own right. This was a welcome fringe benefit of getting out of the REIT structure.[3]

The brothers worked long hours, often going to their nearby Des Moines office after supper, as their father had done many years earlier when he owned the grocery store. To finance new centers, the Bucksbaums often sold older properties, just as they had done when they were first starting out.

After one such sale—in Minot, North Dakota—their staff decided it was time the Bucksbaum brothers got some recognition from them. They cooked up a scheme with the brothers' wives to get Martin and Matthew to go to a public park on a pretext. At the time, Matthew was driving a Volkswagen, and Martin was driving a well-worn Lincoln.

There in the park, wrapped in big red ribbons, were two brand-new luxury cars: a Jaguar for Martin, and a Mercedes for Matthew. When the Bucksbaum brothers opened their trunks, they found that one was full of champagne, and the other was full of food. It was, by all accounts, a great party.

Next Steps: Another REIT

Meanwhile, Martin focused on the company's next steps. At Equitable's request, the Bucksbaums purchased Equitable's management company, which was handling those centers the Bucksbaums were not already managing. They inherited a sizable leasing and operating staff centered in Minneapolis.

Martin also began thinking again about going public (that is, forming a new REIT). This time, the new money would be put to a different use. Martin had concluded that the United States was becoming over-malled in some areas, and that henceforth, the best opportunities were likely to be in acquisition rather than development. Many of the institutions that had bought shopping centers in the preceding decade were now becoming sellers. By taking advantage of this reversal of an earlier trend, the Bucksbaums would be able to make good money, and also achieve greater scale, which remained an important priority in the retail and financial climates of that time.

Along with Bernie Freibaum, their chief financial officer, and Bob Michaels, their chief financial operating officer, the brothers spent three years exploring their options. Finally, they felt ready to take the plunge. Goldman Sachs made an offering that raised $400 million for the new REIT, which was called General Growth Properties. After contributing its properties, the family retained a 45 percent interest in the new entity.

Working in concert with another REIT, General Growth soon purchased a package of 16 regional malls and 3 power centers from Prudential Life. (A *power center* is anchored by a number of big-box retailers such as Home Depot.) Martin's perception as to what would happen in the industry proved prescient: Acquisitions were where the money was to be made at that point in time, but being in a partnership with another REIT was another story. The other REIT with whom General Growth had partnered had emerged as the manager of the properties, and the Bucksbaums preferred to control what they owned. After only two years in the partnership, therefore, General Growth sold its interest to the other REIT at a good profit.

Shortly thereafter, the vast Homart property portfolio came on the market. Homart had been the development arm for Sears, and owned a large number of centers. In most of these, Sears was one of the anchors. After a spirited bidding process, General Growth was able to purchase the portfolio for what was then a staggering sum: $1.6 billion. The Bucksbaums worried that they had paid too high a price. They told themselves, however, that they could make it up by upgrading some of the centers and by developing some of the extra parcels on their peripheries.

Dealing with Tragedy

Then came the ultimate X factor: Martin died of a sudden heart attack. This upset the existing dynamics in a major way. Matthew, who had been more involved with the inside operations, now became committed to completing the purchase his brother started. He took on the CEO role.

Matthew's son John, then 39, also took on a more prominent role. He had been in the family business for about 15 years. After college, he started as an assistant and became a project manager on malls under development. He then moved to California, where he supervised the setup of a West Coast development office. More recently, he had moved back to assist his uncle Martin in negotiating the terms of their new REIT, and selling the idea to investors.

Martin's sudden departure prompted the company to rethink how it organized itself. A powerful leader, Martin had surrounded himself with followers, and had created a top-down, centralized, informal organization. But the sheer scope of the Bucksbaums' operations now demanded more structure, more procedures, better processes, and—most of all—more people capable of making decisions. The office in Des Moines had become a small one, in relative terms, with management now being centered in Minneapolis. With the acquisition of Homart, the company had a large presence in Chicago, which was selected as the new headquarters for the company.

Matthew began to address the necessary organizational changes. The firm hired a counselor to work not only with the senior leadership team, but also with another 20 individuals in the organization's middle ranks, with an eye toward building the company as a national player. Matthew embraced the notion that there might be more than one "best solution"—an idea that Martin had difficulty subscribing to. Matthew and John focused on learning to delegate, and on rewarding their employees and shareholders. They encouraged their senior leaders to spend less time arguing among themselves and more time looking for joint solutions.

At the same time, John and CFO Bernie Freibaum played the financial cycles masterfully, continuing to expand through acquisitions, upgrading of existing malls, and selected new development. These purchases were financed by borrowing on a short-term basis, which could be obtained at more favorable rates than the capitalization (or "cap rate") on their purchases.

Eventually, these short-term loans would be replaced by longer-term loans—albeit at slightly higher rates. By that time, the company hoped to have improved the cash flow of the centers to more than cover the increased mortgage costs.

Of course, this strategy could leave the company exposed to short-term interest rate swings. Fortunately for them, however, interest rates did not spike up. From time to time, they issued new REIT equity or preferred shares to help pay down debts. In short, the company combined skill *and* luck in managing the liability side of its balance sheet. The Bucksbaums understood that there were times to buy and to sell income-producing property. They felt comfortable playing the real estate cycles, and hedging their risks.

Following the Cash

As it had throughout its history, the company adapted its strategy to shifts in the public-market versus the private-market demand for investing in real estate. Following the source of the cash had proved to be a very profitable game both for the Bucksbaums and their partners. They also built new "life-style centers" without an enclosed mall and with fewer anchors. These centers provided a lower-cost option for many retailers.

Yet the core of the business remained where it had been for decades: in regional malls. The Bucksbaums were not only skilled acquirers and developers; they were also skilled operators. They worked to make the extra $1 or $2 per square foot from operating their malls, and often succeeded. Meanwhile, they tried to take advantage of their size and their understanding of what drove traffic to their centers to sign up the most appropriate retailers. They realized that the mall business was one in which scale could be beneficial—although in their wildest dreams, they couldn't have imagined the scale that they would ultimately achieve when they first set out to expand the family grocery store in Iowa.

Trammell Crow: A Strong Offense, a Weak Defense

For most of its first 30 years, the Trammell Crow Company's growth trajectory was upward—*straight* upward. True, it went through one major financial crisis in the 1970s, but all the partners chipped in to get the company through it.

Name: Trammell Crow

Start-up location: Dallas

Scale-up location(s): Multiple across the United States, Central America, Europe, and Asia

Hedging-the-risks challenges: Coping with a mismatch between the business model and a changing marketplace, "salvaging the remains," and searching for a new niche

The Crow family business was involved in a variety of property types: office, industrial, shopping centers, residential, hotel, and distribution. At its height, the Crow empire of companies controlled more than 140 million square feet of space. Each product type had its own legal and financial structure, with partners at the top, at the regional level, and at the local project level. Even the individual projects had separate legal and financial structures. Trammell Crow himself was the glue that held it all together. His passion, optimism, drive, and willingness to reinvest his earnings—and to guarantee personally the borrowings of all his ventures—made it work.

A *Flawed Structure*

Unfortunately, when the tide turned, this wasn't enough to keep the huge empire from spinning out of control. The crash came for a number of reasons. First, an incentive system that paid a small salary and little in the way of cash bonuses, and depended on equity participations in local projects, encouraged local partners to keep developing even when markets were overbuilt. The willingness of the company's top officers to guarantee notes personally for these local projects also fanned the flames.

In addition, transferring virtually all power to the local level resulted in the central office not always knowing what had been committed. A decentralized accounting system compounded the flow-of-information problem. The junior partners' loyalty was to their local and regional partner, rather than to the center.

As times grew tough, moreover, Trammell's desire to keep a large share of the profits for himself and his family, and to turn over future leadership to his own offspring, did not sit well with those in the field.

As the management issues tied to growth worsened, the response from those at the top was formulaic, and ill advised: *Restructure, reduce the number of reports at the top,* and *install new layers of management.* These organizational tweaks, although well intentioned, only served to further isolate those at the top and to create "winners" and "losers."

Many of these winners had a great deal of clout at the local market level. They had financial interests in existing properties, which they wanted to monetize to separate themselves from the pack. Many had reputations that enabled them to go out on their own, which meant that they no longer needed the Crow name or backing. In Chicago, San Francisco, and Atlanta—all key markets for the firm—managing partners departed, taking most of their staff with them. Disputes over valuation, who was entitled to what, and who owed loyalty to whom resulted in confrontations and, in many cases, lawsuits.

The high levels of leverage in most of the Crow deals also hurt badly in this downturn, because a small change in operating income often made the difference between a profitable or money-losing deal.

As lenders began to close in—demanding repayment, threatening to foreclose on personal guarantees—a major weakness in the ownership structure of the properties surfaced. Because each property had different partners, with some properties more or less solvent, conflicts arose as to whether the more successful properties or partners should bail out the less successful. Many lenders required an amalgamation of properties as a condition of advancing new money—a step that was nearly impossible to take under the existing decentralized structure.

Finally, the junior partners found that many of them had personal guarantees on their projects in proportion to their equity participation. And that wasn't the worst of it: Many would have substantial tax liabilities if the properties were foreclosed upon, regardless of whether there was any residual value in the property.[4] Ultimately, Crow's management team and its lawyers worked out a way for the junior partners to avoid their tax liability—but only in exchange for giving up their ownership interests. The difficult outcome undermined much of the trust that had been built up and accounted for much of the subsequent fractionalization of the company.

Many of the former partners still thought kindly of Trammell personally, and appreciated the opportunities he had given them, but they lost their faith in the organization. A culture of togetherness and trust had been destroyed.

A New Beginning

Despite this collapse, many still thought there was considerable value in the thousands of *people* who remained in the organization. Although opportunities for development were limited, there were many local offices staffed with talented people who were skilled at building, leasing, and managing properties, and who could provide a high level of services. In fact, the firm already had begun to go in that direction, providing services for third parties to offset some of its substantial overhead costs.

Several of the remaining senior partners decided to form a new corporation. The Crow family would still be the primary shareholder, but the other partners would own the balance of the company. The new corporate framework would protect the stakeholders from personal liability—a weakness in the old corporate structure that they now understood all too well.

Although the new entity would have some potential to undertake development, it would primarily be a service operation for commercial properties. With most of the physical assets already given back to the lenders—or divided among the Crow family and a few of the senior officers—the service business would be run differently. Decision making would be centralized. Standardized financial statements, investment guidelines, salary levels, and job descriptions would be developed. There would be a central pool for bonuses, which would be determined by the overall profitability of the company, and then allocated to reflect individual performance.

The new company started with the Crow legacy properties as its prime client. Gradually, however, it built a niche by persuading corporations to outsource to them many (or all) of their real estate functions, both in the United States and globally. It also undertook build-to-suit structures on a fee basis for owner/users, and continued to do a limited amount of new development under the auspices of the local offices.

Funds were launched to attract money from institutions anxious to invest in real estate. As was the case with many former developers at that time, everyone was scrambling, looking for new ways to make a living or to complete their projects.

A Public Incarnation

Approximately seven years after forming the partnership, the partners made the decision to take the company public. This gave some liquidity to the original shareholders, and allowed a transition of ownership away from those shareholders to individuals who had become more active in the company. It was a successful offering, with the initial stock price of $17.50 more than doubling over the next few years.

Then another financial crisis hit the real estate industry, this time as a result of the 1999 technology bubble collapse. The commission and fee business dropped off dramatically, and the stock price plummeted to under $9 per share.

At the same time, there was also increasing confusion about how to integrate those in development with those in leasing and management. Especially at the local office level, struggles arose over personalities, compensation practices, and reporting arrangements. The solution eventually arrived at was to divide the company into two separate divisions: one for service operations, and one for development.

As the market improved, the company began to make strategic acquisitions, buying local or regional brokerage/management firms to expand its presence in certain markets. At first, there were problems in integrating the new firms into the parent company's operations—taking advantage of cost-saving options, retaining key players, and focusing the new employees on the types of businesses the parent was interested in. The company learned from its mistakes, however, and in its later acquisitions did a better job of integration.

As the business grew, the board increasingly faced strategic decisions. For example, how big did they have to be to compete in what had become global markets? Should they stay public or attempt to go private? It was becoming clear that there were disadvantages in Crow's being a public company, as earnings were affected by the irregularity of the profitability of development activities. Wall Street, as a result, had trouble evaluating the company, even though the core service business income was reasonably stable. Led by Bob Sulentic, who had become CEO four years after the company went public, the board now had to decide whether to go private or to sell out to an even larger firm.

The Decision to Sell

The decision to sell became easier when a new player came on the scene. At that time, publicly held CB Richard Ellis was already the world's largest commercial real estate services firm. It was known for its high-quality people. It was also recognized for having effectively managed the integration of other firms into its operations, and for giving substantive positions to qualified newcomers. From CB Richard Ellis's point of view, Trammell Crow was an especially attractive acquisition target, because the company was strong in the integrated management of the real estate functions of a large stable of corporate accounts, an area in which CB Richard Ellis wanted to expand.

By this time, the Crow family had sold virtually all its stock, so most of the profits from this sale went to the existing management. The price—$49.51 per share, or $1.9 billion—was more than respectable for a company that had been started 16 years earlier with a capitalization of $18 million! In this case, the service company had created a value independent of the underlying value of its physical assets.

The "Trammell Crow" name was retained, but it was used only for the development division of the combined company. That division was headed by Bob Sulentic, and staffed mainly by Crow people. Bob also headed up all the Asian activities of CB Richard Ellis.

What's in a name? Although Trammell Crow's name is less prominent in the real estate world, his personal legacy and that of the company will be an enduring one. He helped train and inspire legions of people who are now shaping the industry that he once dominated. His influence will continue to be profound, even if his legend as a financial wizard diminishes.

Gerald Hines: Building a Market-Based Sustainable Business

When we last saw Gerry Hines in Part II ("Scaling Up"), his company was in the middle of a major transition: from being a company driven by an entrepreneur to an entrepreneurially driven company.

Name: The Hines organization

Start-up location: Houston

Scale-up location(s): National

Hedging-the-risks challenges: Finding and embracing alternatives to development, welcoming in the next generation (with its different skills), building the management business, and finding new markets, both in the United States and overseas

Hines had expanded from his Houston base to develop quality office buildings nationally. This provided him with the opportunity to retain and motivate partners who otherwise would go out on their own. Although major decisions were still made by Gerry, his partners in the field were given considerable local operating authority. An executive committee of Gerry and his key associates was set up to meet quarterly, to discuss general strategic issues and project- or people-specific problems.

The geographic diversification proved to be a plus for the company. Falling oil prices had a major negative impact on the Houston economy. Meanwhile, the company benefited tremendously from new office projects in cities such as Chicago and San Francisco.

The Tide Turns

Soon, though, the Houston market problems became a national problem, as a building spree fueled by excess lending decimated the financial institutions. There was little mortgage money to be had, especially for development deals. The question for Hines—as for many of us—became, *how do you survive a bear market and still create a sustainable business?* Or does the cyclicality of the real estate business preclude this from happening?

For Trammell Crow, as we've seen, the firm's very survival was at stake. In Hines's case, the situation was dire but not deadly. Many of his leases were with quality tenants and extended for many years to come. Some timely sales had provided the company with a reserve of free cash, and most of the company's properties were not highly leveraged, at least in relative terms. With ownership control centralized in the well-regarded Hines family, it was easier to renegotiate problem deals with lenders, cross-collateralizing as necessary. Where possible, projects in the pipeline were cancelled or deferred. The company's industrial division, which had been operating semiautonomously, was closed and the properties sold off, in part because Gerry did not see where he could differentiate or add value to that product class.

In spite of this downturn, Hines wanted to preserve his organization for the next upturn. With that end in mind, he took on a number of third-party service assignments and construction projects to cover overhead. At the same time, keeping his organization intact helped him to do a better job leasing his existing projects. He also named his son, Jeff, president of the company. This move sent a signal that Gerry and the Hines family were in it for the long haul.

His strategy paid off. As the market improved, his firm was ready to seize opportunities at a time when many of his competitors were temporarily or permanently out of business.

Rethinking the Business

At this point, however, the opportunity set looked very different for Hines, as it did for many of the protagonists in this chapter. The new market posed a difficult question: *Why build new, when you can acquire properties at below reproduction cost?*

Gerry initially opposed the idea of buying other people's buildings. He liked to hold for the long term, and he didn't see why he should own properties that he considered inferior to the ones that he had built. His partners impressed on him the fact that money was available for acquisitions, but not necessarily for new developments. Large pension funds such as CALPERS and General Motors were anxious to deploy more of their endowment assets into real estate. The Hines organization was precisely the type of real estate entity that these institutions wanted to do business with.

On the other hand, these institutional investors wanted a say in major decisions. Also, because their projects were less leveraged, they wanted more of the cash flow and upside. As this was the only real game in town, Hines had to play by the house rules. The company also started funds of its own, amalgamating money from institutional investors that were not large enough to warrant separate accounts.

This new corporate strategy carried with it potential conflicts. How should deals be allocated among the various investors? How do you ensure that the local partner's focus on an individual project, and on the fees charged to that project, does not adversely affect the over-all fund? To solve this dilemma, the company created the position of "asset manager" to serve in the central office as, in effect, the client representative. The internal negotiations were not always easy, but the clients appreciated the effort.

The additional processes and controls did not fit well with the entrepreneurial spirit that traditionally had driven the firm. Still, most realized that given their size and the nature of their investors, they had little choice.

The company also had to rethink its incentive system, with the Hines family reducing its share of the overall pie to allow others to participate. There had to be more of a share for the increasingly powerful central staff, and for local partners. Hines was willing to lend them their share of the equity needed, but only on condition they take downside as well as upside risk. As the property markets improved and investors paid higher prices for the same cash flows, there were few downsides. For the time being, almost everyone was happy.

Going International

At the same time, however, Gerry and many of his senior people still thought of themselves as—and got their kicks from being—*developers*. They liked to *build* things. Obviously, there were fewer such opportunities in the United States, so Hines began to think internationally. With the acceleration of globalization, Hines saw his company as having a potential niche: providing Hines-quality buildings and services to expanding multinational companies in both developed and emerging markets overseas.

The first version of the plan was to consider launching a separate "international division" that wouldn't involve the U.S. partners directly. That didn't fly, mainly because those partners wanted to be in on the action. As a result, Hines divided up the international markets in such a way that each of the senior partners became responsible for setting up and supervising offices in a designated area overseas, while continuing to run their own U.S. divisions. It was a highly unusual structure, but there was a logic to it. By keeping the senior partners involved, Gerry and Jeff Hines hoped they would not only support the global efforts, but also encourage many of their talented younger associates—who knew the Hines's expectations and practices—to go abroad to staff these offices and help find local partners. Although these overseas offices often took a long time to become profitable, the partners could afford to wait: a clear case where being a private company proved extremely helpful.

The international initiative became even more central to the focus of the organization when Gerry himself moved to London. This allowed him to do the new development projects that excited him and to give his son, Jeff, and Hasty Johnson, the chief financial officer, more freedom to run the show in the United States.

As the company expanded internationally, it began to target other property types. It seized on whatever opportunities it saw in local markets. As an example, Hines owned some land in Moscow. It donated a central parcel of the land to the best English-language school catering to foreigners, and then built residential units around the school. The project was an immediate success. In Mexico, the firm developed not only office buildings, but also residential condominiums and industrial projects. They raised pools of money in funds that gave them the capital and flexibility to invest quickly and wherever they wanted.

The resulting growth was spectacular. Fifty years after Gerry first went out on his own, his company had become one of the largest developers and property owners in the world—and one of the few that has successfully expanded internationally. Today, it has more than 100 offices in 14 countries, with more than 3,000 employees.

Given its size, its culture was bound to change, to some extent. However, its mission has remained the same: to provide quality buildings and great service in an ethical, customer-oriented manner. Hines has proven that a large company can maintain its entrepreneurial spirit. It continues to build what the market wants, and to create a sustainable business for its partners. It does so by being successful in adapting the company to both internal and external environmental changes—a rare feat in this demanding and cyclical industry.

Looking Forward

If you think back over the players we've "updated" in this chapter and the preceding chapter, it's clear that there are many ways to hedge your risks in real estate. It's also clear that

- Smart people can get it wrong.
- Luck can play a critical role in determining outcomes.
- It helped to be a player in the United States in the second half of the twentieth century, where, despite some down cycles, opportunity abounded and cheap money was (generally) available.

We have seen our protagonists remain small, start funds, form REITs, stay private, go public, and go private again. X factors (mostly man-made) benefited some and destroyed others. It's not clear which of the businesses we've looked at will ride out future cycles and emerge as long-term survivors. Most likely, not all of them will be interested in doing so. Some of their principals may move on to the next phase of their professional and personal lives.

This is the subject of Part IV "Taking Stock." Assuming you've achieved some degree of success in real estate, what are you going to make of that success? By this point, you probably won't be surprised to learn that there are a multitude of "right answers" to that question.

Endnotes

[1] An UPREIT is a legal entity formed to own shares in a particular REIT. Generally, shares in the UPREIT are given in exchange for a property which is then owned by the REIT. The recipient of such shares defers any taxes due while still maintaining full economic rights in the REIT, such as the receipt of dividends. The disadvantage is that the owners of UPREIT shares have no voting rights in the REIT. To vote their shares, they have to convert them into regular shares of the REIT, which triggers the tax.

[2] An 80 percent loan-to-value ratio requires one half as much equity as a 60 percent loan.

[3] In a public REIT, it is difficult to motivate employees with stock options, because most of the REIT's cash flow must be distributed to its shareholders, which in turn puts a damper on increases in the stock price. There is also less money left in the company to invest in new projects that might grow earnings.

[4] The reason is that if the owner's current basis for tax purposes is below the amount owed under the mortgage being foreclosed, the difference is considered a forgiveness of debt, and thus becomes taxable.

Part IV

Taking Stock

This fourth and final section of this book deals with the later phases of your real estate career—a period of transition, although not necessarily closure.

The good news is that depending on your specific circumstances, you probably have a wealth of options. The same wide-open, fragmented nature of the real estate field that drew you in and provided opportunities in the first place is now providing an equally broad range of possibilities later in your life. Your success in real estate—at whatever scale you've achieved—now gives you numerous choices, most of them good.

You need to figure out not only what to do with your business, but also what you want to do with the rest of your life. What about the assets you've accumulated? How will they benefit you, and how will they benefit other people? Should you involve your children in the business, and if so, how?

Taking stock is something we often associate with the later stages of one's career. The difference for today's generation is that what used to be a 40-year career span might now be 50 or 60 years for those lucky enough to be in good health. Deciding what is right for you can be an exciting challenge, and one that has the potential of adding years to your life.

10

Your Business and You

Some real estate careers don't end until the central character finally is forced to exit from the scene.

Maybe such characters just love the work too much to quit. Maybe they have achieved a comfortable lifestyle—good income from the properties, and minimal need for active oversight—and there's no compelling reason to make a change. If so, more power to them.

Some real estate careers wind up with the central players cashing out and turning their attention to entirely different activities. This isn't unique to real estate, of course; entrepreneurs in all kinds of businesses choose to leave their enterprises behind. They move on to other moneymaking ventures, philanthropic interests, baseball teams, sailing, politics, or other pursuits.

Finally, some real estate entrepreneurs achieve a certain kind of immortality—or at least forestall the inevitable—by involving their children in the business, thereby creating a "family business."

These are all very different paths, obviously. But in every case, the individual needs to take stock, make a plan, and *act* on that plan. Just as there are lots of ways to break into the real estate business early in your career, and to scale up and ride the waves in later years, there is an almost infinite variety of ways to exit (or not exit) the business. The point is to chart the course that's right for you—and to realize that whatever your plan, it may take years to implement it.

From reading the first three parts of this book, you know that "taking stock" is something that we do throughout our real estate careers. We are constantly evaluating where we've been, where we are, and where we might go next. Now I'm encouraging you to do more of the same—although this time with a different focus, and perhaps in a more systematic and sustained way. At this stage of your real estate career, I want you to take stock first of your *business*, and then of *yourself*.

Taking Stock of Your Business

Thinking systematically and objectively about your business game plan is hard to do because you're so close to it. But try asking yourself a number of questions that collectively add up to a broader perspective. For example

- What business am I really in?
- What are my goals for the business? Have they changed? What unmet commitments do I have?
- What's my time frame?
- Do I have a succession plan? If not, what would it take to put one in place?
- Does the business have a value beyond that of the individual assets?
- Do other family members in my generation want to stay (or get) involved?
- What obligations do I have to those who have worked with me?
- Is this a good time in the market to consider selling?
- How much should I be influenced by tax or inheritance problems?

Note that these questions deal primarily with business issues, although some business issues inevitably shade into the personal realm. Note, too, that most of these questions don't address the challenges of including (or not including) the next generation in the business. I think of that as a complicated enough issue to be the subject of a separate chapter (Chapter 11, "Your Business and Your Family"). For now, let's consider these business questions, and then—in the second half of this chapter—move on to more personal issues.

What Business Am I Really In?

Maybe this question surprises you. By this stage in your life, you should know what business you're in, right?

Yes and no. Over the course of their existence, most businesses change in two ways: dramatically, and incrementally. We discussed the X factors earlier in this book—the bolts from the blue that can create the kinds of dramatic changes that are impossible to overlook. But there's a whole other universe of subtle, incremental changes that occur over time, by degrees. Therefore, taking stock in a comprehensive way—perhaps with the help of a trusted outside advisor with some degree of objectivity—can be extremely helpful.

What property type or types have I settled into? What's my geographic base? What are the strengths and weaknesses of the various members of the management team? What does the ownership structure look like? What implicit or explicit commitments have I made: to specific projects, to my investors, to my coworkers? Does my business go beyond managing the assets I have in place? What flexibility do I really have? Am I wedded to a particular property type and geographic area when there is no longer a demand? Can I compete with new competition in my niche? What are my goals for the business?

As you answer these questions and others that are important in your particular situation, try taking a longitudinal slice, too: How would you have answered these questions differently a decade ago? Are you more or less willing to take on longer-term developments or purchase property that has substantial vacancy or needs considerable renovation? Are you willing to change the focus of your business?

It is not a given that as you age, you become more risk averse. Sometimes, you may feel that you have enough excess assets that you are more willing to take a flyer, either by yourself or perhaps by backing someone you trust.

Don't think of this as an exercise merely for the Big Fish. For the person whose family has lived from the cash flow of two or three small, self-managed, income-producing properties, much is riding on the future of these assets.

Ed Mank—the Boston developer who ultimately recovered nicely from his adventure in the ski business—feels no great compulsion to take on any major new projects. He's leading a very comfortable existence, living off his Harvard Square property. He still enjoys negotiating leases and being part of the game, though. Because Ed likes running a low-maintenance enterprise, which he can control and manage, he will probably do so indefinitely. His business lends itself to that approach. He is not forced to retire. My experience is that Ed's case is typical of many in real estate.

Hasu and Hersha Shah are not in the same category. The presence of their sons in the business complicates their equation, as does being in a business with public shareholders. The parents support their sons' goal to grow the business and continue to serve as advisors to the business, becoming involved in occasional projects that interest them. They realize that growth is essential to succeeding in the hotel business.

Gerry Hines has sought to have it both ways. He has turned over the operating core of the business to his son, Jeff, and Hasty Johnson, the CFO. He realizes that both the large size of his organization and its wide scope require strong controls and interventions. He himself has relocated to London, where he can indulge his passion for developing in new parts of the world. Although he serves (like the Shahs) as elder statesman to the enterprise that still bears his name, he also gets dirt under his nails on a regular basis—successfully, it seems—without becoming a nuisance to the next generation.

What's My Time Frame?

Organizations usually don't change overnight. When they do, it's often due to an X factor, and it's usually not for the better. Positive change takes time.

As you develop your business goals, you have to be thinking about how long it's likely to take to implement them, and how that fits with your personal planning. (I repeat this question in the "personal" section, later in this chapter.) If you have multiyear projects underway, you likely aren't comfortable leaving them in midstream. If you have personal guarantees or capital calls outstanding, you have to honor your commitments.

Maybe you have to invest a certain amount of time in developing your leadership team to the point where you can turn over the reins. That, too, will take time.

Is There a Succession Plan?

This question grows directly out of the preceding one. If you simply want to put someone in place who will manage the assets you leave behind, this can be done. You find an asset manager—as opposed to an entrepreneur—and set up all the necessary structures. Assuming that your properties are rented, in good condition in a stable neighborhood, you might be able to put them on maintenance mode. They can generate income for you and your family indefinitely. You can even outsource the property management functions.

On the other hand, if your goal is to have the firm continue as an active developer or trader in your wake, you have to answer two key questions: *Do you have the right people in place,* and, *where will the money come from?* Are you willing to bankroll others indefinitely—even after they make a couple of costly mistakes? (Remember: Everyone makes a few costly mistakes, especially when just starting out.) When it's all or mostly all your money that's on the table, how much will you really be willing to delegate? If you have been the entrepreneur in your organization, are others prepared and equipped to play that role?

If your goal is to help the business continue as an active development or trading entity, but you're unwilling to delegate most of the authority to the new generation—in other words, if you're unwilling for whatever reason to put most of your eggs in someone else's basket—it probably won't work. And think about it from their point of view, too: If you are expecting them to raise their own capital, what are *you* still bringing to the table?

Does the Business Have a Value Beyond That of the Individual Assets?

This is a question that some entrepreneurs, as they take stock, have a hard time coming to grips with. Entrepreneurs tend to tell themselves that they're going to live forever. If they admit to their own mortality, sometimes they give themselves comfort by telling themselves that their *business* will last forever.

It's probably not true. Very few businesses have a value beyond their individual assets. In other words, 2 + 2 tends to equal 4, not 5. There are some cases—for example, the shopping center or hotel worlds—where it's arguable that the operating skill sets of management are important, which means that if the business is sold, it might well be preserved as a whole (or mainly whole) entity. But if the assets can be sold individually with no penalty—or if the individual sale of assets actually commands a premium—the business is very likely to be broken up.

There's another dynamic at work here, too. For you to arrive at the level of success you currently enjoy, you had to hire really good people, some with entrepreneurial talents. Well, it's simply unrealistic to imagine that those great people are going to hang around forever managing *your* properties. They are unlikely to pay you much for the use of your name after you have gone. They have the option of starting their own companies, or finding other, more dynamic settings that afford them greater opportunities.

For these reasons and others, it's unrealistic to think that many nonfamily companies will outlive the founder for very long. True, some firms in this category carry on the founder's name and just redirect the income streams from the assets to a new generation of owners. But, this tends to be a very different kind of company from the one the founder created all those years ago.

So if your goal is immortality, you may want to look somewhere other than your business.

Do Other Family Members in My Generation Want to Stay (or Get) Involved?

As you've already seen, and as you'll see again in the next chapter, real estate is often a family enterprise. The ability to structure each real estate deal as a freestanding entity serves as a natural point of entry for other family members. And although many books and movies have focused in recent years on dysfunctional family businesses, there's a lot to be said for being able to turn to your grown offspring, your siblings, or cousins for help or guidance.

But what if you are looking to step out of the business, and your sibling or siblings want to carry on without you? Are you willing to leave your assets under their control? Conversely, and more negatively: Are you willing to shut down the business by forcing a sale of assets?

The answers to these questions are situation specific. After all those years as the more involved sibling, can you take on a lesser role?

Moreover, perhaps your sibling—who's been patiently waiting in the wings for years, perhaps even working with you—believes he or she is an even greater real estate talent than you are. If you or other family members don't see it that way, who decides?

From my ongoing study of real estate families, my sense is that there's a lot of doubt hanging in the air. Giving everybody enough liquidity to lead his or her own life is very often the best course of action—assuming you can afford it, which is a big assumption. Yes, it may pain people—you, more than anybody!—to see the family name coming down off those buildings, but that might ultimately be the best way to go. More on that later.

What Are My Obligations to My Employees?

What do you owe your high-level, trusted employees—in other words, the ones who helped get you here?

Possibly, they already have equity stakes in one or more of your projects, so they're somewhere along the path toward financial security. Depending on your circumstances, that's probably a good and equitable outcome.

But what do you owe them beyond financial rewards? I think you owe them candor about where things are headed: what the company is likely to look like in the future and whether there will be development opportunities. If those opportunities are not forthcoming, they might want to make other plans. You might be in a position to help them by opening doors, by making a personal investment in their new company, or by giving them some other vote of confidence that lends your reputation and credibility to their projects.

Is This a Good Time to Sell?

It's pretty unlikely that an urgent *need* to sell will coincide with the perfect time in the cycle to sell. (One never knows for certain the perfect time to sell, except in retrospect.) Quality properties, especially those you know well, are difficult to replace. Unless you have other more profitable investments to make or a desire to diversify your assets, selling for pure market timing rarely makes sense in the long run.

If a circumstance arises that makes one member of the family really determined to sell, you might find that it's very difficult *not* to cash this person out. Believe me, anyone who's involved in the active management of the business isn't going to want a dissatisfied person, especially a relative, hanging around complaining about whether the company is going overboard on tenant improvements or whether it's really necessary to replace an expensive mansard roof *now*. Assuming there is a reasonable mechanism to establish the price, *cashing out* might mean a buyout by one party or the other. As noted previously, if you have personal liquidity, or if you can get cash by remortgaging the property at a higher level, such changes are easier to swallow. If not, you might have to resort to a buy/sell agreement whereby the anxious seller gives the buyer first rights to acquire his or her interest based upon a pre-agreed-upon process. If not, the property can be sold in the open market. (I find it dysfunctional to then give the other party a formal right of first refusal at the final sales price. It tends to discourage potential buyers.)

In any case, what if, like most of us, you don't have enough cash lying around to buy out someone's share in the enterprise? What happens if you have to sell assets to accomplish the buyout? And what happens if you have to sell those assets into a down market?

Planning ahead is the best course of action. Have a binding procedure for the breakup. Look at an up-cycle in the market as an opportunity to amass cash for such a buyout—but of course, you don't always have the luxury of long-term planning when a near-term crisis emerges. Sometimes you simply have to muddle through.

What Are the Income Tax Implications?

Closely related to the preceding question are the tax issues inherent in the disposition of property. If you've held on to the property long enough, it's likely that you have a very low cost basis in that property, and a sale will trigger significant tax consequences. You can quantify the impact:

Consider this hypothetical example. Suppose, for instance, that I bought a building 25 years ago for $400,000. Today it's worth $1 million. If I sell it today, I'd probably have to pay a capital gains tax at a 15 percent federal rate and a 5 percent state rate. So, that's roughly a 20 percent tax on $600,000, or $120,000.

But let's suppose that I've depreciated my $400,000 investment down to $100,000. That means that for tax purposes, my total gain is $300,000 greater. The recapture of this depreciation is taxed at a 25 percent rate. Combined with the 5 percent state tax, another $90,000 is due.

Now let's assume that I've put a $500,000 mortgage on this property. If I sell the building for $1 million, after I pay back the $500,000 mortgage and pay $210,000 in taxes, I'm only going to net around $290,000. I may wind up wishing I had held on to the building!

There is, of course, the option of tax-free Section 1031 exchanges, which defer the tax. (Consult your accountant and attorney if you don't know these specifics.) The problem is often in finding equivalent properties with similar quality and growth potential. You also have to be able to identify that property close to the time of the sale.

In addition, if you're in a deal with other people and you have a limited partnership interest, when you appraise that asset, you often will have to take a sizable reduction in value because of the lack of liquidity of that limited partnership interest. (The property is worth less because it's not totally within your control.) It might be that you are better off gifting or selling to your heirs at the lower price. I cite these specifics only to make the point that all sorts of tax complexities enter into these calculations. With the help of creative lawyers and accountants, you can actually do a great deal—legally—to minimize your tax obligations and (as I reiterate in the next chapter) transfer real estate values to the next generation.

In many cases, an overriding consideration in making such transfers is how much income you need for yourself. Depending on how you answer that question, you may be able to structure a sale or gift so that you and your spouse receive some income for the balance of your lifetime (or for a specific numbers of years).

Professional advisors can help, and good ones definitely earn their keep. As you make your decisions, draw on their skills to help you balance financial realities with personal priorities.

Taking Stock of Yourself

This leads to the second main focus of this chapter: taking stock of yourself. Start with a few key questions. By definition, these are likely to be personal and person-specific, but they should include subjects such as these:

- What do I want my personal involvement in the business to be?
- What else might I do with my time and money?
- What's my time frame?
- What can I learn from others (in or out of real estate)?
- What are my health, age, and spouse telling me?

Let's look at each of these in turn.

What Do I Want My Personal Involvement in the Business to Be?

Having looked at this question from the business side, let's consider it from the personal side. There are really two issues to be factored into your answer:

- First, how much are you willing to delegate? If you've never been particularly good at delegating, you're not likely to get good at this at, say, age 60 or beyond. If you continue sitting in on meetings, even if you only perceive of yourself as a bystander, others might not see it that way. They will still regard you as the ultimate decision maker.
- Second, where do you get your kicks? If, like Gerry Hines, you'll always be a developer in your bones, then maybe it's a question of *where* and *how* to be involved actively in development. If you are still good at running your business, why not continue?

Maybe for you there's some sort of middle ground. Is there something you can do that helps the business and gives you satisfaction, but still leaves room for new operators to put their own stamp on things? Can you be a prospector? A goodwill ambassador? A continuing point of contact for key accounts?

If you go this route, think seriously about putting a time limit on the activity—perhaps in the form of a formal or informal contract that is renewable at the option of both parties. Things will change. Your contacts will inevitably thin out. You will lose your fastball, sooner or later. Don't linger.

Walter Shorenstein makes the point that one of the reasons he thought it sensible to change the focus of his San Francisco–based business and turn over management to his son, Doug, was the aging of his own financial relationships. New, younger people were running Bechtel, IBM, and Met Life—that is, his original financial partners. Doug's institutional contacts had become more relevant.

In my own business, many of our tenants have been in our buildings for decades. Yet the people now running these companies have changed. My son, Jonathan, has relationships with the new generation. He is therefore the appropriate person to negotiate our lease renewals. It is a crucial function. Retaining good tenants is the best way I know to maintain the value of your property.

Also, think about how you and your colleagues will present your new status to the world. Think about Marlon Brando's Don Corleone in *The Godfather* persuading his business associates to take the new boss (his son Michael, played by Al Pacino) seriously. True, that was a fairly unusual family situation, but there are definitely corresponding challenges in the real estate world.

One last caveat, I have seen too many examples of people retiring to a warm climate but still trying to manage their business from afar or through short site visits. Unless handled carefully, your staff can be easily discouraged if decision making gets tied to your schedule. The quality of your decision making may also suffer.

What Else Might I Do with My Time and Money?

Most people can't decide the degree of personal involvement they want in their business without being able to weigh it against a clear alternative. What might you do *instead* of doing what you've done every day for the past four or five decades?

Maybe you have a ready answer: *Play golf. Travel. Take courses. Do nothing.*

My observations of the recently and not-so-recently retired suggest to me that you shouldn't be quick to embrace doing nothing. There are a lot of books on this subject; you might want to pick up a few and see what people who've already been there have to say. If you're the kind of high-energy, task-oriented, sociable person who is often involved in real estate, my guess is that you're likely to continue to need an outlet for all that energy.

Walter Shorenstein, in his early 90s, has more or less redirected his still-abundant energy away from business in favor of a new pursuit. This change came in part because Walter decided that the nature of the business today (as described previously) made it a game for younger people—like his son, Doug. But there were pulls away from the business, as well. He loves politics, and this led him to fund the Shorenstein Center for Press and Politics at Harvard. Because he's interested in what is happening in Asia, he also funded centers specializing in that region both at the University of California at Berkeley and at Stanford. I'm sure it's enormously satisfying for him to see the fruits of his many years of labor embodied in prestigious academic centers on both coasts. You may not be in a position to establish a center, but maybe you can, for instance, volunteer your time at a local not-for-profit, or perhaps help a political candidate you support.

Wilford Cardon was quite happy to step back from the family land-development business in Phoenix, relegating decision making to his son. Missionary work had been an important part of his Mormon upbringing. *Retirement* for Cardon meant that he could channel his still-abundant energies into living much of the year in Brazil and helping young people there get a head start in life.

To some extent, the examples cited here aren't typical, because in each case there is a qualified family member ready to step in to continue the business. Without a logical successor, the decision to move on becomes much more complicated. However, I think my central point still holds: If you have an inquiring, active mind, there is never a shortage of outlets.

What's My Time Frame?

As you get older, time speeds up, and every year becomes more precious. Maybe you still think of yourself as invulnerable and immortal, but you'd probably agree that past the age of 50 or 60, you've lived more than half of your life. So how do you want to spend the second half of your life?

One technique some people consider useful is to look forward in discrete blocks of time. What do you want to get done, in the next one, two, and three blocks ahead of you? Of course, the real estate entrepreneur doesn't always have total control over what will happen. Still, the alternative—no planning at all—is worse. Strike your own balance.

What Are My Health, Age, and Spouse Telling Me?

When planning ahead, you should ask yourself this: Do I want to spend less time working and more time traveling? If so, when am I going to start? The healthier you are, the more you'll enjoy your travels. Do it when you can. When your health goes, all bets are off; you'll march (or more likely, *not* march) to the tune of a different drummer.

If you're married, you have to factor in your spouse's health and interests, too. Are you in a situation where your significant other's career is growing while yours is winding down? Do you have an aging parent or in-law to whom you or your spouse have obligations? My friend and colleague Howard Stevenson points out that there's not a tombstone in the world that reads, "I wish I had spent more time at the office."

If you want to spend more time—and more relaxed time—with your grandchildren, will you have to relocate? What does that mean for your business? What's a realistic time frame within which to accomplish that? Do you want to be near your children so that they can take care of you? Keep in mind that according to the statistics, people who live near their daughter are more apt to keep living independently.

Both at Once

I separated out the business and personal aspects of taking stock simply to make things easier to discuss. But of course, these two aspects of taking stock are really two sides of the same question.

Now we'll move on to an issue that arises in real estate more than it does in most other fields of business: Should you look to create a family business, and thus involve the next generation in it (assuming your kids are both able and interested)?

11

Your Business and Your Family

A few years ago, one of my aunts—who was then in her 90s—approached me at a family gathering. From the look on her face, I could tell she was furious. She proceeded to tell me exactly what was on her mind.

The story dated back to the early 1950s. Much of our family was then living in various units at a six-unit apartment house that had been in the family since the mid 1930s, and which my grandfather owned outright. Sometime around 1951, my grandfather transferred his ownership in the building to his three children, giving my father a 50 percent interest and each of my two aunts a 25 percent interest.

A half-century later, this perceived inequity was still eating away at my aunt. "It should have been *equal*," she proclaimed vehemently. By this time, my grandfather had been dead for 45 years, and my father close to 15 years. My aunt didn't really need the money—she was living comfortably in Philadelphia—and the actual *value* of the apartment house in the 1950s had not been all that substantial, so she really hadn't been "cheated" out of very much, in terms of dollars. The fact that my father was in business with his father at the time, and was involved in the operation of the property, was totally irrelevant to her. "Fair is fair," she concluded, wagging a finger at me.

I was reminded, once again, that *family dynamics* have consequences that last—sometimes as long as memory endures.

Because no two families are alike, there is no one preferred code of behavior for families doing business together. The potholes almost always turn up in different places. Still, from my research and experience with countless students and their families, I can venture some suggestions as to where you and your family are likely to encounter potholes, and what you might do to avoid falling into them.

Kids in the Business: Sometimes a Win-Win-Win

Why do kids get into the real estate game in the first place?

Maybe they've grown up visiting your office and job sites, listening to your dinner-table talk about how exciting your work is. Well, now they can do all that interesting stuff themselves. They can carry on your legacy, and incidentally provide a place for you to have an office, and perhaps give you the opportunity to play the role of senior advisor as you wind down the scope of your activities.

Another answer, as explained in earlier chapters, is that this is a field in which there are hundreds of thousands of properties, each of which can become the basis for a separate business. As the ownership structure of each project is determined on a case-by-case basis, you can allocate as you wish. It is unlikely your kids will have similar opportunities in other businesses they may be considering.

From the parent's side, there can be tremendous psychic benefits to working with your offspring, and transferring to them what you've learned over the years. You trust them. You can pass on your experience and your contacts. You can often lend them money at favorable rates to acquire an interest in a project. You can give them a head start in life.

And finally, from the standpoint of other interested parties, having the next generation in the business can be enormously reassuring. In some cases—but of course not *all*—employees welcome the continuity that comes with a son or daughter entering the business. (It signals that the business is going to stay active and continue.) If your long-term tenants are satisfied with the way you've run your business over the years, they, too, will probably take comfort from continuity. Finally, all those people you've done business with over the years, ranging from builders to banks, may also be glad to hear that some version of the business will continue. In many of our public Real Estate Investment Trusts (REITs), having a competent second-generation successor is considered a plus by the analysts. In other words, having a new generation enter the business may be a win-win-win situation.

Not So Fast!

If everybody stands to benefit from family involvement in business, then why do we read of so many family businesses that end up as train wrecks, characterized by intrafamily lawsuits and major rifts among the siblings? There are a number of answers. Before I start listing them, however, I want to put a universal caution on the table: *If your relationship with your son, daughter, son-in-law, or daughter-in-law is not a happy one, bringing him or her into the business will only make it worse.* I've seen a lot of strained parent-child relationships. I can't think of a single one that was made better by putting it under the additional pressure of a business relationship.

Even assuming that the relationship is okay to start with, things can still go wrong. Why? First, we parents too often assume that our offspring—who are made of the same clay as we are—must have all the talents that we have, and "success" for them is simply a matter of listening to us and following dutifully in our footsteps. Wrong! Earlier, I pointed out that not everybody wants to be Donald Trump. By the same token, not all kids are, or want to be, like their parents. The harder we try to make them so, the more annoying we become. More important, to the extent that we succeed in overpowering them, and making them "just like us," we almost certainly end up hampering their growth. Ultimately, they have to become who they are—not who we were, or wanted to be.

In that spirit, don't spend a lot of time talking about the "good old days," or about how you had to overcome long odds to succeed. The good old days probably weren't that good when you were living in them. And if your kids don't have to struggle as hard as you did just to make a living, that's not their fault. Don't hold it against them.

In addition, we have the challenge of the entrepreneurial parent. I said "challenge" rather than "problem" because in fact, it's the energy and determination of the entrepreneur (as well as his or her skill and luck) that has created much of the value in the business up to this point. Many entrepreneurs, even old ones, want to continue to *run the show* as they always have—to dominate the meeting, close the deal, hire and fire, and so on. It's a proven formula; why mess with it?

Many entrepreneurs are not good delegators to begin with, and with their kids in the vicinity, they may be even worse. They may look at a 30-year-old man and see an immature and insecure 15-year-old boy. Some may take modest steps toward sharing some authority— but in reality, they don't want to turn over the keys to the kingdom to anyone.

As a result, the kids—even the fully grown kids—never get a chance. My son, Jonathan, refers to this as the "Prince Charles syndrome": having to wait around too long to be king. (He's talking about other people's families, of course.) Boredom and impatience set in, and sometimes mischief takes root. Rent the DVD of *The Lion in Winter*, and watch Peter O'Toole's portrayal of King Henry II: the dad who just won't quit, and the sons who can't come to grips with that fact.

As you'd expect, having multiple offspring in a business complicates the situation even further. It *can* work—but only if the siblings have sorted out their relationships with one another prior to entering the business, and each has real responsibilities. For example, one can be the hunter, the other the skinner. One can be the deal maker, the other in charge of operations. One can be perceived by the outside world as the leader, while the other stays more in the background. They can split their business geographically or by product type. It works best if they're both serving useful purposes and are happy with their respective roles.

Absent those critical prerequisites, you're likely to start seeing what I call the "president's brother's syndrome," in which the under-employed brother gets seduced by flatterers anxious to capitalize on his relationship to power. Jimmy Carter's younger brother, Billy, is one of many who come to mind.

Then there's the problem of siblings not in the business (such as my aunt) and sometimes even their spouses or children. Jealousies and concerns over financial matters—such as the ownership of assets, the reinvestment or pay-out of profits, the payment of salaries, the distribution of perks for running the business—can easily turn into family donnybrooks.

Control over decision making is another potential topic for a fight. Who gets to "vote" (formally or informally) on key management issues? Is it enough to have an ownership stake? Or do you have to be actively engaged in management to get a vote on these issues? Does the older child or the leader get more votes (generally a *bad* idea)? Either give that person real power or keep it equal. Primogeniture may be the easy way out, from the family's standpoint, but for your business, it may be a bad solution.

If you really do want the last word, don't pretend to be running a participatory democracy. Your kids probably understand you better than you think, and they will know the difference between being a consultant and being a decision maker.

All of these issues get even more complicated in the next generation: the "cousins' generation." For the most part, cousins haven't had the benefit of growing up around the same kitchen table—an idea that I borrowed from Wilford Cardon. Think about it: Even if your nuclear-family dinner conversations weren't always tranquil events, everyone around that table (you hope!) learned how to be a part of a community. They learned how to communicate even when passions ran high and tempers were flaring. They learned the outer limits of acceptable discourse. In most cases, cousins don't have the opportunity to build these bonds and internalize these limits. By and large, they are less skilled at problem solving with one another than siblings, and this deficit carries over into the business.

Don't underestimate the power of spouses. They can provide doses of realism and good advice. They can also become fierce competitors, pushing their spouses to demand a greater role in the business or a greater share of the profits. I have seen situations in which the spouse in the business is driven to make unrealistic demands so as not to appear inadequate at home. Second marriages can compound the problems even further, especially if there are children from both sides. Be careful with in-laws in the business. It could work—but if it doesn't, it could affect not only your relationship with your own children, but their relationship with one another, too.

What emerges, therefore, is a picture of great potential—both for good and for harm. Oftentimes, the potholes of families in business together can be avoided as long as you, the founder, are around. But what's going to happen after you're gone? How can you maximize the good, over the long term, and minimize the damage? The answer starts with *you:* with your thorough understanding of your family, warts and all; with your commitment to carving out an appropriate role for yourself in your remaining time with the business; and with your embrace of long-term planning.

How to Be Helpful

What steps can you take to make the transition from one generation to the next smoother, and to increase the odds that your son or daughter will succeed in the business?

Perhaps most important is to get the relevant members of your family focused on the issue of *value.* How is value created, and who creates it? A young person entering the organization isn't necessarily adding much to the bottom line at the outset. Eventually, he or she gains skills and experience, and becomes an increasingly important creator of value. And then, at the other end of his or her career, he or she may become less valuable to the business.

Nonfamily businesses act on this basic truth in fairly predictable and cutthroat ways: They reward the people who are creating (or who *appear* to be creating) the most value. This makes good economic sense. (Identify the golden goose, and then feed it well.) Logically, families in business should look for ways to do the same thing. But as you can imagine—or as you might already have experienced—this can be hugely difficult in a family context. Should one sibling "get more"—either in terms of control, or assets, or both? Is the sibling who finds and runs new projects worth more than the one doing day-to-day management?

In many cases, the answer is "yes," and it's your job to explain why, and to introduce the process whereby that can be accomplished. Unless your family consists solely of saints and angels, it won't be easy. There's a large body of family-business literature out there that you may want to consult. If there's someone who can play the "Dutch uncle" role in your family—the outsider who knows the family intimately, and who speaks to members of the different generations with equal ease—this may be a good juncture to press that person into service.

Meanwhile, you also have to take steps to ensure that the young person who's supposed to be adding this value is both equipped and positioned to do so. Let's assume that it's your daughter. Listen hard to what she's saying about her vision of the business. Together, envision the kinds of training that might prove useful in getting her from here to there.

Although it's risky to generalize here, I'll venture to say that the chances are that *the particular kinds of education, formal or informal, which served you so well are unlikely to be anywhere near as useful to your son or daughter.* The world has changed. You've amassed assets. Your success has created obligations and opportunities for your kids that you never had. Work with your children to figure out what's right for them in the *here and now.*

An extension of this prescription is to *identify the best possible apprenticeship* for your kid. Is it outside the business entirely? (The answer, in many cases, is "yes," if only for the development of self-confidence.) Is it in a corner of the business that sets him or her up for a particular kind of success—say, at a bank, or a construction site, or a brokerage agency? Assuming your business is large enough, can you put together some sort of rotational system? Even smaller firms have a variety of functions through which your kid might be rotated—for example, marketing, leasing, operations, deal making. In the early stages, the more hands-on your kid's experience, the better. This can mean showing space, dealing with tenant complaints, doing renovations, interacting with regulators, and so on. If your kids are to be effective later, they should understand the details of what this business is really about.

Is your relationship one in which he or she will feel free to take a risk, and possibly make a mistake, during this apprenticeship? If not, think about involving an intermediary as your kid's direct supervisor.

This raises a final point. Eventually, your offspring coming into the business will have to earn his or her own stripes. But, you can and should take steps to make sure that he or she is walking into the most supportive environment possible. When you talk to nonfamily members about Junior, speak both positively and realistically. Don't shut down criticism of your offspring, but don't actively seek it out. Ultimately, your seasoned veterans may not choose to shift allegiances to your kid. Meanwhile, help keep options open for your son or daughter.

Death and Taxes: Some Prescriptions

Like many people, I like to make lists. The following offers some prescriptions about legacies, financial and otherwise. You'll almost certainly add to my list when you make your own. But I'd be surprised if doing the *opposite* of what's prescribed here would ever serve your family well:

- **Be transparent.** We talked about this in the Chapter 10 ("Your Business and You"), in the context of employees. Your kids will not like surprises. Suppose, for instance, that you may have good reasons not to treat them equally when it comes to dividing up assets. If so, be prepared to explain why you've reached that "inequitable" conclusion. (If my grandfather had been more transparent, my angry aunt might have been spared a half-century of feeling cheated.)

  Until you see how they perform, it might be difficult to determine who should have what power in the business. Again, be prepared to explain yourself.

- **Find out what is important to them, from an inheritance standpoint.** By involving your children in your planning, you might find out things that are important to them that you knew nothing about. It might be that they are at an age that they want anything that they're in line to receive from you to go to their kids—in effect, creative estate planning for them. Conversely, it may be that they need more money to live on now.

  Of course, there are always many sides to this thorny issue. I prefer to start giving grown and responsible children money *earlier.* I believe it fosters a better attitude and behavior (and makes them less likely to look forward to your funeral).

- **Start your planning early.** There are ways to transfer assets to your children through gifts, loans, and sales; to take full advantage of them, however, you have to start planning early.

  In Chapter 10, I gave a hypothetical example of a building that was purchased 25 years ago for $400,000 that today is worth $1 million. If the property is in your name, you might be better off leaving it in your estate so that you don't pay both a capital gains tax now and an estate tax later. The goal, in this case, might be to wind up paying only one tax.

  This raises the further question of whether you really want these assets in your name. If you think that there's going to be growth in the value of the assets, you might want to either gift or sell that asset to a trust for your children now. If you go that route, all future values over what the property is appraised at would go to them rather than to you.

Carrying the example forward, I could put my $1 million building into a trust out of which, for all practical purposes, the cash flow from the building comes to me or my spouse for the next 10 or 15 years. After that, the income from the trust could be redirected to my children. Alternatively, I could sell it to them at market value and take back a mortgage for most of the purchase price at a low interest rate. In that case, I am making an installment sale, deferring much of the capital gains.

You also have your personal exemptions to use up in giving gifts to children and grandchildren. Good tax lawyers and accountants are valuable. Take the time to make sure that they know you well, understand your view of your current options, and help you to broaden them.

- **Update your plan periodically.** No plan is forever. Estate tax laws at both the federal and state levels will be revised. Your circumstances and those of your children will likely change, especially if you live to a ripe old age. Remember the first prescription in this list: *Be transparent* about your review process. Schedule discussions with your advisors periodically. Make it clear to your children that this is part of doing business as usual, not some emergency intervention by an angry (and possibly erratic!) parent.

  When the update is completed, share it and explain it. What's changed, and why?

- **Reward those family members in the business with disproportionate equity shares in projects in which they're involved.** Relate it to the value they have created. The goal here is to start building their equity early and to help them feel rewarded for their active and positive contributions to the business.

  That said, it's a good idea to bring them along slowly, making them "earn their stripes." Watch the way they are perceived and treated by their coworkers. If you start seeing a pattern you don't like, try to get to the bottom of it.

  A sidebar to rewarding the family member in the business is the effect it will have on other siblings not in the business. They may say that it is not their fault they went another route, or that you are over-rewarding that sibling even while you, the founder, are still the rainmaker. The one response I find useful is that you have divided the ownership in earlier projects equally, and that they still will have ownership in future projects, just in less equal proportions.

- **Don't "lock in" your heirs so that they must hold on to your properties forever.** In Chapter 10, I explained how liquidity can go a long way toward soothing jangled nerves and smoothing ruffled feathers. In your estate planning, try to give your heirs the flexibility they need to sell or split up the assets.

  This is especially important in your grandchildren's generation—in which the family ties are generally weaker and the number of people involved is almost always greater.

- **Pick your executors and trustees wisely.** These are the people who will speak for you after you're gone. They can be either family members or outsiders; the most important qualifications are that they have good real estate judgment and that they command the respect of the potential beneficiaries. Do you want your family's wishes to prevail over those of your trustees; should those two worldviews ever diverge? Are your trusts really set up to ensure that outcome? If you don't know the answer, ask a good lawyer to help. Keep in mind that changing the structure to this end might offend (and possibly even drive out) your successor in your business, whether a family member or outsider, so this isn't something you should undertake lightly. They might not want to share decision making with or take orders from your designee.

  I am not big on banks or large law firms serving as long-term trustees because the person assigned to your account is very likely to turn over, sooner or later, and the new person coming in is likely to be less qualified along one or both of the dimensions previously described. Trust offices also may be limited in the investments they make or the risks they take. That may or may not be what you want.

  In this context, I won't get into the design of trusts: a hugely complex issue. Suffice it to say that it's sometimes a good idea to have a formal committee—composed of either family members, trusted outsiders, or both—with the power to occasionally change trustees if some predetermined percentage of the beneficiaries request it.

- **Think carefully about the general partners who will succeed you in the various partnerships or limited liability corporations that are responsible for the actual properties in which you are involved.** Chapter 10 covered the key issue of succession. The fact is, your successor in these kinds of business relationships may hold the *real* power over the disposition of your assets. Are his or her interests congruent with those of your beneficiaries? Will they be congruent ten years down the road?

Of course, any changes that you make in this area have the potential to be irritating, or even inflammatory, in the eyes of your successor or your nonfamily partner. (Do your actions reflect a lack of trust in me? Why? What have I done wrong?) This is not a good enough reason to refrain from acting to solve a potential problem; it's just a reason to tread carefully.

- **Consider diversifying your assets so that your wealth is not totally tied up in your real estate.** The reason is obvious: Real estate is a less-liquid asset class.

On the other hand, there is the tendency to want to stay with a business you understand, where you can add value. You don't want to make the mistake of many who go into deals they don't understand because others are doing it. Be conservative in what you invest in outside your business. Take your risks in the business you understand. Remember, cash or cash equivalents, such as short-term government securities, can be an excellent investment, and a good diversifier. You might need it.

- **Find positive ways over the years to bring your family members together.** Family holidays and vacations can and should be fun. (If they're not, change something to help make them fun.) In addition, they can create and reinforce the kind of bonds that will serve the family well if the business comes under pressure.

Let the kids help set the agenda for where you go and what you do. Be careful to remember that as your kids grow older, they will almost certainly start to diverge from each other, and from you, in terms of their social preferences, pastimes, and economic circumstances. How can those differences be bridged in a way that's comfortable for all?

Grandparents can be the great unifiers. When they play their roles well, they're unselfish, and their love is unconditional. Nothing sets a good example—or puts people on their best behavior—like unconditional love. They also can help bring cousins together.

- **As your children get older, involve them in your charitable giving.** This is not only a good way to share values, it's also an effective way to help your offspring get involved and established in their communities. Many families teach their kids to allocate part of their allowance to charity, even from a very early age. Later, they might give their children a sum of money to give away every year, attaching only one string: *Tell us why you're giving to that cause.*

By the way, if you set up a charitable foundation and you want your grown-up children to keep on giving to certain causes through that foundation after you're gone, *make that wish explicit.* Your children may have moved away or have different priorities. In my experience, there are all too many foundations out there dispensing money in ways that the founder never intended or would have wanted. Yes, build flexibility into the foundation—don't tie the trustees' hands—but make sure the spirit of your generosity is honored. It may be that the best way to ensure that is to give it all away in your lifetime.

The bottom line is, whether your gift is $100, $1,000, or $1 million, there are a lot of needs out there. Your recipients will appreciate whatever you can do.

• **Protect your spouse's interests.** If you are a hard-charging, Type A entrepreneur, your spouse will likely outlive you. Depending on your spouse's financial and medical circumstances, he or she may need greater or lesser assets to live on. Overzealous tax advisors might try to persuade you to give away too much, in an effort to minimize your inheritance tax burden. That's their job. Your job is to protect your spouse's interests.

Remember also that if something goes wrong either before or after you've gone, your spouse may be caught in the middle—with people on all sides trying to win him or her over to their particular point of view. This can result in permanent damage to relationships, and cause much grief for all concerned. I've seen this happen too often: A parent (usually the wife/ widow) gets caught in the middle of a sibling fight, not uncommon if that parent has a history of being the mediator in earlier family disputes. Try to stay out of these kinds of traps through planning that protects your spouse's autonomy under most scenarios. In the last analysis, there is only so much you can do. Once you and your spouse become parents, you have that job for life.

• **Assume that smaller stakes sometimes mean bigger fights.** It's often said that academic politics—where nothing very important is at stake—are the most ferocious.

I don't want you to think, as you read about foundations and advisors, that the issues I'm discussing pertain mainly to the rich and super-rich. Naturally, the more money that is at stake, the more these types of issues get discussed. At the same time, it's often true that *families with the smallest holdings have the greatest need for good planning.* The limited amount of money involved is likely to make more of a difference to each individual's life, and may inspire the kinds of emotions that lead to bad outcomes.

So, even if the stakes seem to be small, plan carefully for their disposition.

- **Remember the outsiders.** In Chapter 10, I encouraged you to think about what you owe to the people who helped make you successful. In this context, I simply encourage you to make sure you take care of them. All too often, they are treated as members of the family without getting any of the financial benefits of being a family member. If *you* don't address this problem, who will?

- **Build great relationships.** No business is a good business if the people inside it are miserable. I suspect that a miserable family business is the worst kind of business in the world.

What do you really want out of life? You probably want, most of all, a great relationship with your kids and grandkids. So do everything you can—inside and outside the business—to make that happen. Never let business concerns overwhelm personal relationships; if you do, neither the family nor the business will thrive.

Finally, keep in mind that one great relationship can serve as a powerful model for more great relationships. Unfortunately, the opposite also holds true. Hitting it off with one of your kids but not the other is likely to complicate, and even sour, all kinds of relationships within the family. Therefore, try your hardest to build consistently positive relationships.

Kids in the Business: Five Approaches

In this section, I want to speak directly to the next generation. Earlier in this chapter, I argued that the stock-taker (your parent) has an obligation to think again about the definition of the business: *What's this business all about?*

I now argue that you have the same obligation and opportunity. If you want to be involved, what are *your* goals? What skills and other resources do *you* bring to the table? How much flexibility do *you* have, in terms of the expectations of other family members? How do you see the family dynamics? Keep in mind that this is anything but a static definitional exercise. The business you're stepping into almost certainly will have to change under your leadership. In which direction(s) do you want it to change?

Which of the following do you want to be?

- The investor
- The sustainer
- The extender
- The transformer
- The breakaway

Let's look at these five categories, which—with the exception of the breakaway category—represents a spectrum of gradually increasing "activism": a commitment to reshaping or expanding the business. Many of you fit into more than one category. You may evolve from one category to another throughout your career. Your role might change when the founder is out of the picture. Remember, it is rarely possible for the founder to manage effectively from the grave.

The Investor

If you're a young person thinking of stepping into the family real estate business as an *investor* or limited partner, that probably means that 1) there are assets at stake, and 2) most likely, you have other activities that command most or all of your time. At the same time, you've learned a good deal, somewhere along the line, about the various asset classes. You've come to believe that real estate has a role to play in the family portfolio—and you may be lucky enough to have an equity interest in some of these assets already.

Your job is to make sure that you have skilled managers on the ground who can represent your interests, and who will bring the big problems (and opportunities) to your attention. Don't neglect the capital expenditures necessary to keep up your property. Keep in mind that you might need to reposition the property, which will also require money.

You also have to think about *asset* management, not just property management. Asset management involves larger questions, such as whether to hold, refinance, or sell the property. How does the asset fit into the total family investment portfolio? How should you deal with your partners in the venture, whether family or outsiders?

The Sustainer

Another category is what I call the *sustainer.* Suppose you've grown up in and around the family real estate business. Suppose further that you think Dad (or Mom) figured things out pretty well, and that the family investments are in a reasonably stable property class. Even so, they still demand significant management attention. You are willing to spend the time to fulfill that role, perhaps even on a full-time basis.

Think about whether and how to involve other family members in new deals. One approach that some families take is that if one person sees an opportunity to invest—in other words, you—that opportunity is extended to other family members. This can be a good way to promote a healthy level of involvement, and family solidarity, without inviting *too much* involvement. But it can also present problems of its own—for example, if you decide that you want a special benefit for yourself for finding/shaping the opportunity. That is often fair, but can lead to arguments unless the principle is agreed on in advance.

Sometimes "real estate kids" are limited to an investor role because there's no family consensus behind any other model. This is particularly likely to happen in the cousins' generation. Wil Cardon, the grandson, originally thought that he could create a "cousins' consensus" behind his development vision; when that didn't material-ize, he had to scale back his expectations and separate the family assets. Only then could he find a way to turn himself into an extender (discussed next).

This lack of consensus can also bedevil the siblings' generation. When Trammell Crow's empire came crashing down, it fell to his son Harlan to pick up the pieces. He became the manager of the family's remaining assets, and has done it well enough that additional family members (and more recently some outsiders) have invested their money with him. Others went their own way.

Real estate is all about *change*. Almost no property type sits outside of the cycle. Almost no location is safe from everything forever. So if you're a sustainer, make sure that you're also sustaining your *current industry knowledge* and your *contacts*. If you have to get deeper into the game in a hurry, you'll need these resources.

Finally, don't get nostalgic about holding the family jewel forever. It might or might not be a good idea. It might be tempting to keep a property just to give yourself something to do. On the other hand, having multiple properties may permit you to hire better people and build an organization that will enhance your ability to manage your assets.

The Extender

If you're an *extender*, you're someone who's going to build on the foundation that's been put in front of you, but also keep your eye out for ways to create new opportunities. Maybe it's new property types in your current location, or familiar property types in a new geographic area.

John Bucksbaum in General Growth was thrust into a leadership role by the death of his uncle Martin, and—in my view—he's an extender: well aware of the role he has stepped into, but also aware of the need to invent new approaches in a changing retail market. After splitting up the family assets, Wil Cardon became an extender of his branch of his family's land-development business.

I think of Neil and Jay Shah as extenders, in the sense that they've moved the family hotel business into more and bigger hotels, many in larger cities.

The Transformer

Suppose you've sized up the family business, and you've decided that significant changes—wholesale changes—are needed. This would make you a *transformer*.

Doug Shorenstein, in my view, is a transformer. While respecting his father's amazing accomplishments in San Francisco, Doug decided that there were fewer opportunities in development; he believed there were more in establishing funds to acquire existing properties.

Jeff Hines also could be put in this category. The Hines Company had already started shifting its business model under Gerry Hines's leadership; Jeff continued that change—and greatly accelerated it. While his father continued developing internationally, Jeff focused (as did Doug Shorenstein) on acquiring properties using institutional money. Another way of looking at this is to ask, *what's the core competence?* I'd argue that for these two families, their core competence has expanded in the financial arena, while both firms still maintain high standards in operating their properties.

And this raises another key point: *You enter the family business at a specific stage in its growth.* Had Jeff Hines come into the business hoping to mimic or re-create his father's early successes, he would have been frustrated in the short run and destroyed in the long run. Those opportunities were no longer there. Jeff had to find new opportunities for a large company, and he did. John Bucksbaum at General Growth took what already was a major regional mall developer and, to remain competitive, more than doubled its size.

The Breakaway

Let's imagine that you've grown up steeped in real estate—living and breathing it. Perhaps your father, or your grandfather, or both, were household names in the real estate business—either in your home town or nationally. Perhaps you've found that legacy to be, well, *confining*—and yet, you still want to carve out a niche in real estate, but separate from the family business. If so, I'd call you a *breakaway.*

We haven't met any breakaways so far in this narrative. However, my research into real estate families turned up a surprising number of breakaways. Will Zeckendorf—grandson of Bill, the foremost urban developer of the 1960s—is a case in point. Will grew up in the long shadows of his grandfather and father, and very much wanted to break out of the family mold, with its history of financial ups and downs.

Working with Kent Swig—grandson of Ben Swig, another prominent developer who also in his later days had financial problems—
they bought Brown, Harris and Stevens, a residential New York
brokerage firm. They've used the company as a point of entry into
building condominium apartments, sometimes together, sometimes
separately. Part of their bonding came from their mutual experiences
in seeing what could go wrong in a family business. When doing new
development, they were willing to reduce their ownership share to
bring in deep-pocket investors who take much of the financial risk.

A second example is another former student of mine, Scott
Malkin, who comes from a long line of New York real estate titans.
You may not know the Malkin name, but you know some of the properties his grandfather syndicated, including the Empire State Building. Scott's father, Peter, carried on the tradition, and Scott learned
the business as a representative of the third generation. Scott, looking
to do his own thing, eventually moved to London and started a chain
of value retail centers throughout Europe—a very different business
from the one he had grown up in. These centers not only offer a new
retail experience for Europe, they also require considerable marketing skills to operate. You can't just put up the physical structure and
let the retailers take it from there. Scott also had to find a whole new
set of investors. His younger brother, Tony, stayed in New York, coming into the business after Scott had left, and extended the syndication business his grandfather and father had started.

A third breakaway example arises in the Jinich family—this time
in the second generation. Roberto and Ricardo Jinich moved to San
Diego with their parents from Mexico, after some reversals in their
father's family construction business there. The two brothers saw a
niche in developing land and building moderately priced homes for
the tremendous influx of Hispanic families into Southern California.
Because of their background, they understood what differentiated
that market, and designed and sold their product accordingly.

Again, I'm not advocating one of these five roles over another.
You have to be motivated by your own situation. Our breakaways (for
example) had both the vision and drive to start afresh. This impulse
isn't inherently good or bad; it's just aimed at producing something
different and more appropriate to the next generation's needs.

Today and Tomorrow

There are three more components of "taking stock" that we still need to consider.

The first two involve taking stock of our industry. What has changed over the years, and what hasn't?

Finally, and perhaps most important: How do you want to be remembered? What has given you the most satisfaction over your career in real estate? What will do so today, and tomorrow?

These are the topics of the next and final chapter.

12

Looking Forward, Looking Back

Real estate is all about change. Change, as we've seen in previous chapters, creates opportunity. I've argued that even though change can upset your applecart, you have to be prepared to embrace it and move forward.

But real estate is also all about *continuity*. This is clearly important on the individual level. Most of the characters in this book achieved their successes (on various scales, in very different niches) by developing a particular kind of expertise and then applying it relentlessly, paying attention to every salient detail, year after year. Continuity is also a key concept when you go up one "power of magnification" and look at real estate careers in general. Throughout this book, I've argued that most real estate careers follow a typical arc: starting out, scaling up, hedging your bets, and taking stock. I've also made the implicit case—which I make explicit in this chapter—that a successful real estate *venture* involves bringing together *people*, *properties*, and *deals* in creative and mutually beneficial ways, and that a successful real estate *career* involves adding value through great execution over time. Vision alone is not enough.

Toward the end of this chapter, I want to return to an idea that I first raised in the Introduction ("The Many Paths to Success"): the idea that "wealth" is a moving target. Starting out, most of us, when we heard the word *wealth,* thought in terms of our "bank account." What we learned over the course of our careers is that there are other kinds of wealth that are critically important to our success along the way. Your reputation, for example, is also a kind of wealth. In this chapter, I want to encourage you to think about wealth as broadly as possible. I want you to think about the places in your life where financial wealth, satisfaction, and responsibility intersect.

Back to the Future: Shanghai 2007

If the subject is *change,* what better place to start than in China—and specifically, in Shanghai, China's number-one city for business?

I first visited Shanghai in the mid-1990s, principally as a tourist, but also as an interested observer of Chinese city planning. The Chinese government had plans to build a new community in the historic city of Suzhou, just west of Shanghai. The plans were nothing if not ambitious: The government intended to conjure up a new community about the size of Boston with 600,000 residents and 300,000 jobs, with the explicit goal of attracting investments and jobs from multinational corporations. It seemed unlikely to me (as well as to others) that this ambitious vision would be realized anytime soon.

Not only was I wrong; I was *spectacularly* wrong. When I returned to Shanghai in the spring of 2007, I made a point of stopping by Suzhou to see what had happened. What I encountered there was a booming, gleaming, brand-new city—in fact, everything the planners had planned for, and much more. It turns out that somewhere along the line, the Taiwanese had decided that Suzhou would be a great place to manufacture computers. The result was an economic boom of astounding proportions, with thousands of Taiwanese engineers and managers flocking to take up residence there.

And Suzhou's dynamism is representative of the bigger Shanghai picture. Back in the 1990s, Shanghai was a city of bicycles. Today, it's a city of automobiles. Shanghai now boasts more than 16 million residents (up from 13 million in 1990), many of whom hold down multiple jobs while they learn to speak English in their spare time.

The pace of construction—the noise, the dust, the detours—is staggering. I was shown a room, about the size of a basketball court, which was nearly filled with a model of the entire city of Shanghai—*every single building*—and how it will change between now and the Shanghai World's Fair (2010). In anticipation of this highly visible event, the city is building roads, airports, housing, and other infrastructure elements at an unprecedented rate. People joke that the national bird of China is the (construction) crane; nowhere is this truer than in Shanghai.

Shanghai, in turn, is part of a bigger picture. China is undergoing truly mind-boggling changes: large-scale migrations from the countryside to the cities, enormous influxes of capital, a rapidly expanding (although still volatile) stock market, and dramatic increases in personal wealth (especially at the top rungs of the economic ladder). The central government is focusing on education, job creation, and stimulation of exports.

Although generalizations about 1.3 billion people are always risky, I think it's safe to say that the Chinese population is *on the move.* The Chinese are optimistic about their future. They are embracing a difficult new language—English—with their characteristic determination, because they believe this will open new doors for them down the road. With property rights becoming more secure in their country, they are increasingly entrepreneurial. Businesses are springing up on every scale, aimed at the internal market, the export market, or both. Consumerism has supplemented communism as the national religion.

Déjà vu All Over Again

At several points on my recent visit, I was struck by a strong sense of déjà vu. Yes, Shanghai and Suzhou are smashing their molds and leaping energetically into an unknown future, with dazzling results. But I kept asking myself, *where have I have seen this before*—governments on all levels building infrastructure, cities passionately embracing the automobile, people moving from farms to cities and seeking out educational opportunities, and entrepreneurs investing in the future with optimism and a "big picture" in mind?

The answer, of course, is the United States in the 1950s, when Americans belatedly realized that they were in the middle of a century of national dominance on the world stage. We built the interstate highway system, thus accommodating and reinforcing a broadly based migration from rural to urban areas, and from cities to suburbs. With a huge boost from the FHA and the VA, we built public and private housing on a scale not matched before or since. We filled these houses with the latest appliances. We expanded our universities. Under perceived pressure from the Russians and their Sputniks, we made huge investments in science and technology. A strong country made itself stronger.

At the same time, of course, we set ourselves up for the frustrations and disappointments of the 1960s. A decade later, we were tearing down many of those same public-housing projects, and a few decades after that, we were attempting to deal with the crumbling bridges and road surfaces of our aging and heavily trafficked interstate highways, and with the negative consequences of the ill-placed roads and ramps that had divided and blighted many of our urban neighborhoods. Belatedly, we began upgrading the standards of both our products and our workplaces.

Meanwhile, we had to come to terms with the kinds of social unrest that grew out of economic disparities, frustrated expectations, and various kinds of institutionalized racism. Our very successes were responsible for a host of unanticipated problems, including overpriced housing markets that effectively excluded large segments of the population from home ownership. The riots in urban America in the 1960s had many causes, but surely they were rooted in the close proximity of the haves and the have-nots, and the widening gulf between those two groups.

Finally, we faced the need to start paying the huge environmental bills that came due after many years of abusing our air, land, water, and other natural resources. Today, new construction must pay much closer attention to the green revolution that is gaining strength in the developed world.

China, too, will eventually have to come to grips with the costs of its current exuberance. The Chinese may find it even harder than we have to keep the social fabric from unraveling. Back in the 1950s, our leaders had to speak only one language to communicate with 200-million-plus Americans. But the Chinese have to deal with hundreds of distinctive dialects in use across the country. So, in the coming years, the knitters of the social fabric in China will have their work cut out for them. Balancing their desire for a strong, central government with a dispersed and heterogeneous population that is demanding more independence will not be an easy task.

Meanwhile, it's an amazing place to do business. During my stay in Shanghai, I looked up Melissa Lam, one of my former teaching assistants. While she and her husband Steve lived in Boston, they bought and fixed up a three-unit brownstone in the South End neighborhood—much as Pete and Sara, introduced in Chapter 2,

"Finding a Focus," did in a Boston suburb—as a way to improve their living conditions and start building equity. When Melissa and Steve moved to Shanghai with their two small children, they bought and creatively fixed up an old "lane house," the Shanghai equivalent of a brownstone, in the former French Concession, which is one of the few older sections of the city that still survives more or less intact.

Melissa is not a real estate professional, per se; in fact, she is currently the chief administrative and financial officer of a Swedish company that specializes in teaching English as a second language. (A few years ago, the company had 150 employees; today it has more than a thousand.) Yet Melissa's story underscores the fact that real estate wealth can be accumulated everywhere, under a wide variety of conditions, both by people who are in the industry full time and by savvy nonprofessionals. As Melissa and Steve well understood, by creatively improving run-down housing in a neighborhood that is on the upswing, you can end up creating considerable wealth.

I also looked up another old acquaintance then living in Shanghai, Ben Wood. Ben was a partner in Ben Thompson's firm, back when that firm created the Design Research Building next to one of my properties in Cambridge. Thompson's firm had several specialties, including one pretty unique niche—the "festival marketplace"—which he perfected along with developer James Rouse. (Think Faneuil Hall Marketplace in Boston, South Street Seaport in New York, Bayside Marketplace in Miami, and so on.) Ben was invited by one of the leading Chinese developers to do something similar in Shanghai. Today, several years later, he has approximately 30 architects working for him, collectively capitalizing on the Chinese Miracle. Here again you see someone who spotted opportunity in China and moved to take advantage of it.

Throughout this book, I've talked about change as both a threat to real estate entrepreneurs and—paradoxically—as the source of many of the opportunities in real estate. A frontier is inherently a confusing and messy place. While in Suzhou, I visited a brand-new museum in the older area of town which was designed by Chinese-American architect I. M. Pei as a gift to the community where his family had its roots. It was beautifully designed and built, and it included all the latest air-handling systems. It turned out, however, that the grates installed to facilitate air distribution were confusing to some of the museum's patrons, who thought they might serve other useful purposes (which I won't specify here).

Clearly, moving into the twenty-first century in a hurry—practically overnight—entails its complexities. In such a dynamic context—with the old crashing into the new, with the countryside overwhelming and being overwhelmed by the city—you see great wealth being created.

Is the day of broad-based wealth creation behind us in the United States? In several important senses, the answer is "yes." In this country, we're no longer knocking down whole city blocks in favor of public housing, or damming huge rivers for hydroelectricity. We no longer have the huge influx of capital flowing into new development that's fueling much of the change in today's China. We've already been through the revolution in mortgage financing that's sweeping China today and spurring the rapid rise in home ownership.

So, should we all move to China to take advantage of the great opportunities there? Of course not. For one thing, there is no shortage of local talent or capital in China, which means that an outsider with no special competitive edge—and no local network or language skills—will have a hard time jumping into the Chinese boom.

Besides, opportunity still abounds in our own economy, which remains by far the world's largest. It is no accident that hundreds of thousands of immigrants still clamor to come to work and live in our country. And *new opportunities arise every day*. Real estate is no exception. Each building is different. It sits in its own neighborhood, and its own market, and is priced individually. It is an opportunity waiting to arise.

Together, these two stories—China today, the United States a half-century ago—lead me to two somewhat contradictory themes that sit at the core of this final chapter: embracing change and understanding some "eternal truths" of real estate.

A Changed and Changing Industry

Some of the characters in this book—including me—went into the real estate business a half-century ago. The world has changed a great deal since then: *Real estate is an industry that is in a constant state of turmoil.* We have to acknowledge this continuous change, and recalibrate and retool our individual careers accordingly. Someone getting into the game today has to understand at one level just how different things are from what they were in the recent past.

For example, the real estate business is much more professionalized than it was a few decades back. Most of the people in it are better educated. Thanks in part to technology and the public markets, there's much more information generally available to people. The kinds of secrets or contacts that used to benefit the small, privately held firm are no longer as important as they used to be. Properties are sold or developed in more transparent ways.

The financial markets, too, are much more sophisticated. The good news is that there are many more types of financing available; the bad news is that this requires people in the business to be more financially sophisticated. Securitization of individual loans, grouped into packages and divided not by property but by overall risk in the portfolio, has become the norm even if the risk is not always understood by the parties involved. The tradition of securing financing based on personal relationships as opposed to being transactionally focused isn't dead; but it's no longer the dominant way of doing business in the real estate field.

Fifty years ago, almost all sales and other types of real estate transactions were handled by local brokers. Today, regional and national financial institutions have become more prominent players in this game. The financial institutions have invaded corners of the market that were formerly more localized. The investment banks are also realizing and exploiting the benefits of being both brokers and principals. Much of their profits are coming from the investment of their own money.

Investment banks have started funds to cater not only to wealthy individuals, but also to pension funds, endowments, foundations, international investors, and other institutions that take a broader view of asset classes in which they might invest. For many of these institutions, real estate has become an asset class: nothing more, nothing less—a portfolio of properties to be traded over short time horizons for financial gain. And for better or worse, most institutions prefer and expect to deal with firms experienced in such relationships.

Many of the old-line local and regional firms have felt compelled for competitive reasons to "go national," primarily through merging with similar firms. Even a national service firm such as Trammell Crow agreed to be merged into CB Richard Ellis. (For its part, CB Richard Ellis wanted the Crow organization's strength in serving international corporations that were looking to centralize their real estate functions.)

From a different perspective, tenants on every level have become more sophisticated, and more demanding. In the past, the landlord's broker was normally the only intermediary in a deal. Today, tenants often have their own broker, and this changes the whole dynamic of the landlord/prospective tenant negotiation, as well as the cost. Now, not one, but *two* brokers have to be paid. And not surprisingly, tenants—with the benefit of their own advisors—are focusing much more intensely on what you (as a landlord) propose to provide for them in the way of services and improvements.

From a landlord's perspective, you must take a more professional approach. For example, if your tenants are primarily retailers, and if retailers today are more national than in the past, you will only succeed if you understand their markets, know where they want their stores, and correctly identify what stores grouped together provide the kind of shopping experience that their customers demand. Moreover, existing shopping centers, even successful ones, periodically need remodeling and refurnishing to remain competitive.

The regulatory process has become much more rigorous. Community groups have become both more active and more demanding in what they expect from a developer. Long gone are the days when a real estate entrepreneur could simply invoke "property rights" and blast ahead! Today, developers have to be willing and able to invent the kinds of trade-offs that will protect both the environment (or whatever else is the issue in contention) and the viability of the proposed development. Energy efficiency, handicapped accessibility, and life-safety concerns are integral to the design process. Attention to scale, to how a development fits in its environment, becomes even more important as advances in technology permit architects to experiment with new shapes and new materials. Obviously, it takes a more experienced owner to operate in this environment. It also takes a developer with deep enough pockets to carry a project through an approval process that can stretch out for years.

Inevitably, developers are becoming less the traditional bucca-neering entrepreneurs and more the managers of other people's money. They may be expected to put up some money of their own—their partners may demand that they have "skin in the game"—but increasingly, developers are becoming promoters, with a share of the upside. They might be the instigators of the project and put in a certain amount of their own money, but they're not on the line as much *financially*.

In the old days, depending on the nature and scale of the project, the developer might have convinced some wealthy investors to put up virtually all the equity. But, in all likelihood these developers would have been obligated to cover construction overruns and operating losses in return for which they might have received 50 percent or more of the upside. Today's developers generally receive less of the upside—say, 20 percent—in exchange for less risk. A close analogy to the deal between today's developers and their investors is hedge fund managers, who get a 1 to 2 percent annual fee plus 20 percent of the profits with or without much of their own money in the fund.

For all of these reasons, and more—such as the maturation of certain property types and markets, and the increasingly high cost of new construction—we're seeing more emphasis being put on financial structuring—that is, the trading of existing pools of properties and mortgages. This is neither "good" nor "bad." It's just one of the opportunities in today's real estate industry, in which there has been an ample supply of relatively inexpensive debt and equity financing. When that changes, as it inevitably will, investors will demand higher return for their risk, and the opportunity set in the resulting correction will look very different.

Eternal Truth 1: Your Career Arc Is Predictable

So there you have it: a picture of an industry undergoing constant change with an ever-changing cast of characters either using new or old tools in dramatically new ways.

At the same time, as made clear in previous sections, *the basic phases and realities of a real estate career are relatively unchanging.*

There *is* an underlying structure, a rhythm, and logical sequence of activities that you're likely to be engaged in over the course of your real estate career. There *are* typical challenges that you are very likely to face. No matter how much the industry twists and turns, you still have to get in the game, scale up your business, attempt to deal with the cycles, and—eventually—take stock.

Let's review those phases briefly here.

In the starting-up phase, the central decision is how, when, and where to break in. All of our protagonists started out in different ways, in different types of jobs and disciplines. Some used their training as engineers or accountants. Others used contacts: their own or those of their families or friends. (Almost nobody hung out a shingle right out of school and announced he or she was in the real estate business.) Other kinds of decisions tended to impinge upon the real estate career decision—for example, their desire or their spouse's desire to live in a particular part of the country.

In Part II, "Scaling Up," we saw a number of examples of people who decided they wanted not only to stay in the field, but also to take the next step and grow a more substantial real estate business. At that point, the decision became *how* and *where* to grow. Some decided to take on larger, more complex projects on their own home territories—whether it was Boston, Atlanta, or San Francisco. Others in the retail and hotel sectors decided to try to replicate a successful product across a range of geographic areas—either because they saw opportunity beyond the horizon, or because they were worried about saturation of their local markets, or both. Some, such as Gerry Hines, decided to do it all: intensify the local efforts, broaden the product line, and expand geographically.

Note how different the scaling-up decisions are from the starting-out decisions. But note, too, that in both phases, the *context* of the decision is all-important. As you scale up, yesterday's decisions inevitably shape today's and tomorrow's decisions. Yes, you can decide to step sideways into something substantially different, but your existing reputation and resources will strongly influence how and where you can move. Taking stock of where you are, and *what* you want to become, is critically important.

You have to make decisions about the size and nature of your organization. These grow in part out of your ambition, your vision, your ability to raise and deploy capital, and what functions you prefer to perform in-house versus outsource.

At regular intervals, you have to decide whether to keep your organization small and flexible or to expand—taking on new people, costs, and responsibilities. Again, there's no one "right way." And the "right solution" for one phase of the cycle may become the wrong solution for the next.

The need for more capital to expand led some of our protagonists to set up public Real Estate Investment Trusts (REITs), which is about as thoroughgoing an organizational change as you can embrace in real estate. (Going public has major implications for every aspect of your business.) Other characters in previous chapters formed private funds with new groups of investors, and others established alliances with potential tenants for their buildings. Many still financed their projects separately. Sometimes, they sold properties to free up money for the next deal.

Part III, "Hedging Your Bets," included a number of cases in which the passage of time tested the business model, and led to a reassessment of how the protagonist's business could and should be run.

In a cyclical industry, there are always downturns, which may be local, regional, or national in scope. Any of these can be extremely challenging to the real estate player who is highly leveraged. At the same time, these downturns provide opportunities. Rich Erenberg looked at his options carefully and decided that if he could combine his extraordinary personal energy level, his experience, and some additional hours, he could buck the downward trend in Pittsburgh-area property absorption. As a result of this assessment, he bought a vacant building at a very favorable price, retrenched in other areas to free up the necessary time and resources, and moved his office into the building.

John Dewberry, too, assessed his position, and decided that he had sufficient assets to construct a new office building in an overbuilt Atlanta market, even if (as was likely) he would incur short-term cash shortfalls. He was willing to bet on the future of Midtown Atlanta. The Shah family saw they needed to expand their central operations to service their growing portfolio of motels. Gerry Hines's firm developed service businesses to fund their overhead, as did the remaining partners in the Crow organization after its reorganization. They wanted to keep together the teams they had spent so much time assembling.

Sometimes these kinds of reassessments come at a high cost. The Cardons in Phoenix learned the hard way that they could not expand into multiple types of real estate businesses in which they had minimal expertise and over which they exercised minimal control. Their subsequent soul-searching led them to conclude that they should return to their land-banking and land-developing roots and refrain from constructing "anything higher than a curb." Once they did that, they were able to rebuild the family fortune.

Finally, you have the taking-stock phase. One important point to remember about this phase of your career is that you still have ample opportunities to *add value* and create wealth. It is more than just cashing in your chips. True, if you are scaling back your business life, you may not be transforming cityscapes or further enlarging your personal fortune. Even so, you can continue to do new deals either as an active or passive partner. You can also concentrate on building new kinds of relationships—inside and outside the family. You can spend more time teaching and mentoring young people. You can also become more involved in volunteer activities, using your wealth, wisdom, and time in different ways. As I define the term, these are all ways of *adding value.*

Eternal Truth 2: It's About Adding Value Through Great Execution Over Time

In my real estate classes, I used to tell my students that success in real estate is all about bringing together *people, properties,* and *deals.* For an individual project to work, you have to negotiate in all of these areas, more or less simultaneously:

- **People.** You have to have the right people to perform the many functions needed to make a real estate deal happen. Ours is a fragmented, localized industry, dependent upon many ad hoc sets of relationships. Many entrepreneurs enjoy the people challenge. They are "people people," by and large—interested in and skilled at building good relationships. But their most challenging problems often arise when they must start bringing in partners, delegating responsibility, and sharing control. It is not easy to align the interests of all those on whom you are dependent to complete your project.

- **Property.** There are literally millions of properties out there. Most are custom designed. They come in all shapes, sizes, and intended uses. Some are already built; others are still on the drawing board. They might be conceived of as relatively impermanent, or they might be built for the ages. They might be mass-produced or handcrafted. They sit (or are expected to sit) within a particular context, in a larger market that is fragmented, subject to local controls, and always at the mercy of regulators at all levels of government.

  Yet, properties exist (or are created) to meet similar human needs. People will always need places to live, work, shop, and play. Although the particulars might change—movie theaters, malls, bowling alleys, and McMansions experience their ups and downs—those underlying needs will never go away. New properties will be brought on line in response to those needs, and existing properties that successfully meet one or more of those needs will tend to be long-lived assets—assuming, of course, that they are well built and well maintained.

- **Deal.** For the people and the property to come together, you need some combination of debt and equity financing, which in the case of an income property depends primarily on the cash flow generated by the property. It is also affected by the cost and availability of funds in the underlying financial markets, and by the income tax implications of a transaction. Finally, the legal entity in which a property is held—such as a corporation, partnership, or joint venture—impacts the way relationships are structured.

  In the last analysis, you affect the value of the underlying asset not only by what you do with the property, but also by how you structure the transaction. One of the great joys of real estate is the ability to structure each deal independently, create incentives, and distribute equity project by project.

But there's another, equally valid way to look at people, properties, and deals. This involves taking the long view. Simply put, creating substantial real estate wealth in most cases involves *adding value through great execution over time.* Rather than taking a "snapshot" of a deal, this is more like making a movie. It's about *improving a property over the long run, and thereby increasing its ability to generate cash flow, and thus increase its value.* This is a key real estate truth that tends to get overshadowed when individual markets heat up and the "flippers" come out to play (those who buy properties speculatively, hold them briefly, and hope like crazy that a rising market will continue to rise). If you want to create substantial real estate wealth, *you need a long-term strategy, rather than a speculative outlook.* You need to develop very specific skills of execution in a particular niche or niches, and then you have to implement like crazy. You have to pay attention to the details, on every level. You have to sweat the small stuff, year after year.

True, you'll probably be compelled to sell properties to free up the necessary cash to make an even better investment, especially early in your career. But as a rule, you want to *buy and hold and improve.* This is the best way to maximize your control over your own destiny. As many flippers have found out to their dismay, markets collapse just as easily (and as often) as they inflate. In the long run, it's the value players—rather than the momentum players—who end up in the winner's circle.

Let's run through our cast of characters again, in this light:

The Bucksbaums brought their retail expertise to the shopping center context, which helped them figure out the intricacies of being a landlord to multiple retail tenants. They adjusted their product and adapted their financial structure to become leaders in the transformation of retailing in the United States.

Susan Hewitt got really good at exploiting a specific regulatory context, and actively evolved that expertise as the competitive and economic climates changed.

The Cardons, out in Phoenix, were experts in selecting and permitting land. (It was when they ventured out of their wheelhouse that they got into trouble.)

Gerry Hines grasped the power of great architecture and complemented that skill with a focus on unparalleled tenant services. His reputation as a straight shooter also served him well. (Reputation is a form of wealth.) It's not an accident that the Hines organization is a consistently successful development firm.

The Shahs applied their culturally based notion of hospitality to U.S. motels, building an operation motel by motel, at first by leveraging their Indian expatriate contacts. Eventually, they had to change their model to accommodate rapid growth, but the fundamentals remained in place. They involved their two sons, who have maintained the tight corporate culture of the organization even as they expanded their base significantly.

Ed Mank, one of the more complicated figures in our cast, did extremely well in Boston residences and commercial properties. Even when his more far-flung ventures (such as his ski resort) got him in trouble, he continued to make money close to home as he worked his way back out of trouble.

Trammell Crow carried to a new level at least one real estate niche—a merchandise mart for wholesalers in Dallas—and also emerged as a player in a number of other product types before he and his organization got into trouble on the grand scale. Along the way, he provided a great ride for hundreds of real estate professionals who learned the trade in his shop.

Rich Erenberg initially became an expert in foreclosed Houston apartments. Not incidentally, he and his partner did all of their early rehabbing work themselves—making themselves expert in the hands-on value-creation process. He then applied some of the same strategies to other distressed projects. True, they were in new locales and they were less hands-on, but his expertise and attention to details remained applicable.

Walter Shorenstein, at first an outsider in the clubby real estate community that was San Francisco in the 1950s, simply made himself the smartest kid on the block when it came to commercial real estate in his adopted city. As a result, he saw things that no one else could see. Arguably, his son Doug has accomplished the same thing on the deal-making side of the business.

Finally, John Dewberry continues to focus on Atlanta, especially the Midtown area. Although the jury is still out on his new office building, Two Peachtree Pointe, it's clear that One Peachtree Pointe would never have happened without his vision for and understanding of that area.

A 30-Year "Deal": The Brattle Walkway

Allow me to present a personal case in point. This particular story both reiterates some of my previous observations and leads naturally into the final topic of this chapter: measuring your career in terms of the value that you have created.

Back when I first got the opportunity to invest in Harvard Square—when a family that owned a key, but underdeveloped, parcel in the square decided to go along with my proposal of a 75-year ground lease as the first step in the development that I envisioned for this property—I knew that I had a fundamental problem I would someday have to resolve.

The parcel sat between two major streets that run roughly parallel: Mount Auburn Street and Brattle Street. My existing frontage was on Brattle Street. A third street, Church Street, ran from the subway stop near the heart of the Square, dumping out onto Brattle directly across from my property.

In short, a great location! But, my property was an elongated one, with the short side on Brattle Street. The long side only reached halfway to Mount Auburn Street. If I put the main entrance on Brattle Street, I would have to run a hallway the length of each floor using up rentable space and reducing my flexibility to subdivide the floors—not a great solution. Putting the entrance in the front, moreover, would chew up valuable retail frontage on Brattle Street.

But, what if I created an outside walkway alongside my building? I could then put the entrance to the offices off the walkway in the middle of my building, thus making the office floors more efficient and flexible. Eventually, if I got my neighbors to go along, I might be able to extend the walkway all the way to Mt. Auburn Street, making it, in essence, an extension of Church Street.

Thus began a 30-year process of trying to persuade my neighbors to share in this vision and getting them to help me make it a reality. To start off, I was willing to take the risk that tenants would accept, at least at the beginning, a dead-end walkway as the access to their front entrances.

Over time, I was able to acquire some of the abutting properties. Eventually, as the remaining abutters developed their sites, they went along with extending the walkway. We put in trees and other plantings, built overhangs to shield pedestrians from the rain, and installed a brick sidewalk. Today, as you walk down our passageway in the summer, you can hear birds chirping, and even at times the occasional cricket.

You May Well Be Asking: 30 Years to Do *That?*

Yes, 30 years to do that. And although it doesn't look like much on a map of Cambridge, down at ground level, it's a major improvement. Over those same 30 years, office rents on my Harvard Square properties have risen from $6.50 per square foot to more than $30 today—primarily because of the overall rise in the local market, but also due to the efforts that my neighbors and I have made to make our properties more valuable.

Let me say it again, for emphasis: Although buying wholesale and selling retail can sometimes serve you well, *owning, maintaining, and improving good, well-located real estate over long periods of time is a great way to create long-term financial wealth in real estate.* This is especially true if you're a taxpaying individual (as opposed to a nontax-paying institution) who doesn't like paying the 15 percent of the gain you'll realize if you sell the property. All things being equal, 1) hold your property, 2) make it more valuable through steady improvements, and 3) use your resulting cash flow to refinance the property, giving yourself the opportunity to take out cash on a tax-deferred basis.

The *Boston Globe's* architecture critic, Robert Campbell, recently wrote a complimentary piece about my 30-year quest to complete my urban walkway, which he dubbed the Brattle Walk:

> The Brattle Walk isn't an important place or, even, a remarkably beautiful one. It's not going to appear in any books about great architecture. That's not the point. It's not about fame or fortune or what's called "signature architecture." It's about how you make good cities by getting the small things right.

In a sense, "getting the small things right" is one of the key underlying messages of this book—as is *taking the time to get it right.*

What's Wealth?

You undoubtedly approached this book with one specific kind of wealth in mind: *financial* wealth. And I'm the first to say that financial wealth is indeed good and useful. It feels great to be able to feed, clothe, house, and educate your family, not to mention indulge yourself now and then. (Every year, it seems, tickets to the Red Sox get more expensive.)

It also feels great to succeed according to a generally accepted benchmark, such as having "money in the bank" or a robust personal balance sheet. Even if you don't care what other people think of you, it's very gratifying to set a financial benchmark, and then surpass it.

And then there are all those things that money makes possible indirectly. You can be helpful to other people and institutions. You can make decisions that, in the short term, may cost you financially, but in the long term create all kinds of other benefits. For these and other reasons, I've argued throughout this book that embracing and pursuing a successful, moneymaking strategy with a long term perspective is the *sine qua non* of real estate. Without it, you will be like those condominium flippers in Miami today: successful in the short term but unsuccessful in the longer term.

Here I want to make the case that there are other kinds of wealth you may want to enter on your scorecard as you take stock.

The first is the kind of wealth that you create by improving the built environment. As homeowners, we have a responsibility to take care of our properties, and thereby protect and improve our neighborhoods. As real estate developers and professionals, we raise that responsibility up to an even higher level. Max DePree, the former CEO of Herman Miller, once chided some corporate lieutenants who were proposing to put up what he considered to be a bad building. "Gentlemen," he said, "that's a perfectly good cornfield."

In other words, don't venture out into the world with bad plans and no concern for the environment around you. Do it right, and give yourself years of subsequent satisfaction. I live near my Brattle walkway, and I work in the office building I built there. Using the walkway myself each day, and seeing it used as a major pedestrian throughway, is *deeply* satisfying. No, you can't take it to the bank, but it's definitely another kind of real estate wealth.

There are lots of other ways to make a contribution to the world around you, many of which can draw upon the specialized knowledge that you've acquired in your real estate career. Is your favorite nonprofit contemplating a significant rehabilitation of its building, or even putting up a new facility? Most likely, they won't have the necessary skills in house, and will welcome your help.

Look for other kinds of problems that they don't seem able to solve, and which you can help fix. Nonprofits are always in need of people who can contribute one or more of the "three Ws": wealth, wisdom, and work. Figuring out which Ws you can contribute and to whom is one of the great rewards of a successful career. Until the very end of her life, my mother loved to borrow books from the public library in Centerville, on Cape Cod. That library is now undertaking a significant remodeling of part of the building, and I can't think of a better way to honor my mother than contributing to that effort. No, it's not on the scale of Walter Shorenstein's centers for policy research, but I know I'll get great satisfaction from watching that renovation take shape.

Finally, and perhaps most important, there's what might be called *people wealth*. This is wealth that other people give to you, and which you can give to others.

As noted previously, real estate is at its heart a people business, particularly suited to "people people." Each year of my long career has brought a universe of new and interesting people to my doorstep—or brought me to their doorsteps. I've worked with world-class architects, representatives of several major universities, bureaucrats, property owners, and service providers of all types and sizes.

In the early years of your real estate career, you learn to forge strong relationships. Contacts (along with reputation) are equally important to you in the taking-stock phase of your career. To the extent that you want to stay active in the industry, you still have to work through others, and they may be different others. And as described in the first two chapters of Part IV "Taking Stock," you still need to make sure that you have the right people in place to carry on your business, if indeed that's one of your goals.

But now, at this later stage of your career, one of the most important dimensions you can add to your life—and one of the best forms of "wealth" that you can create—involves mentoring young people. I've been particularly lucky in this regard; after all, a large part of being a professor at a professional school involves bringing along young people, not only at the start of but also during their careers. I believe, however, that this is an opportunity that's available to *anyone* who has made a mark in his or her field and is willing to share his or her accumulated experience with younger people. I recently received an e-mail from a 28-year veteran developer in Florida who started a second career of teaching in a college close to his home. There's a demand for knowledge about real estate out there; maybe you can help meet that demand.

Perhaps there are young people in your family or among the non-family members within your organization. Maybe they've come to you via some completely unexpected or roundabout path. In any case, *help them out.* Help them grow and prosper in our industry. Trammell Crow is remembered today less for his contributions to the built environment, and more for his encouragement of the young people around him whom he helped train. For both you and the person you help, this can turn out to be a very special kind of *wealth,* indeed.

INDEX

FINANCIAL TIMES

In an increasingly competitive world, it is quality
of thinking that gives an edge—an idea that opens new
doors, a technique that solves a problem, or an insight
that simply helps make sense of it all.

We work with leading authors in the various arenas
of business and finance to bring cutting-edge thinking
and best-learning practices to a global market.

It is our goal to create world-class print publications
and electronic products that give readers
knowledge and understanding that can then be
applied, whether studying or at work.

To find out more about our business
products, you can visit us at www.ftpress.com.